Symmetric Distributions, Moments and Applications

Symmetric Distributions, Moments and Applications

Editor

Zivorad Tomovski

MDPI • Basel • Beijing • Wuhan • Barcelona • Belgrade • Manchester • Tokyo • Cluj • Tianjin

Editor
Zivorad Tomovski
Faculty of Science and Mathematics,
University of Ostrava
Czech Republic

Editorial Office
MDPI
St. Alban-Anlage 66
4052 Basel, Switzerland

This is a reprint of articles from the Special Issue published online in the open access journal *Symmetry* (ISSN 2073-8994) (available at: https://www.mdpi.com/journal/symmetry/special_issues/Distributions_Moments_Applications).

For citation purposes, cite each article independently as indicated on the article page online and as indicated below:

LastName, A.A.; LastName, B.B.; LastName, C.C. Article Title. *Journal Name* **Year**, *Volume Number*, Page Range.

ISBN 978-3-0365-5847-9 (Hbk)
ISBN 978-3-0365-5848-6 (PDF)

© 2023 by the authors. Articles in this book are Open Access and distributed under the Creative Commons Attribution (CC BY) license, which allows users to download, copy and build upon published articles, as long as the author and publisher are properly credited, which ensures maximum dissemination and a wider impact of our publications.
The book as a whole is distributed by MDPI under the terms and conditions of the Creative Commons license CC BY-NC-ND.

Contents

About the Editor vii

Preface to "Symmetric Distributions, Moments and Applications" ix

Zivorad Tomovski
Special Issue Editorial "Symmetric Distributions, Moments and Applications"
Reprinted from: *Symmetry* **2022**, *14*, 1863, doi:10.3390/sym14091863 1

Robert Frontczak and Živorad Tomovski
Convolutions for Bernoulli and Euler–Genocchi Polynomials of Order (r,m) and Their Probabilistic Interpretation [†]
Reprinted from: *Symmetry* **2022**, *14*, 1220, doi:10.3390/sym14061220 5

Mohamed S. Eliwa, Fahad Sameer Alshammari, Khadijah M. Abualnaja and Mahmoud El-Morshedy
A Flexible Extension to an Extreme Distribution
Reprinted from: *Symmetry* **2021**, *13*, 745, doi:10.3390/sym13050745 21

Kei Nakagawa and Katsuya Ito
Taming Tail Risk: Regularized Multiple β Worst-Case CVaR Portfolio
Reprinted from: *Symmetry* **2021**, *13*, 922, doi:10.3390/sym13060922 39

Jui-Jung Liao, Hari Mohan Srivastava, Kun-Jen Chung, Shih-Fang Lee, Kuo-Nan Huang and Shy-Der Lin
Inventory Models for Non-Instantaneous Deteriorating Items with Expiration Dates and Imperfect Quality under Hybrid Payment Policy in the Three-Level Supply Chain
Reprinted from: *Symmetry* **2021**, *13*, 1695, doi:10.3390/sym13091695 53

Sadaf Khan, Oluwafemi Samson Balogun, Muhammad Hussain Tahir, Waleed Almutiry and Amani Abdullah Alahmadi
An Alternate Generalized Odd Generalized Exponential Family with Applications to Premium Data
Reprinted from: *Symmetry* **2021**, *13*, 2064, doi:10.3390/sym13112064 79

Ehab M. Almetwally, Refah Alotaibi, Aned Al Mutairi, Chanseok Park and Hoda Rezk
Optimal Plan of Multi-Stress–Strength Reliability Bayesian and Non-Bayesian Methods for the Alpha Power Exponential Model Using Progressive First Failure
Reprinted from: *Symmetry* **2021**, *14*, 1306, doi:10.3390/sym14071306 105

Kittisak Chumpong, Raywat Tanadkithirun and Chanon Tantiwattanapaibul
Simple Closed-Form Formulas for Conditional Moments of Inhomogeneous Nonlinear Drift Constant Elasticity of Variance Process
Reprinted from: *Symmetry* **2021**, *14*, 1345, doi:10.3390/sym14071345 125

About the Editor

Zivorad Tomovski

Zhivorad Tomovski has held the position of Full Professor since 2010 at the Ss. Cyril and Methodius University of Skopje, North Macedonia. He held Visiting Researcher and Professorship positions at many prestigious universities and research institutes across Europe. Since, 2022, he has been Associate Professor of Analysis, PDE, Probability and Statistics at the University of Ostrava, Czech Republic. He has published two Springer books and over 100 international papers in the areas of pure and applied mathematics.

Preface to "Symmetric Distributions, Moments and Applications"

Laying the modern axiomatic foundations of probability theory, A. N. Kolmogorov (1903-1987) established his reputation as the world's leading expert in this field. The probability distributions and moments of the random variables are mathematical models in many branches of science, finance, insurance, and any field where stochastic modeling is used. This Special Issue includes eight papers with original results of symmetric random walks and their characterization, stochastic processes, computational number theory, stochastic integrals, probability inequalities, statistics parameter estimation, entropy, Stochastic differential equations, finance mathematics, optimization, information theory, Bayesian methods, Monte Carlo methods, etc. The book is addressed to graduate, PhD students and researchers in statistics and physics, as well as, data sciences, finance and insurance.

Zivorad Tomovski
Editor

Editorial

Special Issue Editorial "Symmetric Distributions, Moments and Applications"

Zivorad Tomovski

Department of Mathematics, Faculty of Science, University of Ostrava, 70103 Ostrava, Czech Republic; zhivorad.tomovski@osu.cz

1. Introduction

In 1933, Kolmogorov published his book, *Foundations of the Theory of Probability*, laying the modern axiomatic foundations of probability theory and establishing his reputation as the world's leading expert in this field. The concept of the probability distribution and the random variables they describe underlies the mathematical discipline of probability theory and the science of statistics. The probability distribution and the random variables serve as mathematical models in many branches of science, complex dynamical systems, population dynamics modeling, finance mathematics, insurance, physical sciences, and any field where stochastic modeling is used. In mathematics, the moments of a function are quantitative measures related to the shape of the function's graph. If the function is a probability distribution, then the first moment is the expected value, the second central moment is the variance, the third standardized moment is the skewness, and the fourth standardized moment is the kurtosis. That is, the moments describe the location (mean), size (variance), and shape (skewness and kurtosis) of a probability density function (PDF). The mathematical concept is closely related to the concept of moment in physics. The classical diffusion equation (heat equation) yields an approximation of the time evolution of the probability density function, associated with the position of the particle going under a Brownian movement under the physical definition.

The continuous time random walk (CTRW) method is the basis for a heuristic explanation of the physical behavior of normal and anomalous diffusion processes. The CTRW method can be characterized by the moments of the random mean motion. If the process is non-local or has a memory waiting time density, then the second moment EX^2 of the random variable X of the jumps is proportional to a power t^α of order α of time, when the time is sufficiently large. This type of stochastic model lets us characterize sub-diffusion, normal diffusion, and super-diffusion, where $0 < \alpha < 1$, $\alpha = 1$, and $1 < \alpha < 2$ respectively. A well-known method to calculate moments is using moment-generating functions or characteristic functions (CF). Since the coefficients of the Taylor expansion of the CF are related to the integer moments of a random variable, we usually state that the probabilistic description of a random variable may also be given in terms of integer moments. In the 1970s, the fractional moments of the type $EX^\rho, \rho \in \mathbf{R}$, were studied, showing that the knowledge of some EX^ρ improves the convergence speed of the maximum entropy method. Fractional moments of a non-negative random variable are expressible by the Mellin transform of PDF, and this fact has been widely used in the literature principally in the field of the algebra of random variables [1]. That is, the Mellin transform is the principal mathematical tool to handle problems involving products and quotients of independent random variables. Another research direction on Mellin applications in probability is represented by the use of special functions such as the Mittag–Leffler, H-Fox, and Maijer's G-functions, due principally to A.M. Mathai and his co-workers. Such functions are indeed representable as Mellin–Barnes integrals of the product of gamma functions and are therefore suited to represent statistics of products and quotients of independent random variables whose fractional moments are expressible as gamma or gamma-related functions.

The stable distributions are a fascinating and fruitful area of research in probability theory; furthermore, nowadays, they provide valuable models in physics, astronomy, economics, and communication theory. The general class of stable distributions was introduced and given this name by the French mathematician Paul Levy in the early 1920s; see Levy (1924, 1925). The inspiration for Levy was the desire to generalize the celebrated Central Limit Theorem, according to which any probability distribution with finite variance belongs to the domain of attraction of Gaussian distribution. Formerly, the topic attracted only moderate attention from leading experts, though there were also enthusiasts, of whom the Russian mathematician Alexander Yakovlevich Khintchine should be mentioned first of all. The concept of stable distributions took full shape in 1937 with the appearance of Levy's monograph (see Levy (1937–1954)), soon followed by Khintchine's monograph (1938). We can now cite the paper by Mainardi, Luchko, and Pagnini (2001), where the reader can find (convergent and asymptotic) representations and plots of the symmetric and non-symmetric stable densities generated by fractional diffusion equations.

This Special Issue includes seven papers with original results of symmetric random walks and their characterization, stochastic processes, computational number theory, stochastic integrals, probability inequalities, statistics parameter estimation, entropy, Stochastic differential equations, finance mathematics, optimization, information theory, Bayesian methods, Monte Carlo methods, etc.

In the paper "Convolutions for Bernoulli and Euler–Genocchi Polynomials of Order (r,m) and Their Probabilistic Interpretation", R. Frontczak and Z. Tomovski [2] introduced a new class of extended Bernoulli and Euler–Genocci polynomials of order (r,m) for which some convolutions, recurrence formulas, and combinatorial sums are presented. By using the concept of moment-generating functions, it is shown that the Bernoulli and Euler–Genocci polynomials can be expressed as moments of order n for some discrete random variables in the standard probability space. A new PDF associated with Bernoulli numbers is defined for which the mathematical expectation is calculated.

In the paper "A Flexible Extension to an Extreme Distribution", published by Mohamed S.Eliwa et al. [3], a new flexible extension of an extreme distribution with three parameters has been proposed, which generalizes the inverse exponential distribution. Furthermore, it can be utilized for modeling asymmetric "positive and negative" as well as symmetric datasets and can be used to model over- and under-dispersed data. Statistical and reliability properties of the extreme distribution, such as quantile function, skewness, kurtosis, incomplete moments, and entropy, are presented. The model parameters have been estimated utilizing the maximal likelihood approach. Finally, four data applications that illustrate the flexibility of the new extension and its excellence over other models have also been analyzed.

The paper "Taming Tail Risk: Regularized Multiple β Worst-Case CVaR Portfolio" published by Kei Nakagawa and Katsuya Ito [4] contains an optimization problem reduced to a linear programming problem, using mixture probability distributions as well as seminonparametric distribution. They performed experiments on well-known benchmarks in finance to evaluate the proposed portfolio. Their portfolio shows superior performance in terms of having both higher risk-adjusted returns and lower maximum drawdown despite the lower turnover rate.

The goal of the paper "Inventory Models for Non-Instantaneous Deteriorating Items with Expiration Dates and Imperfect Quality under Hybrid Payment Policy in the Three-Level Supply Chain" [5] is to determine an optimal replenishment cycle and the total annual cost function by exploring the functional properties of the total annual cost function and showing that the total annual cost function is convex. Theoretical analysis of the optimal properties shows the existence and uniqueness of the optimal solution. Then, the authors obtained simple and easy solution procedures for the inventory system. Moreover, numerical analysis of the inventory model was conducted, and the corresponding examples are considered with the ai of illustrating the application of the supply-chain model that is investigated in this article. The authors have established a sustainable inventory system in which the retailer sells the non-instantaneous deteriorating item that is fully deteriorated close to its expiry date and has imperfect quality such as those in seasonal products, food products, electronic components, and others. In order to manage the quality of the items, an inspection will occur during the state in which there is no deterioration. On the other hand, the supplier demands the retailer a distinct payment scheme, such as partial prepayment or cash and trade credit; in turn, the retailer grants customers partial cash and trade credit. The paper also presents convexity and monotonicity properties to develop efficient decision rules for the optimal replenishment cycle time T*.

In the next paper, "An Alternate Generalized Odd Generalized Exponential Family with Applications to Premium Data" [6] an exponentiated odd generalized exponential (OGE2-G) class of distribution is proposed and studied with some mathematical properties such as ordinary and incomplete moments, mean deviations, Rényi entropy, and generating functions. The maximum likelihood (MLL) approach is used to estimate the model parameters. Then, the authors focussed their attention on one of the special members of the family defined with the Fréchet distribution, called the OGE2Fr distribution. They established the optimized the maximum likelihood methodology in particular, with the goal of effectively estimating model parameters, and validated their convergence by a simulation study, ensuring that the projections have asymptotic properties. The authors evaluated the sensitivity of the method of estimations using the MLL of OGE2Fr distribution parameters using the Monte Carlo simulation technique.

Stress-strength reliability, $R = P(X < Y)$, has been extensively investigated as a stress-strength model, and the research has also been extended to multi-component systems. For numerous statistical models, several scholars have examined the estimation of the stress-strength parameter. Several authors discussed Bayesian and maximum-likelihood estimation methods of reliability for point estimation of the parameter model. The authors Ehab M. Almetwally et al. in the paper "Optimal Plan of Multi-Stress–Strength Reliability Bayesian and Non-Bayesian Methods for the Alpha Power Exponential Model Using Progressive First Failure" [7] considered the inference for multi-reliability using unit alpha power exponential distributions for stress–strength variables based on the progressive first failure. The Fisher information and confidence intervals such as asymptotic, boot-p, and boot-t methods are also examined. Various optimal criteria were found. Monte Carlo simulations and real-world application examples were used to evaluate and compare the performance of the various proposed estimators.

The stochastic differential equation has been used to model various phenomena and investigate their properties, such as the moments, variance, and conditional moments, which are beneficial for estimating parameters that play significant roles in several practical applications. For example, financial derivative prices, such as moment swaps, can be obtained by calculating the conditional moments of their payoffs under the risk-neutral measure.

In "Simple Closed-Form Formulas for Conditional Moments of Inhomogeneous Nonlinear Drift Constant Elasticity of Variance Process" [8], the authors presented closed-form expressions for conditional moments of the inhomogeneous, nonlinear, drift-constant elasticity of variance (IND-CEV) process, without having a condition on eigenfunctions or the transition PDF. The analytical results are examined through Monte Carlo simulations.

This volume will be of interest to mathematicians, physicists, and engineers interested in probability theory, statistics, complex systems, finance mathematics, and insurance.

Funding: The research was supported by the Department of Mathematics, Faculty of Sciences, University of Ostrava.

Conflicts of Interest: The author declares no conflict of interest.

References

1. Tomovski, Z.; Metzler, R.; Gerhold, S. Fractional characteristic functions, and a fractional calculus approach for moments of random variables. *Fract. Calc. Appl. Anal.* **2022**, *25*, 1307–1323. [CrossRef]
2. Frontczak, R.; Tomovski, Z. Convolutions for Bernoulli and Euler-Genocchi Polynomials of order (r,m) and Their Probabilistic Interpretation. *Symmetry* **2022**, *14*, 1220. [CrossRef]
3. Eliwa, M.; Alshammari, F.; Abualnaja, K.; El-Morshedy, M. A Flexible Extension to an Extreme Distribution. *Symmetry* **2021**, *13*, 745. [CrossRef]
4. Nakagawa, K.; Ito, K. Taming Tail Risk: Regularized Multiple b Worst-Case CVaR Portfolio. *Symmetry* **2021**, *13*, 922. [CrossRef]
5. Liao, J.-J.; Srivastava, H.M.; Chung, K.-J.; Lee, S.-F.; Huang, K.-N.; Lin, S.-D. Inventory models for Non-Instantaneous Deteriorating Items with Expiration Dates and Imperfect Quality under Hybrid Payment Policy in the Three-Level Supply Chain. *Symmetry* **2021**, *13*, 1695. [CrossRef]
6. Khan, S.; Balogun, O.S.; Tahir, M.H.; Almutiry, W.; Alahmadi, A.A. An alternate generalized odd generalized exponential family with applications to premium data. *Symmetry* **2021**, *13*, 2064. [CrossRef]
7. Almetwally, E.M.; Alotaibi, R.; Mutairi, A.A.; Park, C.; Rezk, H. Optimal plan of multi-stress-strength Reliability Bayesian and Non-Bayesian methods for the Alpha Power Exponential Model Using Progressive First Failure. *Symmetry* **2022**, *14*, 1306. [CrossRef]
8. Chumpong, K.; Tanadkithirun, R.; Tantiwattanapaibul, C. Simple Closed-Form Formulas for Conditional Moments of Inhomogeneous Nonlinear Drift Constant Elasticity of Variance Process. *Symmetry* **2022**, *14*, 1345. [CrossRef]

Review

Convolutions for Bernoulli and Euler–Genocchi Polynomials of Order (r,m) and Their Probabilistic Interpretation [†]

Robert Frontczak [1,‡] and Živorad Tomovski [2,*]

[1] Landesbank Baden-Württemberg (LBBW), 70173 Stuttgart, Germany; robert.frontczak@lbbw.de
[2] Department of Mathematics, Faculty of Science, University of Ostrava, 70103 Ostrava, Czech Republic
[*] Correspondence: zhivorad.tomovski@osu.cz
[†] Dedicated to Prof. Hari M. Srivastava on the Occasion of his 80th Birthday.
[‡] Statements and conclusions made in this article by R. F. are entirely those of the author. They do not necessarily reflect the views of LBBW.

Abstract: The main purpose of this article is to derive several convolutions for generalized Bernoulli and Euler–Genocchi polynomials of order (r, m), $B_n^{(r,m)}(x)$ and $A_n^{(r,m)}(x)$, respectively. These polynomials have been introduced recently and contain the generalized Bernoulli, Euler and Genocchi polynomials as special members. Some of our results extend the results of M. Merca and others concerning Bernoulli numbers and polynomials. Probabilistic interpretations of the presented results are also given.

Keywords: Bernoulli number; generalized Bernoulli polynomial; generalized Euler–Genocchi polynomial; functional equation; convolution; probability distribution; moment-generating function; moments

MSC: 11B68; 11S40; 05A15; 60E05

1. Introduction

Bernoulli numbers $(B_n)_{n\geq 0}$ are defined by

$$B(z) = \sum_{n=0}^{\infty} B_n \frac{z^n}{n!} = \frac{z}{e^z - 1} \qquad (|z| < 2\pi).$$

A generalization of Bernoulli numbers are Bernoulli polynomials $B_n(x), x \in \mathbb{C}$, defined by

$$B(x,z) = \sum_{n=0}^{\infty} B_n(x) \frac{z^n}{n!} = \frac{z}{e^z - 1} e^{xz} \qquad (|z| < 2\pi).$$

These numbers (polynomials) are fascinating objects, appearing in many mathematical branches such as number theory, combinatorics and analysis. The basic properties of Bernoulli numbers and polynomials are discussed in [1,2].

Closely related to Bernoulli polynomials are the Euler and Genocchi polynomials. These polynomials are defined for $|z| < \pi$ by

$$\sum_{n=0}^{\infty} E_n(x) \frac{z^n}{n!} = \frac{2}{e^z + 1} e^{xz} \quad \text{and} \quad \sum_{n=0}^{\infty} G_n(x) \frac{z^n}{n!} = \frac{2z}{e^z + 1} e^{xz}.$$

Finding recurrences and convolutions for these polynomials is still an active field of research. Many interesting identities for Bernoulli, Euler and Genocchi polynomials can be found in the articles [3–10] for instance. See [11–14] for some properties of generalizations of these polynomials.

The popularity and importance of Bernoulli numbers and polynomials in number theory comes also from their connection to the Riemann zeta function

$$\zeta(2n) = (-1)^{n+1} \frac{(2\pi)^{2n}}{2 \cdot (2n)!} B_{2n},$$

where

$$\zeta(s) = \sum_{n=1}^{\infty} \frac{1}{n^s}, \quad \Re(s) > 1,$$

is the Riemann zeta function [15]. A great deal of proof for this relation has been provided over the years. See [16] for references. Recently, Merca [16] proved the following relation between Bernoulli numbers:

$$\sum_{k=0}^{n} \binom{n}{k} 2^k B_k = (2 - 2^n) B_n. \tag{1}$$

This relation can be used to derive a recurrence relation for $\zeta(2n)$. Moreover, in his next article on the topic, Merca [17] used recurrence relations for Bernoulli polynomials $B_n(x)$ to derive two new infinite families of linear recurrence relations for the Riemann zeta function at positive even integer arguments. Merca's elegant results are based on the following relations (Theorems 2.1 and 3.1 in [17]): Let n be a positive integer and $x, \alpha \in \mathbb{C}$. Then

$$\sum_{k=0}^{n} \binom{n}{k} B_k(x) \left(\alpha^{n-k} - (-1)^k (2x - 1 + \alpha)^{n-k} \right) = 0, \tag{2}$$

and

$$\sum_{k=0}^{\lfloor n/2 \rfloor} \binom{n}{2k} \alpha^{2k} B_{n-2k}(x) = \sum_{k=0}^{n} \binom{n}{k} (-1)^{n-k} \frac{(2x-1+\alpha)^k + (2x-1-\alpha)^k}{2} B_{n-k}(x). \tag{3}$$

In fact, identities Equations (1) and (2) have been widely known and used already in the 19th century as immediate consequences of the simple functional relations

$$B(2z)(e^z + 1) = 2B(z) \quad \text{and} \quad B(x,z)e^{yz} = B(x,-z)e^{(2x-1+y)z}.$$

It may be very difficult to identify the first pioneers who discovered them after all this time. We refer to the notable books by Saalschütz [18], Nielsen [19] and Hansen [20] as a resource in which a large number of classical identities, mainly developed in the 18th and the 19th centuries, can be found. In addition, Equation (1) can be extended to [21]

$$\sum_{k=0}^{n} \binom{n}{k} m^k B_k \sum_{i=0}^{m-1} i^{n-k} = m B_n,$$

valid for all integers $m \geq 1$. Thus, Equation (1) is the special case for $m = 2$. Next, we can define the function $\Phi_n^{(m)}(x,y)$, $m \geq 1$, $x, y \in \mathbb{C}$, by

$$\Phi_n^{(m)}(x,y) = \sum_{k=0}^{n} \binom{n}{k} m^k B_k(x) y^{n-k}.$$

Then, the following identity has been known for a long time:

$$\Phi_n^{(m)}(x,y) = \sum_{k=0}^{n} \binom{n}{k} (-m)^k B_k(x) (2mx - m + y)^{n-k}, \quad m \geq 1. \tag{4}$$

The identity Equation (4) reduces to Equation (2) when $m = 1$ and $y = \alpha$. It is easy to see that $\Phi_n^{(m)}(x,y)$ satisfies the following functional equation.

Proposition 1. *For all $m, n \in \mathbb{N}$ the following functional equation holds:*

$$\Phi_n^{(m)}(x, -(2mx - m + y)) = (-1)^n \Phi_n^{(m)}(x, y). \tag{5}$$

In addition, we can examine a calculation of the sum $\Phi_n^{(m)}(x, y) + \Phi_n^{(m)}(x, -y)$. We have

$$\Phi_n^{(m)}(x, y) + \Phi_n^{(m)}(x, -y) = \begin{cases} 2\sum_{l=0}^{\lfloor n/2 \rfloor} \binom{n}{2l} m^{n-2l} B_{n-2l}(x) y^{2l}, & \text{if } n - k = 2l; \\ 0, & \text{otherwise.} \end{cases}$$

In view of such an identity, we recognize that Equation (3) is an obvious consequence of Equation (2). Finally, we remark that if $n - k$ is odd, then $\Phi_n^{(m)}(x, y) = -\Phi_n^{(m)}(x, -y)$, i.e., the function $\Phi_n^{(m)}(x, y)$ is an odd or asymmetric function with respect to y.

We conclude this section by recalling the definition of $B_n^{(r,m)}(x)$, which comes from [22].

Definition 1. *For integers $r, m \geq 1$ the generalized Bernoulli polynomials of order (r, m) are defined by the generating function*

$$B(r, m; x, z) = \sum_{n=0}^{\infty} B_n^{(r,m)}(x) \frac{z^n}{n!} = \left(\frac{z^r}{e^z - 1}\right)^m e^{xz} \quad (|z| < 2\pi). \tag{6}$$

The numbers $B_n^{(r,m)}(0) = B_n^{(r,m)}$ are called generalized Bernoulli numbers of order r and m.

The polynomials $B_n^{(r,m)}(x)$ belong to the family of Appell polynomials. We mention that they are defined for $n \geq m(r-1)$, i.e., $B_j^{(r,m)}(x) = 0$ for $j < m(r-1)$. From the definition, it is obvious that $B_n^{(1,1)}(x) = B_n(x)$ and $B_n^{(1,m)}(x) = B_n^{(m)}(x)$ are the generalized Bernoulli polynomials of order m. Moreover, $B_n^{(1,1)} = B_n$ are the Bernoulli numbers.

The goal of the present article is to derive several convolutions for generalized Bernoulli polynomials of order (r, m), $B_n^{(r,m)}(x)$. First, we will generalize Merca's results for Bernoulli polynomials to the more general class of polynomials. This will be performed in Section 2. In Section 3, we will prove the analogue identities for generalized Euler–Genocchi polynomials $A_n^{(r,m)}(x)$. A range of additional convolutions for $B_n^{(r,m)}(x)$ and $A_n^{(r,m)}(x)$ will be given in Section 4. Among other things, we will rediscover identity Equation (1) as a special case of our findings. In Sections 5 and 6 we will state some additional remarks concerning applications and future work.

2. Notes on Merca's Identities

Our first result is an extension of Theorem 2.1 of [17].

Theorem 1. *Let r and m be positive integers and $x, y \in \mathbb{C}$. Then,*

$$\sum_{k=0}^{n} \binom{n}{k} B_k^{(r,m)}(x) \left(y^{n-k} - (-1)^{m(r-1)+k} (2x - m + y)^{n-k} \right) = 0. \tag{7}$$

Especially, with $y = m$, we have

$$\sum_{k=0}^{n} \binom{n}{k} B_k^{(r,m)}(x) \left(m^{n-k} - (-1)^{m(r-1)+k} (2x)^{n-k} \right) = 0. \tag{8}$$

Proof. For $|z| < 2\pi$ we have from Equation (6)

$$\left(\sum_{n=0}^{\infty} B_n^{(r,m)}(x)\frac{z^n}{n!}\right)\left(\sum_{n=0}^{\infty} y^n\frac{z^n}{n!}\right) = \left(\frac{z^r}{e^z-1}\right)^m e^{xz}e^{yz}$$

$$= \frac{z^{rm}}{(-1)^m(e^{-z}-1)^m} e^{-xz}e^{(y+2x-m)z}$$

$$= (-1)^{m(r-1)}\left(\frac{(-z)^r}{e^{-z}-1}\right)^m e^{-xz}e^{(y+2x-m)z}$$

$$= (-1)^{m(r-1)} B(r,m;x,-z) e^{(y+2x-m)z}$$

$$= (-1)^{m(r-1)}\left(\sum_{n=0}^{\infty} B_n^{(r,m)}(x)(-1)^n\frac{z^n}{n!}\right)\left(\sum_{n=0}^{\infty} (y+2x-m)^n\frac{z^n}{n!}\right)$$

$$= \sum_{n=0}^{\infty}\left(\sum_{k=0}^{n}\binom{n}{k}(-1)^{m(r-1)+k} B_k^{(r,m)}(x)(y+2x-m)^{n-k}\right)\frac{z^n}{n!}.$$

On the other hand, using Cauchy's rule, it is obvious that

$$\left(\sum_{n=0}^{\infty} B_n^{(r,m)}(x)\frac{z^n}{n!}\right)\left(\sum_{n=0}^{\infty} y^n\frac{z^n}{n!}\right) = \sum_{n=0}^{\infty}\left(\sum_{k=0}^{n}\binom{n}{k} B_k^{(r,m)}(x)y^{n-k}\right)\frac{z^n}{n!}.$$

Comparing the coefficients for z^n in the two power series proves the formula. □

For $(r,m) = (1,1)$ Theorem 1 reduces to Merca's Theorem 2.1. For $(r,m) = (1,m)$ our theorem gives a convolutional relation for generalized Bernoulli polynomials:

Corollary 1. *For $x, y \in \mathbb{C}$ the following relation holds for generalized Bernoulli polynomials:*

$$\sum_{k=0}^{n}\binom{n}{k} B_k^{(m)}(x)(y^{n-k} + (-1)^{k+1}(2x-m+y)^{n-k}) = 0. \tag{9}$$

Corollary 2. *For $x \in \mathbb{C}$ the following relation holds:*

$$B_n^{(r,m)}(x) = \sum_{k=0}^{n}\binom{n}{k}(-1)^{m(r-1)+k} B_k^{(r,m)}(x)(2x-m)^{n-k}. \tag{10}$$

Especially for the generalized Bernoulli polynomials we have the identity

$$B_n^{(m)}(x) = \sum_{k=0}^{n}\binom{n}{k}(-1)^k B_k^{(m)}(x)(2x-m)^{n-k}. \tag{11}$$

Proof. Set $y = 0$ in Theorem 1. □

Next, for $x, y \in \mathbb{C}$, we define the function

$$F_n^{(r,m)}(x,y) = \sum_{k=0}^{n}\binom{n}{k} B_k^{(r,m)}(x)y^{n-k}, \quad r, m \geq 1. \tag{12}$$

Then, we note the following functional equation:

Proposition 2. *For all $r, m, n \in \mathbb{N}$ the following functional equation holds:*

$$F_n^{(r,m)}(x, -(2mx-m+y)) = (-1)^{n+m(r-1)} F_n^{(r,m)}(x,y). \tag{13}$$

Proof. Replacing y with $-(2x-m+y)$ in Equation (12), using Equation (7), we get the result. □

We can also calculate

$$F_n^{(r,m)}(x,y) + F_n^{(r,m)}(x,-y) = \begin{cases} 2\sum_{l=0}^{\lfloor n/2 \rfloor} \binom{n}{2l} B_{n-2l}^{(r,m)}(x) y^{2l}, & \text{if } n-k = 2l; \\ 0, & \text{otherwise,} \end{cases}$$

and

$$F_n^{(r,m)}(x,y) - F_n^{(r,m)}(x,-y) = \begin{cases} 2\sum_{l=0}^{\lfloor (n-1)/2 \rfloor} \binom{n}{2l+1} B_{n-2l-1}^{(r,m)}(x) y^{2l+1}, & \text{if } n-k = 2l+1; \\ 0, & \text{otherwise.} \end{cases}$$

These calculations confirm the following facts.

(i) If $n-k$ is odd, then $F_n^{(r,m)}(x,y) = -F_n^{(r,m)}(x,-y)$, i.e., the function $F_n^{(r,m)}(x,y)$ is an odd or asymmetric function with respect to y.

(ii) If $n-k$ is even, then $F_n^{(r,m)}(x,y) = F_n^{(r,m)}(x,-y)$, i.e., the function $F_n^{(r,m)}(x,y)$ is an even or symmetric function with respect to y.

The above observations lead to the next corollary, which provides an extension of Theorem 3.1 of [17] to the class $B_n^{(r,m)}(x)$.

Corollary 3. *Let r and m be positive integers and $x, y \in \mathbb{C}$. Then,*

$$\sum_{k=0}^{\lfloor \frac{n}{2} \rfloor} \binom{n}{2k} y^{2k} B_{n-2k}^{(r,m)}(x)$$

$$= (-1)^{m(r-1)} \sum_{k=0}^{n} \binom{n}{k} (-1)^{n-k} \frac{(2x-m+y)^k + (2x-m-y)^k}{2} B_{n-k}^{(r,m)}(x) \quad (14)$$

and

$$\sum_{k=0}^{\lfloor \frac{n-1}{2} \rfloor} \binom{n}{2k+1} y^{2k+1} B_{n-2k-1}^{(r,m)}(x)$$

$$= (-1)^{m(r-1)} \sum_{k=0}^{n} \binom{n}{k} (-1)^{n-k} \frac{(2x-m+y)^k - (2x-m-y)^k}{2} B_{n-k}^{(r,m)}(x). \quad (15)$$

We conclude this section with the following results.

Corollary 4. *Let r and m be positive integers and $x, y \in \mathbb{C}$. Then,*

$$\sum_{k=0}^{\lfloor \frac{n}{2} \rfloor} \binom{n}{2k} (-1)^k y^{2k} B_{n-2k}^{(r,m)}(x)$$

$$= (-1)^{m(r-1)} \sum_{k=0}^{n} \binom{n}{k} (-1)^{n-k} B_{n-k}^{(r,m)}(x) \sum_{p=0}^{k} \binom{k}{p} y^p \cos\left(\frac{\pi p}{2}\right) (2x-m)^{k-p} \quad (16)$$

and

$$\sum_{k=0}^{\lfloor \frac{n-1}{2} \rfloor} \binom{n}{2k+1} (-1)^k y^{2k+1} B_{n-2k-1}^{(r,m)}(x)$$

$$= (-1)^{m(r-1)} \sum_{k=0}^{n} \binom{n}{k} (-1)^{n-k} B_{n-k}^{(r,m)}(x) \sum_{p=0}^{k} \binom{k}{p} y^p \sin\left(\frac{\pi p}{2}\right) (2x-m)^{k-p}. \quad (17)$$

Proof. Replace y by iy with $i = \sqrt{-1}$ in Corollary 3 and simplify. □

Corollary 5. Let r and m be positive integers and $x \in \mathbb{C}$. Then,

$$\sum_{k=0}^{\lfloor \frac{n}{2} \rfloor} \binom{n}{2k}(-1)^k m^{2k} B_{n-2k}^{(r,m)}(x)$$

$$= (-1)^{m(r-1)} \sum_{k=0}^{n} \binom{n}{k}(-1)^{n-k} 2^{k-1}(x^k + (x-m)^k) B_{n-k}^{(r,m)}(x) \qquad (18)$$

and

$$\sum_{k=0}^{\lfloor \frac{n-1}{2} \rfloor} \binom{n}{2k+1}(-1)^k m^{2k+1} B_{n-2k-1}^{(r,m)}(x)$$

$$= (-1)^{m(r-1)} \sum_{k=0}^{n} \binom{n}{k}(-1)^{n-k} 2^{k-1}(x^k - (x-m)^k) B_{n-k}^{(r,m)}(x). \qquad (19)$$

Proof. Set $y = m$ in Corollary 3 and simplify. □

3. Analogue Relations for Generalized Euler–Genocchi Polynomials

The definition of generalized Euler–Genocchi polynomials of order (r, m) also comes from the paper [22], where many basic properties of the polynomials are discussed.

Definition 2. Let r and m be integers with $r \geq 0$ and $m \geq 1$. The generalized Euler–Genocchi polynomials of order (r, m), $A_n^{(r,m)}(x)$, $x \in \mathbb{C}$, are defined by the generating function

$$A(r, m; x, z) = \sum_{n=0}^{\infty} A_n^{(r,m)}(x) \frac{z^n}{n!} = \left(\frac{2z^r}{e^z + 1}\right)^m e^{xz} \qquad (|z| < \pi) \qquad (20)$$

with $A_j^{(r,m)}(x) = 0$ for $j < rm$. The numbers $A_n^{(r,m)}(0) = A_n^{(r,m)}$ are called the generalized Euler–Genocchi numbers of order r and m.

We see that $A_n^{(0,m)}(x) = E_n^{(m)}(x)$ and $A_n^{(1,m)}(x) = G_n^{(m)}(x)$ are the generalized Euler and Genocchi polynomials, respectively, where

$$\sum_{n=0}^{\infty} E_n^{(m)}(x) \frac{z^n}{n!} = \left(\frac{2}{e^z + 1}\right)^m e^{xz} \qquad (|z| < \pi) \qquad (21)$$

and

$$\sum_{n=0}^{\infty} G_n^{(m)}(x) \frac{z^n}{n!} = \left(\frac{2z}{e^z + 1}\right)^m e^{xz} \qquad (|z| < \pi). \qquad (22)$$

Finally, we mention that the degenerated case $m = 0$ gives $A_n^{(r,0)}(x) = x^n$ for all $r \geq 0$. The first analogue result of Merca's identities is stated in the next theorem.

Theorem 2. Let r and m be integers with $r \geq 0$ and $m \geq 1$, and $x, y \in \mathbb{C}$. Then,

$$\sum_{k=0}^{n} \binom{n}{k} A_k^{(r,m)}(x)(y^{n-k} - (-1)^{mr+k}(2x - m + y)^{n-k}) = 0. \qquad (23)$$

Especially, with $y = m$, we have

$$\sum_{k=0}^{n} \binom{n}{k} A_k^{(r,m)}(x)(m^{n-k} - (-1)^{mr+k}(2x)^{n-k}) = 0. \qquad (24)$$

Proof. Due to the high degree of similarity in the proofs, we only sketch the proofs. The identity basically follows from

$$A(r,m;x,z)e^{yz} = \left(\frac{2z^r}{e^z+1}\right)^m e^{xz}e^{yz} = (-1)^{mr}\left(\frac{2(-z)^r}{e^{-z}+1}\right)^m e^{-xz}e^{(2x+y-m)z}.$$

□

Corollary 6. *For $x, y \in \mathbb{C}$ the following relations hold:*

$$\sum_{k=0}^{n}\binom{n}{k}E_k^{(m)}(x)(y^{n-k}+(-1)^{k+1}(2x-m+y)^{n-k}) = 0 \qquad (25)$$

and

$$\sum_{k=0}^{n}\binom{n}{k}G_k^{(m)}(x)(y^{n-k}+(-1)^{m+k+1}(2x-m+y)^{n-k}) = 0. \qquad (26)$$

Proof. Set $r = 0$ and $r = 1$ in Theorem 2. □

Corollary 7. *For $x \in \mathbb{C}$ the following relation holds:*

$$A_n^{(r,m)}(x) = \sum_{k=0}^{n}\binom{n}{k}(-1)^{mr+k}A_k^{(r,m)}(x)(2x-m)^{n-k}. \qquad (27)$$

Proof. Set $y = 0$ in Theorem 2. □

Theorem 3. *Let r and m be integers with $r \geq 0$ and $m \geq 1$, and $x, y \in \mathbb{C}$. Then,*

$$\sum_{k=0}^{\lfloor\frac{n}{2}\rfloor}\binom{n}{2k}y^{2k}A_{n-2k}^{(r,m)}(x)$$

$$= (-1)^{mr}\sum_{k=0}^{n}\binom{n}{k}(-1)^{n-k}\frac{(2x-m+y)^k+(2x-m-y)^k}{2}A_{n-k}^{(r,m)}(x) \qquad (28)$$

and

$$\sum_{k=0}^{\lfloor\frac{n-1}{2}\rfloor}\binom{n}{2k+1}y^{2k+1}A_{n-2k-1}^{(r,m)}(x)$$

$$= (-1)^{mr}\sum_{k=0}^{n}\binom{n}{k}(-1)^{n-k}\frac{(2x-m+y)^k-(2x-m-y)^k}{2}A_{n-k}^{(r,m)}(x). \qquad (29)$$

Proof. The proof follows the same arguments as the proof of Theorem 3. □

The special cases where y is replaced by iy and $y = m$ are obvious. We continue skipping the presentation of these explicit results.

4. More Convolutions for $B_n^{(r,m)}(x)$ and $A_n^{(r,m)}(x)$

In this section, several other convolutions for $B_n^{(r,m)}(x)$ and $A_n^{(r,m)}(x)$ are derived. The first two theorems contain convolutions involving $B_n^{(r,m)}(x)$ and powers of 2.

Theorem 4. *Let r and m be positive integers and $x, y \in \mathbb{C}$. Then*

$$\sum_{k=0}^{n}\binom{n}{k}2^k B_k^{(r,m)}(x)y^{n-k} = 2^{m(r-1)}\sum_{k=0}^{n}\binom{n}{k}B_k^{(r,m)}(2x+y)E_{n-k}^{(m)}(0), \qquad (30)$$

where $E_n^{(m)}(x)$ is the generalized Euler polynomial of order m.

Proof. For $|z| < 2\pi$ we have from Equation (6)

$$B(r, m; x, 2z)e^{yz} = \left(\sum_{n=0}^{\infty} 2^n B_n^{(r,m)}(x) \frac{z^n}{n!}\right)\left(\sum_{n=0}^{\infty} y^n \frac{z^n}{n!}\right)$$

$$= \sum_{n=0}^{\infty} \left(\sum_{k=0}^{n} \binom{n}{k} 2^k B_k^{(r,m)}(x) y^{n-k}\right) \frac{z^n}{n!}.$$

On the other hand, we observe that

$$B(r, m; x, 2z)e^{yz} = 2^{rm}\left(\frac{z^r}{e^{2z}-1}\right)^m e^{(2x+y)z}$$

$$= 2^{m(r-1)}\left(\frac{z^r}{e^z-1}\right)^m e^{(2x+y)z}\left(\frac{2}{e^z+1}\right)^m$$

$$= 2^{m(r-1)}\left(\sum_{n=0}^{\infty} B_n^{(r,m)}(2x+y)\frac{z^n}{n!}\right)\left(\sum_{n=0}^{\infty} E_n^{(m)}(0)\frac{z^n}{n!}\right)$$

Comparing the coefficients for z^n in the two power series proves the formula. □

Remark 1. *From the above proof, it is clear that we can also write*

$$\sum_{k=0}^{n} \binom{n}{k} 2^k B_k^{(r,m)}(x) y^{n-k} = 2^{m(r-1)} \sum_{k=0}^{n} \binom{n}{k} B_k^{(r,m)}(x+y) E_{n-k}^{(m)}(x)$$

$$= 2^{m(r-1)} \sum_{k=0}^{n} \binom{n}{k} B_k^{(r,m)}(x) E_{n-k}^{(m)}(x+y)$$

$$= 2^{m(r-1)} \sum_{k=0}^{n} \binom{n}{k} B_k^{(r,m)}(y) E_{n-k}^{(m)}(2x).$$

Corollary 8. *Let r and m be positive integers and $x \in \mathbb{C}$. Then,*

$$2^n B_n^{(r,m)}(x) = 2^{m(r-1)} \sum_{k=0}^{n} \binom{n}{k} B_k^{(r,m)}(2x) E_{n-k}^{(m)}(0), \tag{31}$$

$$\sum_{k=0}^{n} \binom{n}{k} (-1)^{n-k} 2^k B_k^{(r,m)}(x) x^{n-k} = 2^{m(r-1)} \sum_{k=0}^{n} \binom{n}{k} B_k^{(r,m)}(x) E_{n-k}^{(m)}(0) \tag{32}$$

and

$$\sum_{k=0}^{n} \binom{n}{k} (-1)^{n-k} B_k^{(r,m)}(x) x^{n-k} = 2^{m(r-1)-n} \sum_{k=0}^{n} \binom{n}{k} B_k^{(r,m)}(0) E_{n-k}^{(m)}(0). \tag{33}$$

Proof. Set $y = 0, y = -x$ and $y = -2x$ in (30), respectively. □

Evidently, the sums in the Corollary contain some interesting special cases. The evaluations with $(r, m) = (1, 1)$, and $x = 0$ and $x = 1/2$, respectively, yield the following identities for Bernoulli numbers:

$$\sum_{k=0}^{n-1} \binom{n}{k} \frac{2 - 2^{n+2-k}}{n+1-k} B_k B_{n+1-k} = (2^n - 1) B_n, \tag{34}$$

$$\sum_{k=0}^{n-1} \binom{n}{k} (-1)^k \frac{2 - 2^{n+2-k}}{n+1-k} B_k B_{n+1-k} = (2 - 2^n - (-1)^n) B_n, \tag{35}$$

$$\sum_{k=0}^{n-1} \binom{n}{k}(-1)^{n-k}(1-2^{k-1})B_k = (2^n-1)B_n \qquad (36)$$

and

$$\sum_{k=0}^{n}\binom{n}{k}(-1)^{n-k}2^k(2^{1-k}-1)B_k = -2^{n+1}\sum_{k=0}^{n}\binom{n}{k}\frac{(2^{1-k}-1)(2^{n+1-k}-1)}{n+1-k}B_kB_{n+1-k}, \qquad (37)$$

where we have employed the following relations

$$E_{n-1}(x) = \frac{2}{n}(B_n(x) - 2^n B_n(x/2)),$$

and

$$B_n(1/2) = (2^{1-n} - 1)B_n.$$

It is difficult to say whether the Bernoulli identities Equations (34)–(37) are original. We could not find them in the book [20]. Hence, they are maybe not classical. However, they may have appeared elsewhere before. Furthermore, setting $r = m = 1$, $x = 0$ and $y = 1$ in Equation (30) gives

$$\sum_{k=0}^{n}\binom{n}{k}2^k B_k = \sum_{k=0}^{n}\binom{n}{k}B_k(1)E_{n-k}(0) = 2^n B_n(1/2), \qquad (38)$$

where we have used Equation (31). Hence, we rediscover Merca's identity Equation (1).

Theorem 5. *Let r and m be positive integers and $x, y \in \mathbb{C}$. Then,*

$$\sum_{k=0}^{n}\binom{n}{k}2^k B_k^{(r,m)}(x)y^{n-k} = 2^{m(r-1)}\sum_{j=0}^{m}\binom{m}{j}(-1)^{m-j}2^j\sum_{k=0}^{n}\binom{n}{k}B_k^{(r,m)}(0)E_{n-k}^{(m-j)}(2x-m+y), \qquad (39)$$

where $E_n^{(m)}(x)$ is the generalized Euler polynomial of order m.

Proof. The identity follows from

$$\begin{aligned}
B(r,m;x,2z)e^{yz} &= 2^{rm}\left(\frac{z^r}{e^{2z}-1}\right)^m e^{(2x+y)z} \\
&= 2^{rm}e^{(2x-m+y)z}\left(\frac{z^r}{e^z-1} - \frac{z^r}{e^{2z}-1}\right)^m \\
&= 2^{rm}e^{(2x-m+y)z}\left(\sum_{j=0}^{m}\binom{m}{j}(-1)^{m-j}\left(\frac{z^r}{e^z-1}\right)^j\left(\frac{z^r}{e^{2z}-1}\right)^{m-j}\right) \\
&= 2^{rm}\left(\frac{z^r}{e^z-1}\right)^m e^{(2x-m+y)z}\left(\sum_{j=0}^{m}\binom{m}{j}(-1)^{m-j}\left(\frac{1}{e^z+1}\right)^{m-j}\right) \\
&= 2^{rm}\left(\frac{z^r}{e^z-1}\right)^m\left(\sum_{j=0}^{m}\binom{m}{j}(-1)^{m-j}2^{j-m}\left(\frac{2}{e^z+1}\right)^{m-j}e^{(2x-m+y)z}\right) \\
&= 2^{r(m-1)}\sum_{j=0}^{m}\binom{m}{j}(-1)^{m-j}2^j\left(\frac{z^r}{e^z-1}\right)^m\left(\frac{2}{e^z+1}\right)^{m-j}e^{(2x-m+y)z}.
\end{aligned}$$

□

Corollary 9. *For $x, y \in \mathbb{C}$ the generalized Bernoulli polynomials of order (r, m) satisfy the following relation:*

$$\sum_{k=0}^{n}\binom{n}{k}(-1)^{k-m(r-1)}2^k B_k^{(r,m)}(x)y^{n-k}$$
$$= 2^{m(r-1)}\sum_{j=0}^{m}\binom{m}{j}(-1)^{m-j}2^j\sum_{k=0}^{n}\binom{n}{k}B_k^{(r,m)}(0)E_{n-k}^{(m-j)}(m+y-2x). \qquad (40)$$

Proof. Replace x with $m - x$ and use the reciprocal relation (see [22])

$$B_n^{(r,m)}(m - x) = (-1)^{n-m(r-1)} B_n^{(r,m)}(x). \tag{41}$$

□

Setting $r = m = 1$ and using the fact that $E_n^{(0)}(x) = x^n$, we obtain:

Corollary 10. *For $x, y \in \mathbb{C}$ the Bernoulli polynomials satisfy the following relation:*

$$\sum_{k=0}^{n} \binom{n}{k} 2^k B_k(x) y^{n-k} = \sum_{k=0}^{n} \binom{n}{k} B_k (2(2x - 1 + y)^{n-k} - E_{n-k}(2x - 1 + y)) \tag{42}$$

and

$$\sum_{k=0}^{n} \binom{n}{k} (-1)^k 2^k B_k(x) y^{n-k} = \sum_{k=0}^{n} \binom{n}{k} B_k (2(1 + y - 2x)^{n-k} - E_{n-k}(1 + y - 2x)). \tag{43}$$

Inserting $x = (1 - y)/2$ in Equation (42) or $x = (1 + y)/2$ in Equation (43) yields

$$\sum_{k=0}^{n} \binom{n}{k} 2^k B_k \left(\frac{1-y}{2}\right) y^{n-k} = (2 - 2^n) B_n \tag{44}$$

and

$$\sum_{k=0}^{n} \binom{n}{k} (-1)^k 2^k B_k \left(\frac{1+y}{2}\right) y^{n-k} = (2 - 2^n) B_n \tag{45}$$

for each $y \in \mathbb{C}$. We can see that $y = 1$ or $y = -1$ produce Merca's identity Equation (1). It is also worth mentioning the special cases of the above results for y being a power of 2.

We now focus on presenting other types of convolutions. Some types follow straightforwardly from the definitions Equations (6) and (20). For instance, it is fairly easy to deduce that for each integer $p \geq 0$ and $x, y \in \mathbb{C}$

$$\sum_{k=0}^{n} \binom{n}{k} B_k^{(r,m)}(x) B_{n-k}^{(r,p)}(y) = B_n^{(r,m+p)}(x+y)$$

and

$$\sum_{k=0}^{n} \binom{n}{k} A_k^{(r,m)}(x) A_{n-k}^{(r,p)}(y) = A_n^{(r,m+p)}(x+y).$$

Setting $p = x = 0$ corresponds to the representation

$$\sum_{k=0}^{n} \binom{n}{k} B_k^{(r,m)} x^{n-k} = B_n^{(r,m)}(x) \quad \text{and} \quad \sum_{k=0}^{n} \binom{n}{k} A_k^{(r,m)} x^{n-k} = A_n^{(r,m)}(x).$$

Theorem 6. *For $m, p \geq 0$ and $x, y \in \mathbb{C}$ we have*

$$\begin{aligned}&\sum_{k=0}^{n} \binom{n}{k} B_k^{(r,m)}(x) B_{n-k}^{(r,p)}(y) = \\ &\sum_{k=0}^{n} \binom{n}{k} (-1)^{(r-1)(m+p)+k} B_k^{(r,m+p)}(x)(2x + y - (m+p))^{n-k}\end{aligned} \tag{46}$$

and

$$\begin{aligned}&\sum_{k=0}^{n} \binom{n}{k} A_k^{(r,m)}(x) A_{n-k}^{(r,p)}(y) = \\ &\sum_{k=0}^{n} \binom{n}{k} (-1)^{r(m+p)+k} A_k^{(r,m+p)}(x)(2x + y - (m+p))^{n-k}.\end{aligned} \tag{47}$$

Proof. The first identity follows from

$$\left(\frac{z^r}{e^z - 1}\right)^m e^{xz} \cdot \left(\frac{z^r}{e^z - 1}\right)^p e^{yz} = (-1)^{(r-1)(m+p)} \left(\frac{(-z)^r}{e^{-z} - 1}\right)^{m+p} e^{-xz} e^{(2x+y-(m+p))z}.$$

The other one can be proved similarly. □

Theorem 7. For $r, m \geq 1$ and $x, y \in \mathbb{C}$, we have the following convolution

$$m \sum_{k=0}^{n} \binom{n}{k} B_k^{(r,m)}(x) B_{n-k}^{(r,1)}(y+1-m) = (x+y-m)(n)_r B_{n-r}^{(r,m)}(x+y-m)$$
$$- (n+1-r(m+1))(n)_{r-1} B_{n+1-r}^{(r,m)}(x+y-m), \quad (48)$$

where $(n)_r$ denotes the falling factorial defined by

$$(n)_r = \begin{cases} 1, & r = 0; \\ n(n-1)\cdots(n-r+1), & r \geq 1. \end{cases} \quad (49)$$

Proof. Since

$$\frac{d}{dz} \frac{e^{(x+y-m)z}}{(e^z-1)^m} = (x+y-m) \frac{e^{(x+y-m)z}}{(e^z-1)^m} - m \frac{e^{(x+y+1-m)z}}{(e^z-1)^{m+1}},$$

we have the relation

$$m \left(\frac{z^r}{e^z-1} \right)^{m+1} e^{(x+y+1-m)z} = (x+y-m) z^r \left(\frac{z^r}{e^z-1} \right)^m e^{(x+y-m)z} - z^{r(m+1)} \frac{d}{dz} \frac{e^{(x+y-m)z}}{(e^z-1)^m}.$$

□

Replacing x with $m - x$ and using (41), we immediately get the alternating version of Theorem 7.

Corollary 11. For $r, m \geq 1$ and $x, y \in \mathbb{C}$ we have the following convolution

$$m \sum_{k=0}^{n} \binom{n}{k} (-1)^{k-m(r-1)} B_k^{(r,m)}(x) B_{n-k}^{(r,1)}(y+1-m) = (y-x)(n)_r B_{n-r}^{(r,m)}(y-x)$$
$$- (n+1-r(m+1))(n)_{r-1} B_{n+1-r}^{(r,m)}(y-x). \quad (50)$$

For $(r, m) = (1, m)$ the above results reduce to convolutions for generalized Bernoulli polynomials:

$$m \sum_{k=0}^{n} \binom{n}{k} B_k^{(m)}(x) B_{n-k}(y+1-m) = (x+y-m) n B_{n-1}^{(m)}(x+y-m)$$
$$- (n-m) B_n^{(m)}(x+y-m), \quad (51)$$

and

$$m \sum_{k=0}^{n} \binom{n}{k} (-1)^k B_k^{(m)}(x) B_{n-k}(y+1-m) = (y-x) n B_{n-1}^{(m)}(y-x) - (n-m) B_n^{(m)}(y-x). \quad (52)$$

These results generalize the known convolutions for Bernoulli polynomials, which are obtained for $(r, m) = (1, 1)$. The analogue convolution for $A_n^{(r,m)}(x)$ is given next.

Theorem 8. For $r, m \geq 1$ and $x, y \in \mathbb{C}$, the following convolution result holds:

$$m \sum_{k=0}^{n} \binom{n}{k} A_k^{(r,m)}(x) A_{n-k}^{(r,1)}(y+1-m) = 2(x+y-m)(n)_r A_{n-r}^{(r,m)}(x+y-m)$$
$$- 2(n+1-r(m+1))(n)_{r-1} A_{n+1-r}^{(r,m)}(x+y-m). \quad (53)$$

For $r = 0$, the result becomes

$$m \sum_{k=0}^{n} \binom{n}{k} E_k^{(m)}(x) E_{n-k}(y+1-m) = 2(x+y-m) E_n^{(m)}(x+y-m) - 2E_{n+1}^{(m)}(x+y-m). \quad (54)$$

Proof. Use

$$m \left(\frac{2z^r}{e^z+1}\right)^{m+1} e^{(x+y+1-m)z} = 2(x+y-m) z^r \left(\frac{2z^r}{e^z+1}\right)^m e^{(x+y-m)z} - 2^{m+1} z^{r(m+1)} \frac{d}{dz} \frac{e^{(x+y-m)z}}{(e^z+1)^m}.$$

□

Corollary 12. For $r, m \geq 1$ and $x, y \in \mathbb{C}$ the following convolution result holds:

$$m \sum_{k=0}^{n} \binom{n}{k} (-1)^{k-rm} A_k^{(r,m)}(x) A_{n-k}^{(r,1)}(y+1-m) = 2(y-x)(n)_r A_{n-r}^{(r,m)}(y-x)$$

$$-2(n+1-r(m+1))(n)_{r-1} A_{n+1-r}^{(r,m)}(y-x). \quad (55)$$

For $r = 0$ the result becomes

$$m \sum_{k=0}^{n} \binom{n}{k} (-1)^k E_k^{(m)}(x) E_{n-k}(y+1-m) = 2(y-x) E_n^{(m)}(y-x) - 2E_{n+1}^{(m)}(y-x). \quad (56)$$

Proof. This result follows from the reciprocal relation for $A_n^{(r,m)}(x)$ (see [22])

$$A_n^{(r,m)}(m-x) = (-1)^{n-mr} A_n^{(r,m)}(x). \quad (57)$$

□

Theorem 9. For $r, m \geq 1$ and $x, y \in \mathbb{C}$ the following convolution result holds:

$$2^n B_n^{(r,m)}\left(\frac{x+y}{2}\right) = 2^{m(r-1)} (n)_{rm} \sum_{k=0}^{n-rm} \binom{n-rm}{k} B_k^{(r,m)}(x) A_{n-rm-k}^{(r,m)}(y). \quad (58)$$

Proof. Use

$$\left(\frac{(2z)^r}{e^{2z}-1}\right)^m e^{(x+y)z} = 2^{m(r-1)} z^{-rm} \left(\frac{z^r}{e^z-1}\right)^m e^{xz} \left(\frac{2z^r}{e^z+1}\right)^m e^{yz}.$$

□

Upon replacing x with $m - x$ and y with $m - y$ and using Equations (41) and (57), we also get the alternating version of the previous result.

Corollary 13. For $r, m \geq 1$ and $x, y \in \mathbb{C}$ the following convolution result holds:

$$2^n B_n^{(r,m)}\left(m - \frac{x+y}{2}\right)$$
$$= (-1)^{n-m(r-1)} 2^{m(r-1)} (n)_{rm} \sum_{k=0}^{n-rm} \binom{n-rm}{k} B_k^{(r,m)}(x) A_{n-rm-k}^{(r,m)}(y). \quad (59)$$

The case $(r, m) = (1, 1)$ produces relations involving Bernoulli and Genocchi polynomials:

$$2^n B_n\left(\frac{x+y}{2}\right) = n \sum_{k=0}^{n-1} \binom{n-1}{k} B_k(x) G_{n-1-k}(y) \quad (60)$$

and
$$2^n B_n\left(1 - \frac{x+y}{2}\right) = (-1)^n n \sum_{k=0}^{n-1} \binom{n-1}{k} B_k(x) G_{n-1-k}(y). \tag{61}$$

5. Probabilistic Interpretation of Bernoulli and Euler–Genocchi Polynomials

In this section, we indicate a possible application of the polynomials discussed in this work.

Consider a probability measure space $(\Omega, \mathcal{F}, P)$, where Ω is a non-empty space, $\mathcal{F}$ is a σ-algebra of events and P is a probability measure on $\mathcal{F}$. Let X be a random variable which is a measurable real function on the probability space $(\Omega, \mathcal{F}, P)$, and let $p(x)$ be a probability density function of X. Then mathematical expectation and moments of order n of X are defined by

$$E[X] = \int_{-\infty}^{\infty} x p(x)\, dx \quad \text{and} \quad E[X^n] = \int_{-\infty}^{\infty} x^n p(x)\, dx,$$

with $E[X^1] = E[X]$. The moment-generating function of X is defined by

$$\mu(t) = E[e^{tX}] = \int_{-\infty}^{\infty} e^{tx} p(x)\, dx, \quad t \in \mathbb{R}.$$

The relation between the moment generating function $\mu(t)$ and and moments $E[X^n]$ is given by

$$\mu(t) = \sum_{k=0}^{\infty} \frac{t^k}{k!} E[X^k].$$

Suppose that (6), (20), (21) and (22) are moment-generating functions of random variables $X_1, X_2, \ldots, X_5$. Then,

$$E[X_1^n] = \frac{d^n}{dz^n}\left\{\left(\frac{z^r}{e^z - 1}\right)^m e^{xz}\right\}\bigg|_{z=0} = B_n^{(r,m)}(x),$$

$$E[X_2^n] = \frac{d^n}{dz^n}\left\{\left(\frac{z}{e^z - 1}\right)^m e^{xz}\right\}\bigg|_{z=0} = B_n^{(m)}(x),$$

$$E[X_3^n] = \frac{d^n}{dz^n}\left\{\left(\frac{2z^r}{e^z + 1}\right)^m e^{xz}\right\}\bigg|_{z=0} = A_n^{(r,m)}(x),$$

$$E[X_4^n] = \frac{d^n}{dz^n}\left\{\left(\frac{2}{e^z + 1}\right)^m e^{xz}\right\}\bigg|_{z=0} = E_n^{(m)}(x),$$

$$E[X_5^n] = \frac{d^n}{dz^n}\left\{\left(\frac{2z}{e^z + 1}\right)^m e^{xz}\right\}\bigg|_{z=0} = G_n^{(m)}(x).$$

Another interpretation is the next example. Let X be a discrete random variable on $(\Omega, \mathcal{F}, P)$. Then, we can define a probability distribution for X by

$$P(X = k) = \frac{\binom{n}{k} B_k^{(r,m)}}{B_n^{(r,m)}(1)}, \quad k = 0, 1, \ldots, n.$$

Note that

$$\sum_{k=0}^{n} P(X = k) = \frac{\sum_{k=0}^{n} \binom{n}{k} B_k^{(r,m)}}{B_n^{(r,m)}(1)} = \frac{B_n^{(r,m)}(1)}{B_n^{(r,m)}(1)} = 1.$$

Next, replacing k by $n - k$ in the identity

$$\sum_{k=0}^{n} \binom{n}{k} B_k^{(r,m)} x^{n-k} = B_n^{(r,m)}(x)$$

we get
$$\sum_{k=0}^{n}\binom{n}{k}B_{n-k}^{(r,m)}x^k = B_n^{(r,m)}(x),$$

which, upon differentiating with respect to x, yields
$$\sum_{k=0}^{n}k\binom{n}{k}B_{n-k}^{(r,m)}x^{k-1} = nB_{n-1}^{(r,m)}(x).$$

Inserting $x = 1$ gives
$$\sum_{k=0}^{n}k\binom{n}{k}B_{n-k}^{(r,m)} = nB_{n-1}^{(r,m)}(1),$$

which shows that
$$E[X] = nB_{n-1}^{(r,m)}(1).$$

In an analogous fashion, the quantity $A_n^{(r,m)}(x)$ can be interpreted probabilistically.

6. Conclusions and Future Work

In this paper, mainly focusing on convolutions, we established additional properties of the generalized Bernoulli and Euler–Genocchi polynomials $B_n^{(r,m)}(x)$ and $A_n^{(r,m)}(x)$, respectively. These properties provide generalizations of some known facts about generalized Bernoulli and Euler polynomials, respectively. In the future, we intend to work in two different directions. First, it seem desirable to find some new kinds of closed-form expressions for our polynomials (such as combinatorial, integral, hypergeometric and determinantal ones). Such expressions will provide us with new and significant properties of these polynomials. Second, it is possible to study the Apostol-type generalized polynomials $\mathfrak{B}_n^{(r,m)}(x;\lambda)$ associated with the complex parameter $\lambda \neq 0$, which are defined by the generating function

$$\mathfrak{B}(r,m;x,z;\lambda) = \left(\frac{z^r}{\lambda e^z - 1}\right)^m e^{xz} = \sum_{n=0}^{\infty} \mathfrak{B}_n^{(r,m)}(x;\lambda)\frac{z^n}{n!}.$$

Then, it is fairly easy to identify the relations $B(r,m;x,z) = \mathfrak{B}(r,m;x,z;1)$ and $A(r,m;x,z) = (-2)^m \mathfrak{B}(r,m;x,z;-1)$. Therefore, by means of $\mathfrak{B}_n^{(r,m)}(x;\lambda)$ it is possible to discuss both $B_n^{(r,m)}(x)$ and $A_n^{(r,m)}(x)$, at once.

Author Contributions: Conceptualization, R.F. and Ž.T.; Methodology, R.F. and Ž.T.; validation, R.F. and Ž.T.; formal analysis, R.F. and Ž.T.; writing—original draft preparation, R.F.; writing—review and editing, R.F. and Ž.T.; supervision, R.F. and Ž.T. All authors have read and agreed to the published version of the manuscript.

Funding: Ž.T. was supported of the Department of Mathematics, Faculty of Sciences, University of Ostrava.

Conflicts of Interest: The authors declare no conflict of interest.

References

1. Abramowitz, M.; Stegun, I.A. *Handbook of Mathematical Functions with Formulas, Graphs, and Mathematical Tables*; Dover Publications: New York, NY, USA, 1972.
2. Apostol, T.M. *Introduction to Analytic Number Theory*; Springer: Heidelberg/Berlin, Germany, 1976.
3. Agoh, T. Convolution identities for Bernoulli and Genocchi polynomials. *Electron. J. Combin.* **2014**, *21* 65. [CrossRef]
4. Agoh, T.; Dilcher, K. Convolution identities and lacunary recurrences for Bernoulli numbers. *J. Number Theory* **2007**, *124*, 105–122. [CrossRef]
5. Agoh, T.; Dilcher, K. Higher-order recurrences for Bernoulli numbers. *J. Number Theory* **2009**, *129*, 1837–1847. [CrossRef]
6. Agoh, T.; Dilcher, K. Shortened recurrence relations for Bernoulli numbers. *Discret. Math.* **2009**, *309*, 887–898. [CrossRef]
7. W. Chu and C. Y. Wang, Convolution formulae for Bernoulli numbers. *Integral Transforms Spec. Funct.* **2010**, *21*, 437–457. [CrossRef]
8. Chu, W.; Zhou, R. Convolutions of Bernoulli and Euler polynomials. *Sarajevo J. Math.* **2010**, *6*, 147–163.

9. Dilcher, K.; Vignat, C. General convolution identities for Bernoulli and Euler polynomials. *J. Math. Anal. Appl.* **2016**, *435*, 1478–1498. [CrossRef]
10. Srivastava, H.M.; Vignat, C. Probabilistic proofs of some relationships between the Bernoulli and Euler polynomials. *Eur. J. Pure Appl. Math.* **2012**, *5*, 97–107.
11. Dere, R.; Simsek, Y.; Srivastava, H.M. A unified presentation of three families of generalized Apostol-type polynomials based upon the theory of the umbral calculus and the umbral algebra. *J. Number Theory* **2013**, *133*, 3245–3263. [CrossRef]
12. Ozden, H.; Simsek, Y.; Srivastava, H.M. A unified presentation of the generating functions of the generalized Bernoulli, Euler and Genocchi polynomials. *Comput. Math. Appl.* **2010**, *60*, 2779–2787. [CrossRef]
13. Srivastava, H.M.; He, Y.; Araci, S.; Abdel-Aty, M. Higher-order convolutions for Apostol-Bernoulli, Apostol-Euler and Apostol-Genocchi polynomials. *Mathematics* **2018**, *6*, 329.
14. Srivastava, H.M.; Masjed-Jamei, M.; Beyki, M.R. Some new generalizations and applications of the Apostol-Bernoulli, Apostol-Euler and Apostol-Genocchi polynomials. *Rocky Mountain J. Math.* **2019**, *49*, 681–690. [CrossRef]
15. Srivastava, H.M. The Zeta and related functions: Recent developments. *J. Adv. Engrg. Comput.* **2019**, *3*, 329–354. [CrossRef]
16. Merca, M. On the Song recurrence relation for the Riemann zeta function. *Miskolc Math. Notes* **2017**, *17*, 941–945. [CrossRef]
17. Merca, M. On families of linear recurrence relations for the special values of the Riemann zeta function. *J. Number Theory* **2017**, *170*, 55–65. [CrossRef]
18. Saalschütz, L. *Vorlesungen Über die Bernoullischen Zahlen, Ihren Zusammenhang mit den Secanten-Coefficienten und Ihre Wichtigeren Anwendungen*; Springer: Heidelberg/Berlin, Germany, 1893.
19. Nielsen, N. *Traité Ûlúmentaire des Nombres de Bernoulli*; Gauthier-Villars: Paris, France, 1923.
20. Hansen, E.R. Bernoulli, Euler, and Stirling Polynomials and Numbers and Neumann Polynomials. In *A Table of Series and Products*; Prentice Hall: Englewood Cliffs, NJ, USA, 1975; pp. 331–353.
21. Deeba, E.Y.; Rodriguez, D.M. Stirling's series and Bernoulli numbers. *Amer. Math. Mon.* **1991**, *98*, 423–426. [CrossRef]
22. Frontczak, R.; Tomovski, Z. Generalized Euler-Genocchi polynomials and Lucas numbers. *Integers* **2020**, *20*, A52.

Article
A Flexible Extension to an Extreme Distribution

Mohamed S. Eliwa [1], Fahad Sameer Alshammari [2], Khadijah M. Abualnaja [3] and Mahmoud El-Morshedy [2,4,*]

[1] Department of Mathematics, Faculty of Science, Mansoura University, Mansoura 35516, Egypt; mseliwa@mans.edu.eg
[2] Department of Mathematics, College of Science and Humanities in Al-Kharj, Prince Sattam bin Abdulaziz University, Al-Kharj 11942, Saudi Arabia; f.alshammari@psau.edu.sa
[3] Department of Mathematics and Statistics, College of Science, Taif University, P.O. Box 11099, Taif 21944, Saudi Arabia; Kh.abualnaja@tu.edu.sa
[4] Department of Statistics, Faculty of Science, Mansoura University, Mansoura 35516, Egypt
* Correspondence: m.elmorshedy@psau.edu.sa

Abstract: The aim of this paper is not only to propose a new extreme distribution, but also to show that the new extreme model can be used as an alternative to well-known distributions in the literature to model various kinds of datasets in different fields. Several of its statistical properties are explored. It is found that the new extreme model can be utilized for modeling both asymmetric and symmetric datasets, which suffer from over- and under-dispersed phenomena. Moreover, the hazard rate function can be constant, increasing, increasing–constant, or unimodal shaped. The maximum likelihood method is used to estimate the model parameters based on complete and censored samples. Finally, a significant amount of simulations was conducted along with real data applications to illustrate the use of the new extreme distribution.

Keywords: probability distributions; skewed and symmetric data; maximum likelihood estimation; hazard rate function; censored samples

1. Introduction

Data analysis has become of great interest in many fields of science such as health sciences, reliability analysis, industry, environmental studies, and others. The requirement of obtaining suitable models and statistical distributions has become essential, since defining new distributions will enable us to better describe and predict phenomenal and experimental data. See for example [1–9], among others.

Recently, several methods of obtaining new distributions from old ones have been developed. Many generalized classes of life time distributions have been discussed in the literature. It has been proven in many papers that the new generalizations are more flexible in modelling and better fit real-life data. These new distributions also have several desirable properties such as the asymptotic behavior of their probability density function and the hazard rate function's monotonicity, which has made them superior to the original distribution. All of this has encouraged authors to work more on developing new lifetime distributions using different generalization methods. Here, we refer to the papers of [10] for the Marshall–Olkin class, [11] for the Beta and Gamma classes, [12] for the odd exponentiated half-logistic-G (OEHL-G) family, [13] for the flexible Weibull class, [14] for the odd log-logistic Lindley class, [15] for the odd Chen class, [16] for the exponentiated odd Chen class, [17] for a new Kumaraswamy generalized class, [18,19] for the extended Gamma and log-Bilal models, respectively, [20] for type I half logistic odd Weibull-G and [21] for the Poisson transmuted-G family, among others.

Here, we use the OEHL-G family of distributions to build a new flexible model with three parameters. The cumulative distribution function (CDF) of the OEHL-G family with two positive shape parameters α and λ can be reported as

$$\Pi(x;\lambda,\Theta,\alpha) = \left\{\frac{1-e^{-\lambda\frac{G(x;\Theta)}{1-G(x;\Theta)}}}{1+e^{-\lambda\frac{G(x;\Theta)}{1-G(x;\Theta)}}}\right\}^{\alpha}; x \in \aleph \subset \mathbb{R} \quad (1)$$

where $G(x;\Theta)$ is the CDF of the baseline distribution under consideration (for more details, see Afify et al., 2017). In our study, the baseline CDF is the inverse exponential (IEx) distribution. The IEx model can be utilized to model datasets which have inverted bathtub failure rates (see, [22]), but it lacks model datasets that are highly skewed "asymmetric" (see, [23]). Therefore, it is essential to have a skewness property in the IEx distribution so that it would be able to fit asymmetry in the datasets that are heavily skewed. Hence, our goal is to obtain a generalized distribution of the IEx model such that it will extend the IEx distribution and also add more flexible features to this life-time model. Many authors have proposed some inverted models due to their flexibility in modeling various types of datasets in different fields (for instance, [24,25]). The basic motivations for using the odd exponentiated half-logistic inverse exponential (OEHLIEx) distribution in practice are the following:

1. The PDF, CDF, and HRF can be derived in closed-forms.
2. The HRF can be constant, increasing, increasing–constant or unimodal shaped, which makes the proposed model able to be used to analyze different types of datasets.
3. It can be used to model both symmetry and asymmetric datasets.
4. It has more flexibility as compared to well-known models, especially the IEx model.
5. It can be used to model platykurtic-shaped data.
6. It can be used to model over- and under-dispersed data (See Section 6).

2. The OEHLIEx Distribution

A random variable X is said to have the IEx distribution with parameter β if its CDF $G(x;\beta) = e^{-\frac{\beta}{x}}$. Using the CDF of the IEx model in Equation (1), we obtain the CDF of the OEHLIEx distribution, which can be expressed as

$$F(x;\lambda,\beta,\alpha) = \left\{1 - e^{-\lambda\left(e^{\frac{\beta}{x}}-1\right)^{-1}}\right\}^{\alpha}\left\{1 + e^{-\lambda\left(e^{\frac{\beta}{x}}-1\right)^{-1}}\right\}^{-\alpha}; x > 0, \quad (2)$$

where α and λ are the positive shape parameters, while β is the positive scale parameter. The corresponding probability density function (PDF) to Equation (2) is

$$f(x;\lambda,\beta,\alpha) = 2\alpha\lambda\beta x^{-2}e^{-\frac{\beta}{x}}e^{-\lambda\left(e^{\frac{\beta}{x}}-1\right)^{-1}}\left\{1-e^{-\frac{\beta}{x}}\right\}^{-2}\left\{1-e^{-\lambda\left(e^{\frac{\beta}{x}}-1\right)^{-1}}\right\}^{\alpha-1}\left\{1+e^{-\lambda\left(e^{\frac{\beta}{x}}-1\right)^{-1}}\right\}^{-\alpha-1}. \quad (3)$$

The PDF of the OEHLIEx model can be represented as an infinite mixture of an exponentiated IEx (Exp-IEx) distribution:

$$f(x;\lambda,\beta,\alpha) = \sum_{k,l=0}^{\infty} \varphi_{k,l}\, \tau_{k+l+1}(x), \quad (4)$$

where

$$\varphi_{k,l} = 2\alpha\lambda \sum_{j,i=0}^{\infty} \frac{(-1)^{j+k+l}(\lambda(i+j+1))^k}{k!(k+l+1)}\binom{-\alpha-1}{i}\binom{\alpha-1}{j}\binom{-k-2}{l}$$

and

$$\tau_{k+l+1}(x) = \frac{(k+l+1)\beta}{x^2}e^{-\frac{(k+l+1)\beta}{x}},$$

represents the Exp-IEx density with the power parameter $(k+l+1)$. The corresponding reliability function to Equation (2) can be obtained as

$$R(x;\lambda,\beta,\alpha) = 1 - \left\{1 - e^{-\lambda(e^{\frac{\beta}{x}}-1)^{-1}}\right\}^{\alpha} \left\{1 + e^{-\lambda(e^{\frac{\beta}{x}}-1)^{-1}}\right\}^{-\alpha}; x > 0. \tag{5}$$

For the proposed model, the hazard rate function (HRF) and its cumulative can be reported, respectively, as

$$h(x;\lambda,\beta,\alpha) = \frac{2\alpha\lambda\beta x^{-2}e^{-\frac{\beta}{x}}\left\{1-e^{-\frac{\beta}{x}}\right\}^{-2}\left\{1-e^{-\lambda(e^{\frac{\beta}{x}}-1)^{-1}}\right\}^{\alpha-1}\left\{1+e^{-\lambda(e^{\frac{\beta}{x}}-1)^{-1}}\right\}^{-1}}{e^{\lambda(e^{\frac{\beta}{x}}-1)^{-1}}\left(\left\{1+e^{-\lambda(e^{\frac{\beta}{x}}-1)^{-1}}\right\}^{\alpha} - \left\{1-e^{-\lambda(e^{\frac{\beta}{x}}-1)^{-1}}\right\}^{\alpha}\right)} \tag{6}$$

and

$$H(x;\lambda,\beta,\alpha) = -\log\left(1 - \left\{1 - e^{-\lambda(e^{\frac{\beta}{x}}-1)^{-1}}\right\}^{\alpha}\left\{1 + e^{-\lambda(e^{\frac{\beta}{x}}-1)^{-1}}\right\}^{-\alpha}\right), \tag{7}$$

where the cumulative hazard function is the integral of the hazard function. Figure 1 shows the PDF plots and its HRF for different parameter values. It is immediate that the PDF is unimodal shaped and can be used to discuss right- and left-skewed datasets, whereas the HRF can be increasing, constant, increasing–constant, or unimodal shaped. Therefore, the OEHLIEx distribution can be utilized to analyze various types of data in several practical fields.

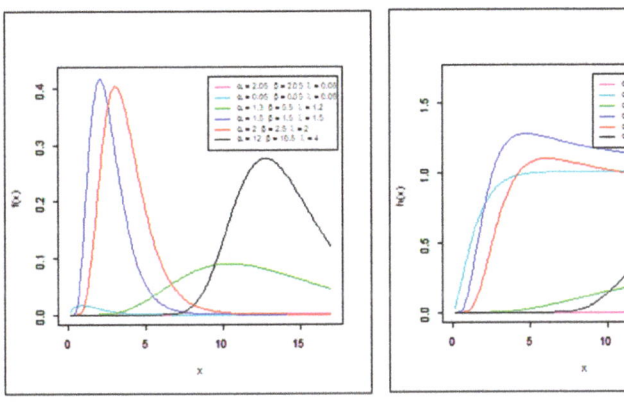

Figure 1. The PDF "left panel" and HRF "right panel" plots.

3. Statistical and Reliability Properties

3.1. Quantile Function (QF), Skewness, and Kurtosis

The QF of the OEHLIEx distribution is given as follows: if U has a uniform random variable on $U(0,1)$, then

$$X_U = -\beta\left\{\ln\left(\frac{-\ln\left(1-u^{\frac{1}{\alpha}}\right)+\ln\left(1+u^{\frac{1}{\alpha}}\right)}{\lambda-\ln\left(1-u^{\frac{1}{\alpha}}\right)+\ln\left(1+u^{\frac{1}{\alpha}}\right)}\right)\right\}^{-1}. \tag{8}$$

Equation (8) can be used to generate a random sample, and the median can be derived at $u = 0.5$. Moreover, it can be used to obtain the skewness and kurtosis, where skewness $= \frac{X_{3/4}+X_{1/4}-2X_{2/4}}{X_{3/4}-X_{1/4}}$ and Kurtosis $= \frac{X_{3/8}-X_{1/8}+X_{7/8}-X_{5/8}}{X_{6/8}-X_{2/8}}$. Tables 1–3 report some numerical values of the quantiles, skewness, and kurtosis of the OEHLIEx model using Maple software.

Table 1. The quantiles, skewness, and kurtosis for $\lambda \to \infty$.

Parameter ↓ Measure →			$X_{1/4}$	$X_{2/4}$	$X_{3/8}$	$X_{5/8}$	Skewness	Kurtosis
α	β	λ						
0.5	0.5	0.5	0.311	0.733	0.491	1.055	0.296	1.268
		0.9	0.238	0.492	0.349	0.678	0.270	1.263
		2.0	0.177	0.314	0.239	0.406	0.221	1.246
		3.5	0.149	0.243	0.193	0.302	0.181	1.229
		100	0.075	0.095	0.085	0.104	−0.007	1.183
		150	0.071	0.088	0.079	0.596	−0.021	1.181

Table 2. The quantiles, skewness, and kurtosis for $\beta \to \infty$.

Parameter ↓ Measure →			$X_{1/4}$	$X_{2/4}$	$X_{3/8}$	$X_{5/8}$	Skewness	Kurtosis
α	λ	β						
0.3	1.5	0.2	0.046	0.093	0.066	0.132	0.345	1.348
		0.8	0.184	0.373	0.264	0.529	0.345	1.348
		1.5	0.345	0.699	0.495	0.991	0.345	1.348
		5.0	1.150	2.332	1.649	3.305	0.345	1.348
		10	2.301	4.664	3.299	6.609	0.345	1.348
		100	23.008	46.639	32.995	66.095	0.345	1.348

Table 3. The quantiles, skewness, and kurtosis for $\alpha \to \infty$.

Parameter ↓ Measure →			$X_{1/4}$	$X_{2/4}$	$X_{3/8}$	$X_{5/8}$	Skewness	Kurtosis
β	λ	α						
1.5	2.0	0.02	0.00	0.00	0.00	0.063	1.000	1.548
		0.05	0.00	0.108	0.076	0.159	0.169	1.784
		0.1	0.108	0.216	0.153	0.318	0.464	1.808
		0.2	0.216	0.429	0.305	0.615	0.393	1.457
		0.8	0.795	1.279	1.027	1.572	0.162	1.242
		1.5	1.231	1.756	1.491	2.056	0.127	1.259

Regarding Tables 1–3, the proposed model is suitable for modelling asymmetric as well as symmetric datasets that are platykurtic shaped.

3.2. Incomplete Moments

The sth incomplete moments can be listed as

$$\omega_s(t) = \sum_{k,l=0}^{\infty} \varphi_{k,l}\, \omega_s^*(t), \qquad (9)$$

where $w_s^*(t) = \int_0^t x^s \tau_{k+l+1}(x) dx$. Thus, the sth incomplete moments of the OEHLIEx model can be proposed as

$$w_s(t) = \sum_{k,l,n=0}^{\infty} \varphi_{k,l} \frac{\{-\beta(k+l+1)\}^n}{n!(s-n-1)} t^{s-n-1}. \tag{10}$$

3.3. Reliability Function of Linear Consecutive, Parallel, Series, and Bridge Type Network Systems

If the random variable X has the OEHLIEx distribution, then the reliability function of the linear consecutive $k - out - of\ n : F$ system can be expressed as

$$\begin{aligned} R_L(t;k,n) &= \sum_{j=0}^{m} N(j;k,n) \{R^{n-j}(t) F(t)\}^j \\ &= \sum_{j,i=0}^{m} (-1)^j \binom{j}{i} N(j;k,n) R^{n-j+i}(t) \end{aligned} \tag{11}$$

$$= \sum_{j,i=0}^{m} (-1)^j \binom{j}{i} N(j;k,n) \left\{ 1 - \left\{ 1 - e^{-\lambda \left(e^{\frac{\beta}{x}} - 1 \right)^{-1}} \right\}^{\alpha} \left\{ 1 + e^{-\lambda \left(e^{\frac{\beta}{x}} - 1 \right)^{-1}} \right\}^{-\alpha} \right\}^{n-j+i},$$

for more details concerning the values of m, $N(j;k,n)$, and j, see [26]. In the special case of the system $k - out - of - n : F$, the parallel and series system when $k = n$ and $k = 1$, respectively.

Consider two systems: one of them is parallel, whereas the other is a series with independent n components. Each component has the OEHLIEx model; thus, the reliability function in the case of the parallel system can be reported as

$$R_{P-S}(x) = 1 - \left[\left\{ 1 - e^{-\lambda(e^{\frac{\beta}{x}}-1)^{-1}} \right\}^{\alpha} \left\{ 1 + e^{-\lambda(e^{\frac{\beta}{x}}-1)^{-1}} \right\}^{-\alpha} \right]^n, \tag{12}$$

where as the reliability function in the case of the series system can be expressed as

$$R_{S-S}(x) = \left[1 - \left\{ 1 - e^{-\lambda(e^{\frac{\beta}{x}}-1)^{-1}} \right\}^{\alpha} \left\{ 1 + e^{-\lambda(e^{\frac{\beta}{x}}-1)^{-1}} \right\}^{-\alpha} \right]^n. \tag{13}$$

In reliability theory, there exists another type of engineering system in the so-called bridge-type network or a complex system, which has many applications in this field. Such systems as these can be evaluated by using many approaches such as conditional probability, a connection matrix, and tree diagrams, as well as cut and tie sets. Assume a bridge-type network consists of five components (A, B, C, D, and E) where each component has the OEHLIEx model, these components can be connected as follows:

Consider the previous network in which success requires that at least one of the paths AC, BD, AED, or BEC is good. To evaluate the reliability function of this network, the conditional probability approach has been utilized. The previous network in Figure 2 can be subdivided into two systems, one with E considered bad, i.e., it always failed, and one with E considered good, i.e., it cannot fail. Thus,

$$\begin{aligned} R_{NW} &= R_{NW}(\text{if E is good}) R_E(x; \lambda, \beta, \alpha) + R_{NW}(\text{if E is bad}) F_E(x; \lambda, \beta, \alpha) \\ &= \{(1 - F_A(x; \lambda, \beta, \alpha) F_B(x; \lambda, \beta, \alpha))(1 - F_C(x; \lambda, \beta, \alpha) F_D(x; \lambda, \beta, \alpha))\} R_E(x; \lambda, \beta, \alpha) \\ &+ \{1 - (1 - R_A(x; \lambda, \beta, \alpha) R_C(x; \lambda, \beta, \alpha))(1 - R_A(x; \lambda, \beta, \alpha) R_D(x; \lambda, \beta, \alpha))\} F_E(x; \lambda, \beta, \alpha), \end{aligned} \tag{14}$$

where $F_* = 1 - R_*$ represents the unreliability function of a component (*). Since $R_A = R_B = R_C = R_D = R_E$, then the reliability R_{NW} can be expressed as

$$R_{NW} = 2\left\{ R(x; \lambda, \beta, \alpha)^2 + R(x; \lambda, \beta, \alpha)^3 + R(x; \lambda, \beta, \alpha)^5 \right\} - 5R(x; \lambda, \beta, \alpha)^4. \tag{15}$$

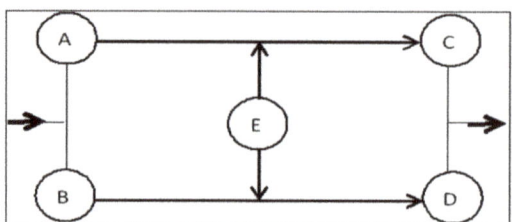

Figure 2. Bridge-type network.

Assume four different systems, namely, parallel, serious, linear consecutive, and bridge network; each system consists of 20 components, except the bridge network which consists of five components. Tables 4–6 list some numerical values of the reliability function for these systems using Maple software.

Table 4. Some numerical values of the reliability for different systems for various values of α.

System ↓ Parameter →	α=1.5		α=5		α=10	
	β=0.5	λ=0.5	β=0.5	λ=0.5	β=0.5	λ=0.5
Parallel	0.4036		0.8215		0.9681	
Series	1.4×10^{-32}		2.2×10^{-22}		9.7×10^{-17}	
Linear Consecutive	0.0157		0.0179		0.0967	
Bridge Network	0.00133		0.01453		0.0551	

Table 5. Some numerical values of the reliability for different systems for various values of β.

System ↓ Parameter →	β=0.5		β=0.8		β=1.5	
	α=0.1	λ=0.1	α=0.1	λ=0.1	α=0.1	λ=0.1
Parallel	0.8041		0.9213		0.9798	
Series	7.5×10^{-23}		3.5×10^{-19}		9.5×10^{-16}	
Linear Consecutive	0.0597		0.0689		0.0794	
Bridge Network	0.0130		0.0309		0.0695	

Table 6. Some numerical values of the reliability for different systems for various values of λ.

System ↓ Parameter →	λ=0.3		λ=0.6		λ=0.9	
	α=0.8	β=0.7	α=0.8	β=0.7	α=0.8	β=0.7
Parallel	0.9873		0.4459		0.0771	
Series	7.3×10^{-15}		1.8×10^{-31}		1.1×10^{-48}	
Linear Consecutive	0.0567		0.0426		0.0411	
Bridge Network	0.0855		0.0017		3.2×10^{-6}	

Regarding Tables 4–6, it is clear that the reliability of parallel, series, linear consecutive, and bridge network systems increases in two cases, one of them for fixed values of β and λ with $\alpha \to \infty$, and the other for fixed values of α and λ with $\beta \to \infty$. Whereas, the reliability of these systems decreases for fixed values of α and β with $\lambda \to \infty$.

3.4. Entropy

The Rényi entropy of a positive random variable X representing a measure of variation of the uncertainty is defined by

$$I_\rho(X) = \frac{1}{1-\rho} \log\left(\int_0^\infty f^\rho(x;\lambda,\beta,\alpha)dx\right); \rho > 0 \text{ and } \rho \neq 1.$$

$$= \frac{1}{1-\rho} \log\left(\sum_{k,l=0}^\infty \Omega_{k,l} \int_0^\infty g^\rho(x) G^{k+l}(x) dx\right) \quad (16)$$

$$= \frac{1}{1-\rho} \log\left(\sum_{k,l=0}^\infty \Omega_{k,l} \frac{\beta^{1-\rho} \Gamma(2\rho-1)}{(\rho+k+l)^{2\rho-1}}\right),$$

where $(2\rho - 1) \neq -1, -2, -3, \ldots$ and

$$\Omega_{k,l} = (2\alpha\lambda)^\rho \sum_{j,i=0}^\infty \frac{(-1)^{j+k+l}(\lambda(i+j+1))^k}{k!} \binom{-\alpha\rho-\rho}{i}\binom{\rho\alpha-\rho}{j}\binom{-k-2\rho}{l}.$$

The binomial coefficients will be computed with the negative values using built-in functions in Maple software. The Shannon entropy is a special case of the Rényi entropy when $\rho \to 1$. Tables 7–9 list some numerical values of entropies using Maple software.

Table 7. Entropies for different values of β.

Entropy ↓ Parameter →	$\beta=0.5$		$\beta=0.8$		$\beta=1.5$	
	$\alpha=0.1$	$\lambda=0.1$	$\alpha=0.1$	$\lambda=0.1$	$\alpha=0.1$	$\lambda=0.1$
Renyi	0.2569		0.3697		0.4302	
Shannon	0.1987		0.1997		0.2159	

Table 8. Entropies for different values of α.

Entropy ↓ Parameter →	$\alpha=1.5$		$\alpha=5$		$\alpha=10$	
	$\beta=0.5$	$\lambda=0.5$	$\beta=0.5$	$\lambda=0.5$	$\beta=0.5$	$\lambda=0.5$
Renyi	2.3694		2.5976		3.6871	
Shannon	2.5364		2.6974		2.7639	

Table 9. Entropies for different values of λ.

Entropy ↓ Parameter →	$\lambda=0.3$		$\lambda=0.6$		$\lambda=0.9$	
	$\alpha=0.8$	$\beta=0.7$	$\alpha=0.8$	$\beta=0.7$	$\alpha=0.8$	$\beta=0.7$
Renyi	3.2168		3.0197		2.4398	
Shannon	3.1020		3.009		2.9578	

Regarding Tables 7–9, it is clear that the entropy increases in two cases, one of them for fixed values of α and λ with $\beta \to \infty$, and the other for fixed values of β and λ with $\alpha \to \infty$. Whereas, the entropy decreases for fixed values of α and β with $\lambda \to \infty$.

4. Parameters Estimation
4.1. Maximum Likelihood Estimation (MLE) Based on Complete Samples.

In this section, we derive the MLE of the unknown parameters λ, β, and α of the OEHLIEx model based on complete samples. Consider a random sample $X_1, X_2, \ldots, X_n$ from the OEHLIEx model; then, the log-likelihood (LL) function can be expressed as

$$L = \sum_{i=1}^{n} \log f(x_i; \lambda, \beta, \alpha). \tag{17}$$

By substituting from Equation (3) into Equation (17), the MLEs of the OEHLIEx parameters can be obtained by maximizing

$$LL = n \log 2\alpha\lambda\beta - 2 \sum_{i=1}^{n} \log x_i - \beta \sum_{i=1}^{n} \frac{1}{x_i} - \lambda \sum_{i=1}^{n} \left(e^{\frac{\beta}{x_i}} - 1\right)^{-1} - 2 \sum_{i=1}^{n} \log\left(1 - e^{-\frac{\beta}{x_i}}\right) + (\alpha - 1) \sum_{i=1}^{n} \log\left(1 - e^{-\lambda(e^{\frac{\beta}{x_i}} - 1)^{-1}}\right) - (\alpha + 1) \sum_{i=1}^{n} \log\left(1 + e^{-\lambda(e^{\frac{\beta}{x_i}} - 1)^{-1}}\right), \tag{18}$$

with respect to λ, β, and α. We used **R** software to obtain the parameters' values. The $(1 - \delta)$ 100% confidence intervals (CIs) of the model parameters can be calculated using the following relations:

$$\hat{\lambda} \pm Z_{\frac{\delta}{2}} \sqrt{var(\hat{\lambda})},\ \hat{\beta} \pm Z_{\frac{\delta}{2}} \sqrt{var(\hat{\beta})}\ \text{and}\ \hat{\alpha} \pm Z_{\frac{\delta}{2}} \sqrt{var(\hat{\alpha})},$$

where $Z_{\frac{\delta}{2}}$ is the upper $\left(\frac{\delta}{2}\right)$th percentile of the standard normal distribution.

4.2. MLE Based on Type-II Censored Samples

The likelihood function for a type-II censored sample can be reported as

$$l = \frac{n!}{(n-k)!} (R(x_k))^{n-k} \prod_{i=1}^{k} f(x_i), \tag{19}$$

where n represents the number of components, and the experiment is stopped when k items failed. If $X_1, X_2, \ldots, X_n$ represent an independent and identically distributed random sample from the OEHLIEx distribution and $X_1, X_2, \ldots, X_k, k \leq n$ represent an ordered sample obtained from a type-II right censoring sample, then the log-likelihood (LL^*) function is

$$LL^* = \ln \frac{n!}{(n-k)!} + (n-k) \ln R(x_k; \lambda, \beta, \alpha) + \sum_{i=1}^{k} \log f(x_i; \lambda, \beta, \alpha). \tag{20}$$

By substituting from Equations (3) and (5) into Equation (20), the MLEs of the OEHLIEx parameters can be obtained by maximizing results of the equation with respect to λ, β, and α.

5. Simulation Results

We assessed the performance of the MLE approach with respect to various samples size. The assessment was based on a simulation study:

1. Generate 1000 samples of size $n = 10, 20, 30, 50, 75, 100, 150$ from the OEHLIEx model under various values of the parameters.
2. Compute the MLEs for the 1000 samples, say $\hat{\theta}_j$ for $j = 1, 2, \ldots, 1000$.
3. Compute the biases and mean-squared errors (MSEs), where

$$\text{Bias}(\theta) = \frac{1}{1000} \sum_{j=1}^{1000} (\hat{\theta}_j - \theta)\ \text{and}\ \text{MSE}(\theta) = \frac{1}{1000} \sum_{j=1}^{1000} (\hat{\theta}_j - \theta)^2.$$

The empirical results for complete data are given in Tables 10–14 using OEHLIEx(1.5, 0.5,0.9), OEHLIEx(2.5,2.5,2.5), OEHLIEx(0.5,0.8,0.9), and OEHLIEx(0.5,0.5,0.5), respectively. Whereas the empirical results for type-II censored data when $k = 20$ are given in Tables 15–17 for OEHLIEx(0.7,0.8,0.9), OEHLIEx(0.5,1.5,2.5), OEHLIEx(0.01,0.5,0.1.5), and OEHLIEx(0.1,1.5,0.5), respectively.

Table 10. The bias and MSE (in parentheses) for schema I.

Parameters ↓ Sample Size →	10	20	30	50	75	100	150
λ	0.12578 (0.15964)	0.11467 (0.15083)	0.11025 (0.14998)	0.11012 (0.14322)	0.09987 (0.10021)	0.04237 (0.06867)	0.01983 (0.01325)
β	0.10361 (0.13555)	0.10318 (0.13200)	0.10251 (0.11036)	0.10112 (0.10998)	0.09876 (0.08655)	0.05217 (0.03524)	0.02649 (0.00145)
α	0.11666 (0.12372)	0.10008 (0.10187)	0.09866 (0.08873)	0.07624 (0.05326)	0.03654 (0.02361)	0.01254 (0.01023)	0.01001 (0.00147)

Table 11. The bias and MSE (in parentheses) for schema II.

Parameters ↓ Sample Size →	10	20	30	50	75	100	150
λ	0.11769 (0.15793)	0.10987 (0.14026)	0.10644 (0.13657)	0.08657 (0.11087)	0.05634 (0.08741)	0.01237 (0.03219)	0.00558 (0.00543)
β	0.10222 (0.11236)	0.10104 (0.10658)	0.10057 (0.09874)	0.08741 (0.05324)	0.05234 (0.01240)	0.03201 (0.00874)	0.00874 (0.00149)
α	0.10984 (0.10037)	0.10567 (0.09759)	0.10111 (0.05687)	0.07876 (0.04217)	0.05234 (0.03217)	0.023264 (0.01007)	0.00951 (0.00188)

Table 12. The bias and MSE (in parentheses) for schema III.

Parameters ↓ Sample Size →	10	20	30	50	75	100	150
λ	0.10998 (0.13067)	0.10756 (0.12361)	0.10564 (0.12248)	0.102341 (0.10252)	0.08764 (0.03101)	0.035418 (0.01097)	0.00429 (0.00574)
β	0.09987 (0.09996)	0.09153 (0.09864)	0.08635 (0.05314)	0.053243 (0.03221)	0.022324 (0.01002)	0.020011 (0.00517)	0.008214 (0.00120)
α	0.076249 (0.057681)	0.075324 (0.056341)	0.063397 (0.042224)	0.048891 (0.033364)	0.039217 (0.02109)	0.011871 (0.00996)	0.003814 (0.00225)

Table 13. The bias and MSE (in parentheses) for schema IV.

Parameters ↓ Sample Size →	10	20	30	50	75	100	150
λ	0.110542 (0.102201)	0.100214 (0.101123)	0.095874 (0.082210)	0.086554 (0.053329)	0.045638 (0.033415)	0.023211 (0.00524)	0.010014 (0.00221)
β	0.085761 (0.065354)	0.056639 (0.032544)	0.0355621 (0.023517)	0.0322624 (0.021030)	0.020132 (0.007461)	0.020100 (0.00712)	0.005624 (0.00230)
α	0.075641 (0.063099)	0.0655327 (0.052201)	0.039640 (0.044671)	0.028634 (0.033249)	0.019652 (0.007956)	0.005536 (0.004310)	0.004187 (0.002140)

Table 14. The bias and MSE (in parentheses) for schema V.

Parameters ↓ Sample Size →	10	20	30	50	75	100	150
λ	0.12578 (0.15964)	0.11467 (0.15083)	0.11025 (0.14998)	0.11012 (0.14322)	0.09987 (0.10021)	0.04237 (0.06867)	0.01983 (0.01325)
β	0.10361 (0.13555)	0.10318 (0.13200)	0.10251 (0.11036)	0.10112 (0.10998)	0.09876 (0.08655)	0.05217 (0.03524)	0.02649 (0.00145)
α	0.11666 (0.12372)	0.10008 (0.10187)	0.09866 (0.08873)	0.07624 (0.05326)	0.03654 (0.02361)	0.01254 (0.01023)	0.01001 (0.00147)

Table 15. The bias and MSE (in parentheses) for VI.

Parameters ↓ Sample Size →	10	20	30	50	75	100	150
λ	0.11458 (0.12694)	0.11536 (0.10083)	0.11256 (0.09844)	0.10123 (0.08436)	0.08563 (0.06369)	0.01326 (0.03698)	0.002366 (0.00743)
β	0.11963 (0.11538)	0.11326 (0.10563)	0.11269 (0.10269)	0.10269 (0.10111)	0.08963 (0.07488)	0.02301 (0.02398)	0.00147 (0.00789)
α	0.17896 (0.13698)	0.16236 (0.12856)	0.14265 (0.10328)	0.12488 (0.09994)	0.08963 (0.09602)	0.03521 (0.05326)	0.00723 (0.00117)

Table 16. The bias and MSE (in parentheses) for VII.

Parameters ↓ Sample Size →	10	20	30	50	75	100	150
λ	0.21653 (0.19691)	0.18856 (0.16136)	0.16456 (0.15452)	0.13698 (0.14236)	0.09856 (0.12013)	0.05602 (0.09695)	0.00147 (0.01369)
β	0.22985 (0.17803)	0.21360 (0.16636)	0.17203 (0.14447)	0.13695 (0.11029)	0.08563 (0.09301)	0.03214 (0.01238)	0.00983 (0.00650)
α	0.10256 (0.09635)	0.09362 (0.08503)	0.07452 (0.06416)	0.03698 (0.03694)	0.00968 (0.01236)	0.00236 (0.00632)	0.00063 (0.00085)

Table 17. The bias and MSE (in parentheses) for VIII.

Parameters ↓ Sample Size →	10	20	30	50	75	100	150
λ	0.12690 (0.11231)	0.12369 (0.11197)	0.11015 (0.11017)	0.10850 (0.10856)	0.10369 (0.10285)	0.06369 (0.07458)	0.00856 (0.00469)
β	0.043028 (0.040695)	0.030258 (0.03312)	0.022136 (0.02635)	0.014369 (0.01802)	0.010236 (0.01132)	0.008896 (0.008309)	0.001539 (0.00239)
α	0.119980 (0.15891)	0.11743 (0.13264)	0.08830 (0.10239)	0.05237 (0.09721)	0.02138 (0.07128)	0.00856 (0.02598)	0.00038 (0.00653)

From Tables 10–17, we can say that the MLE approach can be used effectively to estimate the model parameters for both a small and large sample size. This due to the consistency properties of the estimators when n grows.

6. Data Analysis

6.1. Data Analysis and Discussion Based on Complete Samples

In this section, we illustrate the empirical importance of the OEHLIEx distribution using three applications on real data. These data are used to compare the fits of the OEHLIEx distribution with some competitive models such as the inverse exponential (IEx), exponential (Ex), exponentiated half-logistic (EHL), generalized half-logistic (GHL), and normal (N) models. For the comparison of the models, we should use the values of LL, and Kolmogorov–Smirnov (K-S) test with its *p*-value.

The first data set (I) represents the relief times of twenty patients receiving an analgesic (see, [27]).

The second data set (II) represents the strengths of glass fibers (see, [28]).

The third data set (III) represents the failure times (in minutes) for a sample of 15 electronic components in an accelerated life test (see, [29]).

Tables 18–20 list the MLEs with their corresponding standard errors (in parentheses), and goodness-of-fit (GoF) measures for the datasets.

Table 18. The MLE(s) and GoF statistics for data set I.

Model ↓ Parameter →	MLE(s) [Std-err]			$-LL$	K-S (p-Value)
	α	β	λ		
OEHLIEx	18.389 [12.430]	0.070 [0.175]	0.159 [0.399]	16.327	0.134 (0.863)
IEx	1.724 [0.385]	—	—	32.668	0.387 (0.005)
Ex	0.526 [0.117]	—	—	32.837	0.439 (0.001)
GHL	0.731 [0.163]	—	—	29.464	0.398 (0.003)
EHL	2.780 [0.621]	—	—	22.908	0.281 (0.085)
N	1.90 [0.1535]	0.6863 [0.1085]	—	20.8498	0.2079 (0.3528)

The $(1-\delta)100\%$ CIs of the parameters α, β, and λ are, respectively, [0, 42.752], [0, 0.413], and [0, 0.943].

Table 19. The MLE(s) and GoF statistics for data set II.

Model ↓ Parameter →	MLE(s) [Std-err]			$-LL$	K-S (p-Value)
	α	β	λ		
OEHLIEx	82.594 [41.246]	0.013 [0.003]	0.047 [0.013]	22.602	0.071 (0.887)
IEx	1.526 [0.192]	—	—	92.805	0.468 (<0.001)
Ex	0.618 [0.078]	—	—	93.222	0.472 (<0.001)
GHL	0.896 [0.113]	—	—	82.074	0.446 (<0.001)
EHL	2.278 [0.287]	—	—	65.942	0.396 (<0.001)
N	1.6156 [0.0602]	0.4779 [0.0426]	—	42.8871	0.1774 (0.033)

The $(1-\delta)100\%$ CIs of the parameters α, β, and λ are, respectively, [1.754, 163.435], [0.006, 0.020], and [0.021, 0.073].

Table 20. The MLE(s) and GoF statistics for data set III.

Model ↓ Parameter →	MLE(s) [Std-err]			−LL	K-S (p-Value)
	α	β	λ		
OEHLIEx	0.962 [0.0435]	2.259 [4.711]	0.115 [0.231]	63.946	0.098 (0.996)
IEx	9.559 [2.468]	—	—	69.055	0.263 (0.209)
Ex	0.036 [0.009]	—	—	64.738	0.155 (0.807)
GHL	0.037 [0.009]	—	—	64.592	0.151 (0.833)
EHL	28.874 [7.455]	—	—	367.295	0.799 (<0.001)
N	27.5467 [5.1793]	20.0593 [3.6623]	—	66.2645	0.1897 (0.5885)

The $(1 - \delta)100\%$ CIs of the parameters α, β, and λ are, respectively, [0.437, 2.410], [0, 7.803], and [0, 0.694].

Regarding Tables 18–20, it is clear that the OEHLIEx model is the best model among all tested models. Regarding data set I, it is noted that the TrIEx and EHL models work quite well besides the OEHLIEx model where p-value > 0.05, but we always search for the most fitting model. Thus, we recommend using the OEHLIEx model to analyze data set I. Similarly, for dataset III, it is found that the TrIEx, IEx, Ex, and GHL models work quite well besides the OEHLIEx model, but we also recommend utilizing the OEHLIEx model to analyze these data.

Figures 3–5 show the empirical estimated CDF "ECDF", probability–probability (PP), and fitted PDF "FPDF" plots for data sets I, II, and III, respectively, which support the results of Tables 18–20. Moreover, it is noted that the datasets plausibly came from the OEHLIEx model.

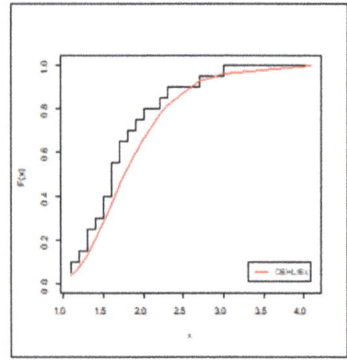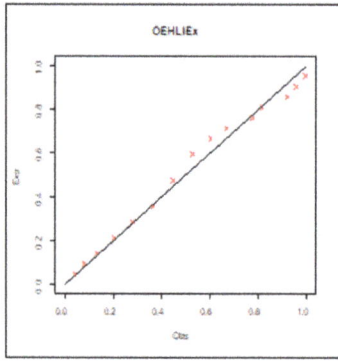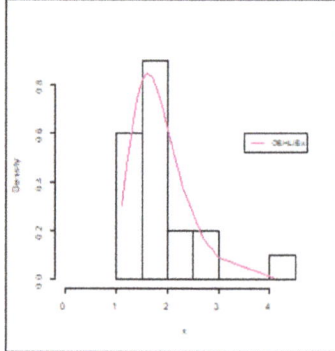

Figure 3. The ECDF "left panel", PP "middle panel", FPDF "right panel" plots for data set I.

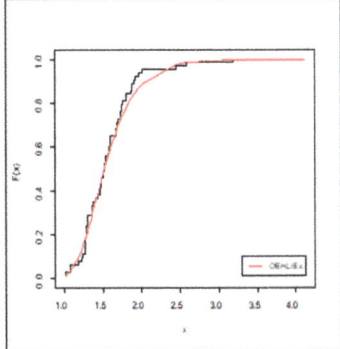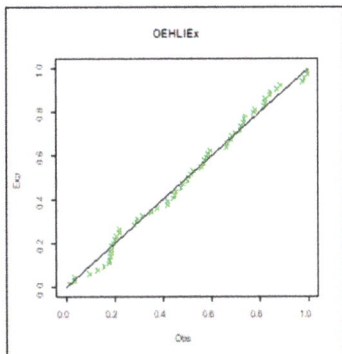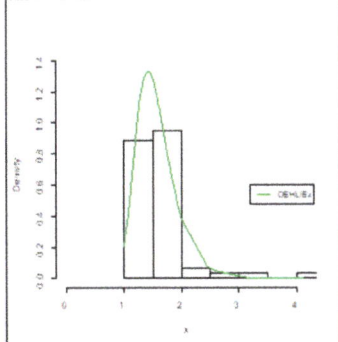

Figure 4. The ECDF "left panel", PP "middle panel", FPDF "right panel" plots for data set II.

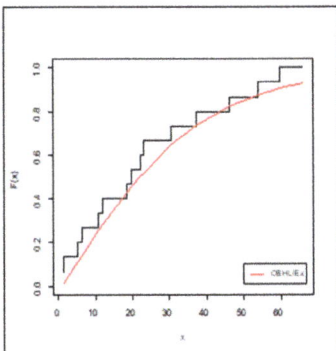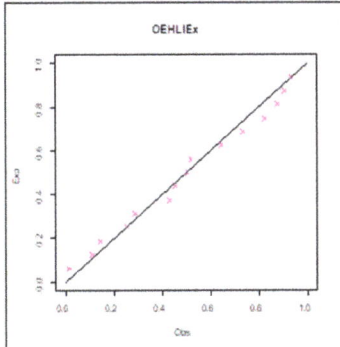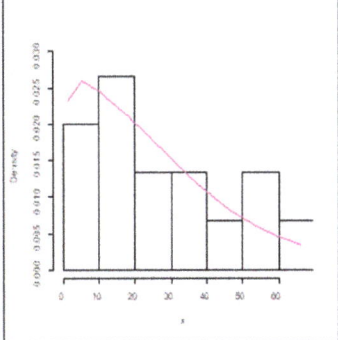

Figure 5. The ECDF "left panel", PP "middle panel", FPDF "right panel" plots for data set III.

Figures 6–8 show the profiles of the LL function "PLLF" based on data sets I, II, and III.

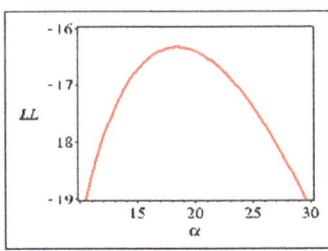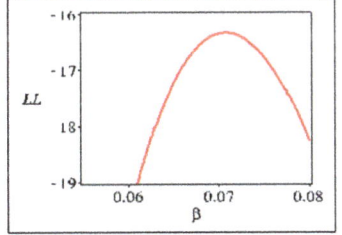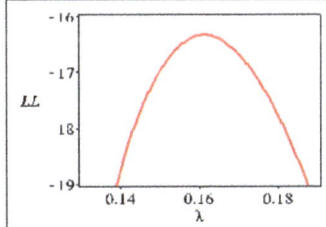

Figure 6. The PLLF for data set I.

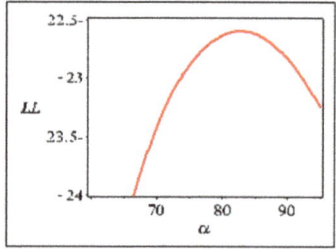 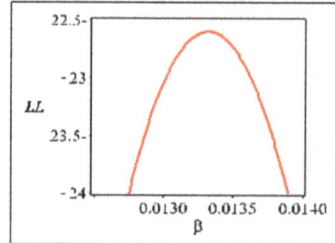 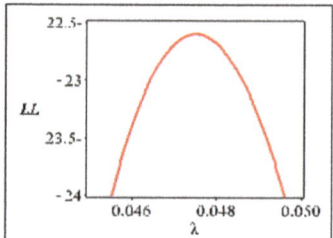

Figure 7. The PLLF for data set II.

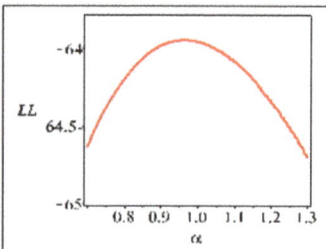 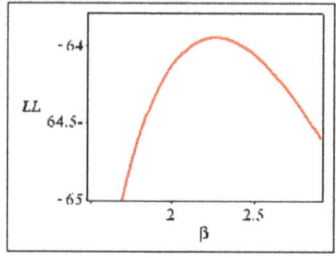 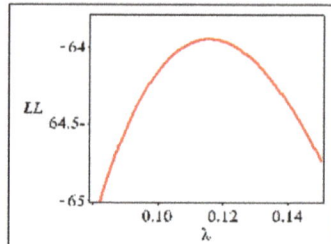

Figure 8. The PLLF for data set III.

Regarding Figures 6–8, it clear that the estimators have a unique solution where the profiles of the LL function are unimodal shaped. Figure 9 shows the total time in test (TTT) plots for data sets I, II, and III. It is clear that the datasets suffer from an increasing hazard rate. Thus, the proposed model can be used to model the HRF for these data sets.

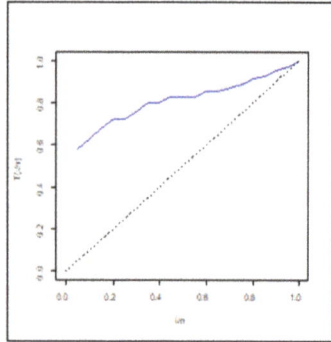 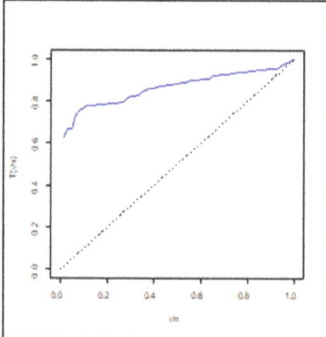 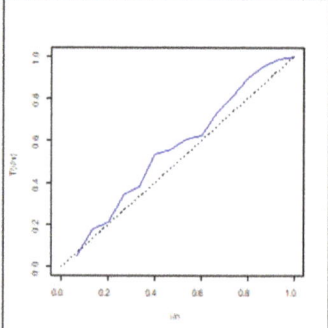

Figure 9. The TTT plots for data I "left panel", data II "middle panel", and data III "right panel".

Table 21 lists some computational statistics for the three datasets by utilizing the OEHLIEx model.

Based on the model parameters, data sets I and II suffer from under-dispersed phenomena (index of dispersion < 1), whereas data set III suffers from over-dispersion (index of dispersion > 1). Moreover, data sets I, II, and III represent positive-skewed data with a platykurtic shape.

Table 21. Some computational statistics for data sets I, II, and III.

Data Set	Mean	Variance	Index of Dispersion	Skewness	Kurtosis	Entropy
I	1.900	0.496	0.261	0.119	1.278	0.756
II	1.615	0.232	0.144	0.118	1.277	0.931
III	27.546	431.116	15.650	0.185	1.239	1.676

6.2. Dataset IV: Analysis and Discussion Based on Type-II Right Censored Samples

The censored data have been obtained from (http://www.biochemia-medica.com, accessed on 6 March 2021). They represent the recovery time of 50 patients suffering from cancer, monthly. The MLEs of the unknown parameters, $-LL^*$, K-S, and p-value for the proposed model are given in Table 22.

Table 22. The MLE(s) and GoF statistics for data set IV.

Model ↓ Parameter →	MLE(s) [Std-err]			$-LL^*$	K-S (p-Value)
	α	β	β		
OEHLIEx	131.228	0.008	0.031	17.691	0.104 (0.611)
IEx	1.575	—	—	75.162	0.463 (<0.001)
Ex	0.599	—	—	75.561	0.526 (<0.001)
EHL	2.388	—	—	52.789	0.394 (<0.001)
GHL	0.862	—	—	66.682	0.501 (<0.001)

Depending on $-LL^*$, K-S, and p-values, it is noted that the OEHLIEx model is appropriate to analyze data set IV. The $(1 - \delta)100\%$ CIs of the parameters α, β, and λ are, respectively, [126.999, 137.201], [0, 0.019], and [0, 0.107]. Figure 10 shows the TTT and PP plots based on the type-II right censored sample.

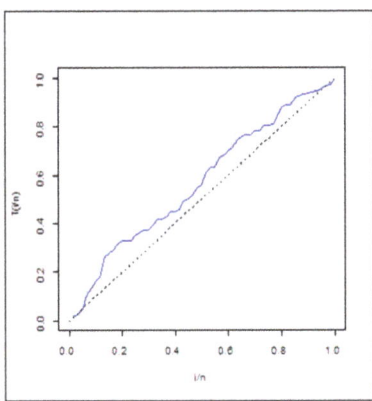
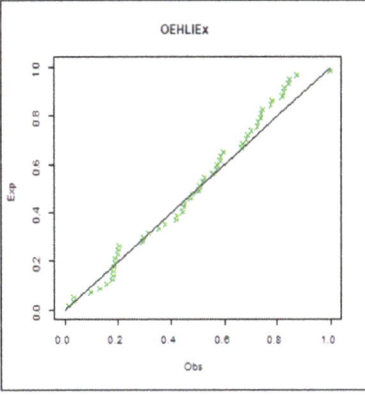

Figure 10. The TTT "left panel" and PP "right panel" plots for data set IV.

According to Figure 10, it is observed that the proposed model fits the data well. Moreover, the shape of the HRF increases. Table 23 shows some computational statistics for data IV utilizing the OEHLIEx model.

Table 23. Some computational statistics for data set IV.

Data Set	Mean	Variance	Index of Dispersion	Skewness	Kurtosis	Entropy
IV	1.667	0.260	0.156	0.324	1.876	1.998

Regarding Table 23, it is noted that the dataset IV suffers from under-dispersed phenomena which are positive skewed and platykurtic shaped.

7. Conclusions

In this article, a new flexible extension of an extreme distribution with three-parameter has been proposed, which generalized the inverse exponential distribution. The HRF of the new extension can be constant, increasing, increasing–constant, or unimodal shaped. Furthermore, it can be utilized for modelling asymmetric "positive and negative" as well as symmetric datasets and can be used to model over- and under-dispersed data. Thus, the new extension can be used effectively to model different kinds of data in several fields. The model parameters have been estimated utilizing the MLE approach. A simulation has been performed for different samples sizes, and it was found that the MLE technique works quite well for estimating the parameters for datasets considered herein. Finally, four data applications which illustrate the flexibility of the new extension and its excellence over other models have been also analyzed.

Author Contributions: Conceptualization, M.S.E. and M.E.-M.; methodology, M.S.E. and M.E.-M.; software, M.S.E. and M.E.-M.; validation, F.S.A. and K.M.A.; formal analysis, M.S.E., M.E.-M. and F.S.A.; resources, F.S.A. and K.M.A.; data curation, M.S.E. and M.E.-M.; writing—original draft preparation, M.S.E. and M.E.-M.; writing—review and editing, M.S.E. and M.E.-M.; visualization, F.S.A. and K.M.A.; project administration, M.S.E. and M.E.-M.; funding acquisition, F.S.A. and K.M.A. All authors have read and agreed to the published version of the manuscript.

Funding: This research received no external funding.

Data Availability Statement: The data was mentioned along the paper.

Acknowledgments: This Research was supported by Taif University Researchers Supporting Project Number (TURSP-2020/217), Taif University, Taif, Saudi Arabia.

Conflicts of Interest: The authors declare no conflict of interest.

References

1. Jehhan, A.; Mohamed, I.; Eliwa, M.S.; Al-Mualim, S.; Yousof, H.M. The two-parameter odd Lindley Weibull lifetime model with properties and applications. *Int. J. Stat. Probab.* **2018**, *7*, 57–68.
2. Eliwa, M.S.; El-Morshedy, M.; Ibrahim, M. Inverse Gompertz distribution: Properties and different estimation methods with application to complete and censored data. *Ann. Data Sci.* **2019**, *6*, 321–339. [CrossRef]
3. Arshad, R.M.I.; Chesneau, C.; Jamal, F. The odd Gamma Weibull-geometric model: Theory and applications. *Mathematics* **2019**, *7*, 399. [CrossRef]
4. ZeinEldin, R.A.; Chesneau, C.; Jamal, F.; Elgarhy, M. Statistical properties and different methods of estimation for type I half logistic inverted Kumaraswamy distribution. *Mathematics* **2019**, *7*, 1002. [CrossRef]
5. ZeinEldin, R.A.; Chesneau, C.; Jamal, F.; Elgarhy, M. Different estimation methods for type I half-logistic Topp–Leone distribution. *Mathematics* **2019**, *7*, 985. [CrossRef]
6. Klakattawi, H.S. The Weibull-Gamma Distribution: Properties and Applications. *Entropy* **2019**, *21*, 438. [CrossRef]
7. Al-babtain, A.A.; Elbatal, I.; Yousof, H.M. A new flexible three-parameter model: Properties, Clayton copula, and modeling real data. *Symmetry* **2020**, *12*, 440. [CrossRef]
8. Yadav, A.S.; Goual, H.; Alotaibi, R.M.; Ali, M.M.; Yousof, H.M. Validation of the Topp-Leone-Lomax model via a modified Nikulin-Rao-Robson goodness-of-fit test with different methods of estimation. *Symmetry* **2020**, *12*, 57. [CrossRef]
9. Bantan, R.A.; Jamal, F.; Chesneau, C.; Elgarhy, M. Type II Power Topp-Leone generated family of distributions with statistical inference and applications. *Symmetry* **2020**, *12*, 75. [CrossRef]
10. Marshall, A.W.; Olkin, I. A new method for adding a parameter to a family of distributions with application to the exponential and Weibull families. *Biometrika* **1997**, *84*, 641–652. [CrossRef]
11. Zografos, K.; Balakrishnan, N. On families of Beta- and generalized Gamma-generated distributions and associated inference. *Stat. Methodol.* **2009**, *6*, 344–362. [CrossRef]

12. Afify, A.Z.; Emrah, A.; Alizadeh, M.; Ozel, G.; Hamedani, G.G. The odd exponentiated half-logistic-G family: Properties, characterizations and applications. *Chil. J. Stat.* **2017**, *8*, 65–91.
13. El-Morshedy, M.; Eliwa, M.S. The odd flexible Weibull-H family of distributions: Properties and estimation with applications to complete and upper record data. *Filomate* **2019**, *33*, 2635–2652. [CrossRef]
14. Alizadeh, M.; Afify, A.Z.; Eliwa, M.S.; Sajid, A. The odd log-logistic Lindley-G family of distributions: Properties, Bayesian and non-Bayesian estimation with applications. *Comput. Stat.* **2019**, *35*, 281–308. [CrossRef]
15. El-Morshedy, M.; Eliwa, M.S.; Afify, A.Z. The odd Chen generator of distributions: Properties and estimation methods with applications in medicine and engineering. *J. Natl. Sci. Found. Sri Lanka* **2020**, *48*, 113–130.
16. Eliwa, M.S.; El-Morshedy, M.; Ali, S. Exponentiated odd Chen-G family of distributions: Statistical properties, Bayesian and non-Bayesian estimation with applications. *J. Appl. Stat.* **2020**, 1–27. [CrossRef]
17. Tahir, M.H.; Hussain, M.A.; Cordeiro, G.M.; El-Morshedy, M.; Eliwa, M.S. A New Kumaraswamy Generalized Family of Distributions with Properties, Applications, and Bivariate Extension. *Mathematics* **2020**, *8*, 1989. [CrossRef]
18. Altun, E.; Korkmaz, M.Ç.; El-Morshedy, M.; Eliwa, M.S. The extended gamma distribution with regression model and applications. *AIMS Math.* **2021**, *6*, 2418–2439. [CrossRef]
19. Altun, E.; El-Morshedy, M.; Eliwa, M.S. A new regression model for bounded response variable: An alternative to the beta and unit-Lindley regression models. *PLoS ONE* **2021**, *16*, e0245627. [CrossRef] [PubMed]
20. EL-Morshedy, M.; Alshammari, F.S.; Tyagi, A.; Elbatal, I.; Eliwa, M.S. Bayesian and frequentist inferences on a new probability generator with applications in engineering. *Entropy* **2021**, *23*, 446. [CrossRef]
21. Handique, L.; Chakraborty, S.; Eliwa, M.S.; Hamedani, G.G. Poisson Transmuted-G Family of Distributions: Its Properties and Applications. *Pak. J. Stat. Oper. Res.* **2021**, *17*, 309–332. [CrossRef]
22. Keller, A.Z.; Kamath, A.R. Reliability analysis of machine tools. *Reliab. Eng.* **1982**, *3*, 449–473. [CrossRef]
23. Abouammoh, A.M.; Alshingiti, A.M. Reliability of generalized inverted exponential distribution. *J. Stat. Comput. Simul.* **2009**, *79*, 1301–1315. [CrossRef]
24. Louzada, F.; Ramos, P.L.; Nascimento, D. The inverse Nakagami-m distribution: A novel approach in reliability. *IEEE Trans. Reliab.* **2018**, *67*, 1030–1042. [CrossRef]
25. Ramos, P.L.; Mota, A.L.; Ferreira, P.H.; Ramos, E.; Tomazella, V.L.; Louzada, F. Bayesian analysis of the inverse generalized gamma distribution using objective priors. *J. Stat. Comput. Simul.* **2021**, *91*, 786–816. [CrossRef]
26. Chang, G.J.; Cui, L.; Hwang, F.K. *Reliabilities of Consecutive-K Systems*; Kluwer Academic: Dordrecht, The Netherlands, 2009.
27. Nadarajah, S.; Bakouch, H.S.; Tahmasbi, R. A generalized Lindley distribution. *Sankhya B* **2011**, *73*, 331–359. [CrossRef]
28. Mahmoud, M.R.; Mandouh, R.M. On the transmuted Frechet distribution. *J. Appl. Sci. Res.* **2013**, *9*, 5553–5561.
29. Lawless, J.F. *Statistical Models and Methods for Lifetime Data*; John Wiley and Sons: New York, NY, USA, 2003.

Article

Taming Tail Risk: Regularized Multiple β Worst-Case CVaR Portfolio

Kei Nakagawa [1,*] and Katsuya Ito [2]

[1] Innovation Lab, NOMURA Asset Management Co., Ltd., 2-2-1 Toyosu, Koto-ku, Tokyo 135-0061, Japan
[2] MITSUI & Co., Ltd., 2-1, Otemachi 1-chome, Chiyoda-ku, Tokyo 100-8631, Japan; Katsuy.Ito@mitsui.com
* Correspondence: kei.nak.0315@gmail.com or k-nakagawa@nomura-am.co.jp

Abstract: The importance of proper tail risk management is a crucial component of the investment process and conditional Value at Risk (CVaR) is often used as a tail risk measure. CVaR is the asymmetric risk measure that controls and manages the downside risk of a portfolio while symmetric risk measures such as variance consider both upside and downside risk. In fact, minimum CVaR portfolio is a promising alternative to traditional mean-variance optimization. However, there are three major challenges in the minimum CVaR portfolio. Firstly, when using CVaR as a risk measure, we need to determine the distribution of asset returns, but it is difficult to actually grasp the distribution; therefore, we need to invest in a situation where the distribution is uncertain. Secondly, the minimum CVaR portfolio is formulated with a single β and may output significantly different portfolios depending on the β. Finally, most portfolio allocation strategies do not account for transaction costs incurred by each rebalancing of the portfolio. In order to improve these challenges, we propose a Regularized Multiple β Worst-case CVaR (RM-WCVaR) portfolio. The characteristics of this portfolio are as follows: it makes CVaR robust with worst-case CVaR which is still an asymmetric risk measure, it is stable among multiple β, and against changes in weights over time. We perform experiments on well-known benchmarks to evaluate the proposed portfolio.RM-WCVaR demonstrates superior performance of having both higher risk-adjusted returns and lower maximum drawdown.

Keywords: RM-WCVaR; tail risk; portfolio optimization

1. Introduction

The problem of finding the optimum portfolio for investors is known as a portfolio optimization problem. The portfolio optimization problem has been an important research theme, both academically and practically as it is a crucial part of managing risk and maximizing returns from a set of investments. The classical portfolio optimization approach is mean-variance optimization (MVO), which mainly concerns the expectation and variability of return (i.e., mean and variance [1]). Although the variance would be the most fundamental risk measure to be minimized, it has a crucial drawback: variance is a symmetric risk measure. Controlling the variance leads to a low deviation from the expected return with regard to both the downside and the upside.

Hence, asymmetric risk measures such as the Value-at-Risk (VaR) measure, which controls and manages the downside risk in terms of percentiles of the loss distribution of portfolio, have been proposed [2].

Instead of considering both the upside and downside of the expected return, the VaR risk measure focuses on only the downside of the expected return as the risk and represents the predicted maximum loss with a specified confidence level β (e.g., 99%). VaR became so popular that it was approved as a valid approach for calculating risk charges by bank regulators such as the Basel Accord II [3].

However, the VaR measure, if studied in the framework of coherent risk measures [4], lacks subadditivity, and, therefore, convexity in the case of general loss distributions. This drawback entails both inconsistencies with the well-accepted principle of portfolio

diversification, i.e., diversification reduces risk. The VaR risk measure is non-convex and not smooth, making it difficult to optimize [5]. To reduce the computational burden of minimizing VaR, ref. [5] proposed a new mixed integer LP optimization based on the symmetric property of VaR. Besides, both variance and VaR ignore the magnitude of extreme or rare losses by their definition. Both risk measures cannot deal with extremely unlikely, but potentially catastrophic, events i.e., managing the tail risk [6].

The Conditional VaR (CVaR) risk measure responds to the aforementioned drawbacks of variance and VaR. CVaR is defined as the expected value of the portfolio loss that occurs beyond a certain probability level β. Obviously, CVaR is a more conservative risk measure than VaR. In [7], it was proven that the CVaR risk measure is a coherent risk measure that exhibits subadditivity and convexity. Additionally, the minimum CVaR portfolio that minimizes the CVaR results in a tractable optimization problem [8,9]. For example, when the portfolio loss is defined as the minus return of the portfolio, and a finite number of historical observations of returns are used in estimating CVaR, its minimization problem can be presented as a Linear programming (LP) optimization and can be solved efficiently. The minimum CVaR portfolio is a promising alternative to MVO for those reasons. In fact, the effectiveness of CVaR in portfolio construction designs has been demonstrated in a large number of recently published contributions, including index tracking and enhanced indexing [10–12].

However, there are three major challenges in the minimum CVaR portfolio. Firstly, when using CVaR as a risk measure, we need to determine the distribution of asset returns, but it is difficult to actually grasp the distribution; therefore, we need to invest in a situation where the distribution is uncertain [13–15]. Secondly, the minimum CVaR portfolio is formulated with a single β and may output significantly different portfolios depending on how the β is selected [16]. In the context of MVO, this is called error maximization, which is the phenomenon that even small changes in the inputs can result in huge changes in the whole portfolio structure [17]. Thirdly, most portfolio optimization strategies do not account for transaction costs incurred by each rebalancing of the portfolio [18]. When buying and selling assets on the markets, commissions and other costs are incurred, such as globally defined transaction costs that are charged by the brokers or the financial institutions serving as intermediaries. Most of these transaction costs are incurred for portfolio turnovers. Transaction costs represent the most important feature to consider when selecting a real portfolio, given that they diminish net returns and reduce the amount of capital available for future investments [19].

The objective of this study is to propose a new tail risk-controlling portfolio construction method that addresses the above challenges and to confirm its performance. In this paper, we propose Regularized Multiple β Worst-case CVaR (RM-WCVaR) Portfolio Optimization. The characteristics of our portfolio are as follows. It makes CVaR robust with worst-case CVaR (WCVaR), which is an asymmetric risk measure and used in situations where the information on the underlying probability distribution is not exactly known [14,15]. Our portfolio is formulated with the multiple probability levels β of WCVaR not to depend on a single β level. Finally, to control transaction costs, we add the $L1$-regularization term on the portfolio as stated in [18,20]. However, unlike these studies, we impose $L1$-norm penalty on portfolio turnovers rather than portfolio weights.

We also prove that the RM-WCVaR Portfolio Optimization problem is written as an LP optimization problem such as the single β-CVaR and WCVaR portfolio. We perform experiments on well-known benchmarks to evaluate the proposed portfolio. Compared with various portfolios, our portfolio demonstrates superior performance of having both higher risk-adjusted returns and lower maximum drawdown despite the lower turnover rate.

In the following sections, we first review the existing methods in Section 2. We formulate the VaR, CVaR, and WCVaR risk measures and the portfolio optimization with them in Section 3 and then, we propose the RM-WCVaR Portfolio in Section 4 and investigate the empirical effectiveness of the our portfolio in Section 5. Finally, we conclude in Section 6.

2. Related Work

MVO assumes that investment decisions on getting a diversified portfolio depend on the two inputs: expected returns and the covariances of asset returns. However, as the estimation errors, mainly in expected return parameters, are amplified by optimization and then propagate into the solution of the optimization, extreme portfolio weights and a lack of diversification are commonly observed. This phenomenon has eventually ruined the out-of-sample performance of MVO [17,21]. To date, many efforts have been expended to handle the estimation risk on the parameter uncertainty. In order to reduce estimation error, the conventional regularization models have been applied for the MVO by [18,20]. They demonstrated superior portfolio performances when various types of norm regularities are combined into the optimization problem. Analogously, ref. [22] considered L1 and L2-norms for the mean-CVaR portfolio and [16] considered L1-norms for the multiple CVaR portfolio. Our paper extends this regularization literature to a multiple WCVaR Portfolio.

Robust portfolio optimization is another approach considering the estimation error and has been receiving increased attention [23]. Recently, ref. [24] proposed a robust portfolio optimization approach based on quantile statistics. Robust optimization also has been adopted on the other portfolio optimization problems. In [13], robust portfolio optimization using worst-case VaR was investigated, where only partial information on the distribution was known. In [15], the concept of WCVaR was introduced for the situation where the probability distributions are only partially known, and the properties of WCVaR are studied, such as coherency. Another approach is using a semi-nonparametric distribution, which may asymptotically capture the true density. This approach has been successfully tested for CVaR [25,26]. Our paper extends this robust portfolio optimization literature to a multiple β WCVaR portfolio.

Another direction to reduce the estimated error is to construct a risk-based portfolio that does not use expected returns. The minimum variance portfolio [27], risk parity portfolio [28,29], and maximum diversification portfolio [30] have been proposed as representative risk-based portfolio construction methods. The risk-based portfolio has the desirable property that the portfolio and its performance do not change greatly in response to changes to inputs [31,32]. Furthermore, an extension of each of them has been proposed such as minimum VaR and CVaR portfolio [33], risk and complex risk diversification portfolio [34,35] and higher order risk based portfolio [36]. Various empirical analyses and backtests of stock portfolios and asset allocations have shown better performance than mean-variance portfolios and market capitalization-weighted portfolios [37]. Our paper adds a minimum WCVaR-based portfolio to this risk-based portfolio construction literature.

3. Preliminary

In this section, we define VaR, CVaR, and WCVaR. After which, we formulate a minimum WCVaR portfolio optimization problem. Let r_j be the return of stock j ($1 \leq j \leq n$) and w_j be the portfolio weight for stock j. We denote $r = (r_1, ..., r_n)^\top$ and $w = (w_1, ..., w_n)^\top$. Here, r_j is a random variable and follows the continuous joint probability density function $p(r)$. $L(w,r)$ refers to portfolio loss function and throughout this paper, we assume $L(w,r) = -w^\top r$. The probability that the loss function is less than α is

$$\Phi(w, \alpha) = \int_{L(w,r) \leq \alpha} p(r) dr \tag{1}$$

When the portfolio weight w is fixed, $\Phi(w, \alpha)$ which is the function of α is non-decreasing and is continuous from the right, but is generally non-continuous from the left. For simplicity, we assume that $\Phi(w, \alpha)$ is a continuous function with respect to α. We can define VaR and CVaR as follows.

Definition 1.
$$VaR(w|\beta) := \alpha(w|\beta) = \min(\alpha : \Phi(w, \alpha) \geq \beta) \tag{2}$$

Definition 2.

$$CVaR(w|\beta) := \phi(w|\beta) \tag{3}$$

$$= (1-\beta)^{-1} \int_{L(w,r) \geq \alpha(w|\beta)} L(w,r) p(r) dr$$

Ref. [4] proposed the coherent risk measure, which characterizes the rationale of risk measure.

Definition 3. *The risk measure ρ that maps random loss X to a real number and satisfies the bellow four conditions is called a coherent risk measure.*

Subadditivity: *for all random losses X and Y, $\rho(X+Y) \leq \rho(X) + \rho(Y)$*
Positive homogeneity: *for positive constant $a \in \mathbb{R}^+$, $\rho(aX) = a\rho(X)$*
Monotonicity: *if $X \leq Y$ for each outcome, then $\rho(X) \leq \rho(Y)$*
Translation invariance: *for constant $m \in \mathbb{R}$, $\rho(X+m) = \rho(X) + m$*

It is well known that CVaR is a coherent risk measure and VaR is not a coherent risk measure as it does not satisfy the Subadditivity [6].

Next, we consider WCVaR. Rather than assuming exact knowledge of the return vector r distribution, we presume that the density function $p(\cdot)$ is only considered to belong to a certain set P of distributions, i.e., $p(\cdot) \in P$.

The concept of the WCVaR is introduced in [15] as follows:

Definition 4.

$$WCVaR(w|\beta) := \sup_{p(\cdot) \in P} CVaR(w|\beta) \tag{4}$$

Ref. [15] have shown that the WCVaR is a coherent risk measure as well as CVaR.

Hereafter, we assume that the return vector's distribution is only considered to belong to a set of distributions that includes all mixtures of any predetermined density distributions, i.e.,

$$P_M = \{\sum_{i=1}^{l} \lambda_i p^{(i)}; \lambda_i \geq 0, \sum_{i=1}^{l} \lambda_i = 1, i = 1,\ldots,l\} \tag{5}$$

where $p^{(i)}(\cdot)$ denotes the i-th density distribution, and l denotes the number of the density distributions.

Since it is difficult to handle when the set P contains an infinite number of $p^{(i)}(\cdot)$, we consider approximating P with a convex linear combination of a finite number of $p^{(i)}(\cdot)$. In this study, the mixture of density distributions P_M is represented by blocks of divided empirical distributions.

To compute the WCVaR, we define the auxiliary function $F^i(w,\alpha|\beta)$ as

$$F^{(i)}(w,\alpha|\beta) = \alpha + (1-\beta)^{-1} \int_{R^n} [-w^\top r - \alpha]^+ p^{(i)}(r) dr \tag{6}$$

where $i=1,\ldots,l$ and $[t]^+ := \max(t,0)$. Then, the following lemma holds.

Lemma 1 (Ref. [15]). *For an arbitrarily fixed w and β, $WCVaR(w|\beta)$ with respect to P_M is given by*

$$WCVaR(w|\beta) = \min_{\alpha} \max_{i \in L} F^{(i)}(w,\alpha|\beta) \tag{7}$$

where $L = \{1,\ldots,l\}$.

Moreover, denote

$$F^L(w, \alpha|\beta) = \max_{i \in L} F^{(i)}(w, \alpha|\beta) \quad (8)$$

Minimizing the $WCVaR(w|\beta)$ overall $w \in X$ is equivalent to minimizing $F^L(w, \alpha|\beta)$ overall $(w, \alpha) \in X \times R$, in the sense that

$$\min_{w \in X} WCVaR(w|\beta) = \min_{(w,\alpha) \in X \times R} F^L(w, \alpha|\beta) \quad (9)$$

From now on, we discuss the computational aspect of minimization of WCVaR. Lemma 1 helps us to translate the minimization problem to a more tractable one. The WCVaR minimization is equivalent to the following problem:

Problem 1.

$$\min_{(w,\alpha,C) \in X \times R \times R} C \quad (10)$$

$$s.t. \quad \alpha + (1-\beta)^{-1} \int_{R^n} [-w^\top r - \alpha]^+ p^{(i)}(r) dr \leq C, \quad (i=1,\ldots,l) \quad (11)$$

We approximate the function $F^{(i)}(w, \alpha|\beta)$ by sampling a random variable $r^{(i)}$, $i = 1, \ldots, l$ from the density function $p^{(i)}(\cdot)$. $r^{(i)}[q]$ is the q-th sample with respect to the i-th density distribution $p^{(i)}(\cdot)$, and $\mathcal{N}_i \subseteq \{1, \ldots, N\}$ denotes the set of corresponding samples. The auxiliary function $F^{(i)}(w, \alpha|\beta)$ is approximated as follows.

$$F^{(i)}(w, \alpha|\beta) \simeq \alpha + (|\mathcal{N}_i|(1-\beta))^{-1} \sum_{q \in \mathcal{N}_i} [-w^\top r^{(i)}[q] - \alpha]^+ \quad (12)$$

Finally, we can formulate the minimum WCVaR portfolio as a linear programming problem, as shown below.

Problem 2.

$$\min_{w,\alpha,t_{iq}} C \quad (13)$$

$$s.t. \alpha + \left(\left|\mathcal{N}^{(i)}\right|(1-\beta)\right)^{-1} \sum_{q \in \mathcal{N}_i} t_{iq} \leq C \quad (i=1,\ldots,l) \quad (14)$$

$$t_{iq} \geq -w^\top r^{(i)}[q] - \alpha \quad (i=1,\ldots,l, \; q \in \mathcal{N}_i) \quad (15)$$

$$t_{iq} \geq 0 \quad (i=1,\ldots,l, \; q \in \mathcal{N}_i) \quad (16)$$

4. Regularized Multiple β WCVaR Portfolio Optimization

In this section, we propose a RM-WCVaR portfolio that takes into account the multiple β WCVaR values and portfolio turnover. Our approach is similar in spirit to that of [38], given that our approach estimates the simultaneously approximating multiple conditional quantiles.

The intuition behind the formulation is to minimize the max margin among multiple β levels of WCVaR (Figure 1). Figure 1 illustrates it where $\beta_k = \{0.97, 0.98, 0.99\}$ and each WC_{β_k} is given as a solution to Problem 1.

Here, $WC_{\beta_k}, k=1,\ldots,K$ is the value of WCVaR obtained by solving Problem 2. Then, we minimized C, considering that WC_{β_k} is a main problem in this paper.

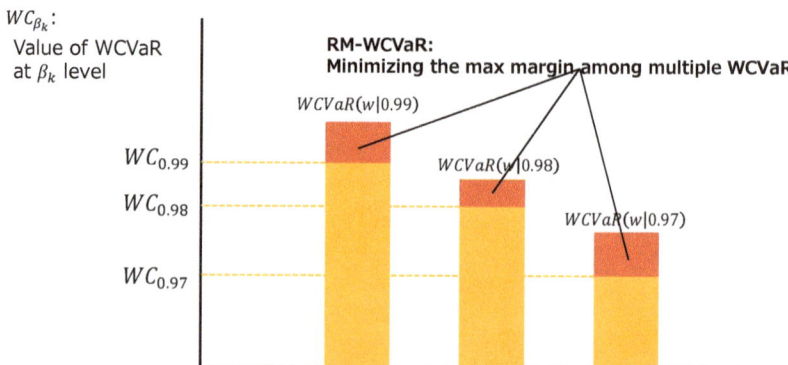

Figure 1. The intuition behind the formulation of RM-WCVaR portfolio (Problem 3).

Problem 3.

$$\min_{(w,C) \in X \times R} C \tag{17}$$

$$s.t. WCVaR(w|\beta_k) \leq C + WC_{\beta_k} \quad (k = 1, \ldots, K) \tag{18}$$

As in Lemma 1, We define $F^L(w, \alpha_k|\beta_k) = \max_{i \in L} F^{(i)}(w, \alpha_k|\beta_k)$. Then, Problem 3 can be written as follows.

Problem 4.

$$\min_{(w,C) \in X \times R} C \tag{19}$$

$$s.t. \min_{\alpha_k} F^L(w, \alpha_k|\beta_k) \leq C + WC_{\beta_k} \quad (k = 1, \ldots, K) \tag{20}$$

Thereafter, we consider the following Problem 5.

Problem 5.

$$\min_{(w,C,\alpha) \in X \times R \times R^K} C \tag{21}$$

$$s.t. F^L(w, \alpha_k|\beta_k) \leq C + WC_{\beta_k} \quad (k = 1, \ldots, K) \tag{22}$$

where $\alpha = (\alpha_1, \cdots, \alpha_K)^\top$.

According to the Lemma 2, Problem 3 and 5 are equivalent.

Lemma 2.
1. If (w^*, C^*) is the optimal value for Problem 4, then (w^*, C^*, α^*) is the optimal value of Problem 5.
2. If $(w^{**}, C^{**}, \alpha^{**})$ is the optimal value for Problem 5, then (w^{**}, C^{**}) is the optimal value for Problem 4.

Proof. Assume that (w^*, C^*) is the optimal value for Problem 4. Given that (w^*, C^*) is a feasible solution of Problem 4, $\min_{\alpha_k} F^L(w^*, \alpha_k|\beta_k) \leq C^* + WC_{\beta_k}$ holds. We defined $\alpha_k^* = (\alpha_1^*, \ldots, \alpha_K^*)^\top$ as $\alpha_k^* := \operatorname{argmin}_{\alpha_k \in R} F^L(w^*, \alpha_k|\beta_k)(k = 1, \ldots, K)$. Then, (w^*, C^*, α^*) became a feasible solution of Problem 5 since $F^L(w^*, \alpha_k^* | \beta_k) \leq C^* + WC_{\beta_k}$ holds. If (w^*, C^*, α^*) is not the optimal solution of Problem 5, there exists a feasible solution $(\hat{w}, \hat{C}, \hat{\alpha})$ satisfying $\hat{C} < C^*$. Then, $\min_{\alpha_k \in R} F^L(\hat{w}, \alpha_k | \beta_k) \leq F^L(\hat{w}, \hat{\alpha}_k | \beta_k) \leq \hat{C} + WC_{\beta_k} (k = 1, \ldots, K)$ holds. Therefore, $(\hat{w}, \hat{C})$ is a feasible solution of Problem 4, thereby contradicting that C^* is the optimal solution of Problem 4. Therefore, (w^*, C^*, α^*) is the optimal solution. Assume that $(w^{**}, C^{**}, \alpha^{**})$ is the optimal value for Problem 5. Then, because $(w^{**}, C^{**}, \alpha^{**})$ is a feasible solution of Problem 5, $F^L(w^{**}, \alpha_k^{**} | \beta_k) \leq C^{**} + WC_{\beta_k} (k = 1, \ldots, K)$ holds. (w^{**}, C^{**}) is a feasible solution for Problem 4 given that $\min_{\alpha_k \in R} F^L(w^{**}, \alpha_k | \beta_k) \leq F^L(w^{**}, \alpha_k^{**} | \beta_k) \leq C^{**} + WC_{\beta_k} (k = 1, \ldots, K)$ holds. If (w^{**}, C^{**}) is not the optimal solution of Problem 4, there exists a feasible solution $(\hat{w}, \hat{C})$ satisfying $\hat{C} < C^{**}$. We defined $\hat{\alpha} = (\hat{\alpha}_1, \ldots, \hat{\alpha}_K)^\top$ as $\hat{\alpha}_k := \arg\min_{\alpha_k} F_{\beta_k}^L(\hat{w}, \alpha_k)$. Then, $(\hat{w}, \hat{C}, \hat{\alpha})$ became a feasible solution of Problem 5, thereby contradicting that C^{**} is the optimal solution of Problem 5. Therefore, (w^{**}, C^{**}) is the optimal solution. □

Here, $r^{(i)}[q]$ is the q-th sample with respect to the i-th density distribution $p^{(i)}(r)$, and $\mathcal{N}_i$ denotes the set of corresponding samples. The function $F^{(i)}(w, \alpha_k | \beta_k)$ is approximated as follows.

$$\tilde{F}^{(i)}(w, \alpha_k | \beta_k) \simeq \alpha_k + \frac{1}{|\mathcal{N}_i|(1-\beta_k)} \sum_{q \in \mathcal{N}_i} [-w^\top r^{(i)}[q] - \alpha_k]^+ \qquad (23)$$

Finally, we derive the RM-WCVaR Portfolio, where the objectives are minimizing multiple WCVaR values and also controlling the portfolio turnover. Controlling the portfolio turnover is realized through imposing the L1-regularization term as $\|w - w^-\|_1 = \sum_{j=1}^n |w_j - w_j^-|$ where w_i^- denotes the portfolio weight before rebalancing.

Based on the above discussion, the RM-WCVaR Portfolio Optimization problem can be formulated as follows:

Problem 6.

$$\min_{(w, C, \alpha) \in X \times R \times R^K} C + \lambda \|w - w^-\|_1 \qquad (24)$$

$$\text{s.t.} \tilde{F}^{(i)}(w, \alpha_k | \beta_k) \leq C + WC_{\beta_k}$$
$$(i = 1, \ldots, l, \ k = 1, \ldots, K) \qquad (25)$$

We can easily prove that Problem 6 is a linear programming problem similar to the usual CVaR minimization problem.

Theorem 1. *The Regularized Multiple β WCVaR Portfolio Optimization problem is equivalent to the following linear programming problem.*

$$\min_{C,w,\alpha,t,u} C + \sum_{j=1}^{n} u_j$$

$$\text{s.t.} \quad u_j \geq \lambda\left(w_j - w_j^-\right)$$

$$u_j \geq -\lambda\left(w_j - w_j^-\right)$$

$$t_{iqk} \geq 0$$

$$t_{iqk} \geq -w^\top r^{(i)}[q] - \alpha_k$$

$$\alpha_k + \frac{1}{|\mathcal{N}_i|(1-\beta_k)} \sum_{q \in \mathcal{N}_i} t_{iqk} \leq C + WC_{\beta_k}$$

$$(i = 1,\ldots,l, \ k = 1,\ldots,K)$$

$$1^\top w = 1$$

$$w_j \geq 0 \quad (j = 1,...,n)$$

Proof. Using a standard approach in optimization, we can replace the absolute value term $\lambda\|w - w^-\|_1$ in the objective function with $u \geq \lambda(w - w^-)$ and $u \geq -\lambda(w - w^-)$ in the constraint. Thereafter, the objective and constraints all became linear. □

The Algorithm 1 summarizes the sequential procedure of the RM-WCVaR portfolio.

Algorithm 1 Regularized Multiple β WCVaR Portfolio Optimization.

Input: K probability levels $\beta_k \in (0,1)$ $(k = 1,\ldots,K)$,
Coefficient of the regularization term $\lambda \in \mathbb{R}_{>0}$,
Number of blocks of a partition $l \in \mathbb{Z}_{>0}$ and
Return matrix $R_t \in \mathbb{R}^{n \times N}$ $(t = 1,\ldots,T)$
Output: Set of optimal weights $\mathcal{W} = \{w_t \in \mathbb{R}^n\}_{t=1}^{T}$
1: **for** $t = 1,\ldots,T$ **do**
2:    Calculate WC_{β_k} via solving Problem 2 $(k = 1,\ldots,K)$.
3:    Randomly divide the set $\{1,\ldots,N\}$ into blocks of a partition $\{\mathcal{N}_i\}_{i=1}^{l}$ s.t. $|\mathcal{N}_i| = \frac{N}{T}$ $(i = 1,\ldots,l)$
4:    $w^- \leftarrow w_{t-1}$
5:    Solve the linear programming introduced in Theorem 1
6:    Add to the output set $\mathcal{W}$ the solution w^* as w_t
7: **end for**
8: **return** $\mathcal{W}$

---

5. Experiment

In this section, we report the results of our empirical experiment with well-known benchmarks in finance.

5.1. Dataset

In the experiments, we use well-known academic benchmarks called Fama and French (FF) datasets [39] to ensure the reproducibility of the experiment. This FF dataset is public and is readily available to anyone (https://mba.tuck.dartmouth.edu/pages/faculty/ken.french/data_library.html). The FF datasets have been recognized as standard datasets and are heavily adopted in finance research because of their extensive coverage of asset classes and very long historical data series. We use FF25, FF48 and FF100 dataset. For example, the FF25 and FF100 dataset include 25 and 100 portfolios formed based on size and book-to-market ratio, while the FF48 dataset contains monthly returns of 48 portfolios representing different industrial sectors. We use all datasets as monthly data from January 1989 to June 2020.

5.2. Experimental Settings

In our experiment, we use the following portfolio models.

- "EW" stands for equally-weighted (EW) portfolio [40].
- "MV" stands for minimum-variance portfolio. We use the latest 10 years (120 months) to compute for the sample covariance matrix [41].
- "DRP" stands for the doubly regularized minimum-variance portfolio [18]. We use the latest 10 years (120 months) to compute for the sample covariance matrix. We set combinations of two coefficients for regularization terms to $\lambda_1 = \{0.001, 0.005, 0.01, 0.05\}$ and $\lambda_2 = \{0.001, 0.005, 0.01, 0.05\}$.
- "EGO" stands for the Kelly growth optimal portfolio with ensemble learning [42]. We set n_1 (number of resamples) = 50, n_2 (size of each resample) = 5τ, τ (number of periods of return data) = 120, n_3 (number of resampled subsets) = 50, n_4 (size of each subset) = $n^{0.7}$, where n is number of assets (i.e., $n = 25, 48, 100$).
- "RMCVaR" stands for the regularized multiple CVaR portfolio [16]. We set $K = 5$ ($k = 1, \ldots, K$) as five patterns of $\beta_k = \{0.95, 0.96, 0.97, 0.98, 0.99\}$ to calculate C_{β_k}. We also set Q (number of sampling periods of return data) as 10 years (120 months). For the coefficient of the regularization term, we implemented four patterns of $\lambda = \{0.001, 0.005, 0.01, 0.05\}$.
- "WCVaR" stands for minimum WCVaR portfolio with β (Problem 2). We implemented five patterns of $\beta = \{0.95, 0.96, 0.97, 0.98, 0.99\}$. We used the latest 50 years' ($N = 600$ months) data and split them randomly into $l \in \{1, 2, \ldots, 10\}$ divisions.
- "AWCVaR" stands for the average portfolio calculated by the simple average of minimum WCVaR portfolio of different $\beta = \{0.95, 0.96, 0.97, 0.98, 0.99\}$ at each month.
- "RM-WCVaR" stands for our proposed portfolio. We set $K = 5$ ($k = 1, \ldots, K$) as five patterns of $\beta_k = \{0.95, 0.96, 0.97, 0.98, 0.99\}$ to calculate WC_{β_k}. We use the latest 50 years' ($N = 600$ months) data and split them randomly into $l \in \{1, 2, \ldots, 10\}$ divisions. For the coefficient of the regularization term, we implement four patterns of $\lambda = \{0.001, 0.005, 0.01, 0.05\}$. The RM-WCVaR Portfolio presented in Algorithm 1 is straightforward in terms of implementation.

We use the first-half period, i.e., from January 1989 to December 2004, as the in-sample period in terms of deciding the hyper-parameters of each portfolio. After that, we use the second half-period, i.e., from January 2005 to June 2020, as the out-of-sample period. Each portfolio is updated by sliding one-month-ahead.

5.3. Performance Measures

The following measures widely used in finance to evaluate portfolio strategies [43] are chosen. The portfolio return at time t is defined as $R_t = \sum_{j=1}^{n} r_{j,t} w_{j,t-1}$ where $r_{j,t}$ is the monthly return of j asset at time t, $w_{j,t-1}$ is the weight of j asset in the portfolio at time $t-1$, and n is the total number of assets.

The annualized return (AR), annualized risk as the standard deviation of return (RISK), and risk-adjusted return (R/R) are defined as follows:

$$AR = \frac{12}{T} \times \sum_{t=1}^{T} R_t, \tag{26}$$

$$RISK = \sqrt{\frac{12}{T-1} \times \sum_{t=1}^{T} (R_t - \hat{\mu})^2}, \quad \hat{\mu} = 1/T \times \sum_{t=1}^{T} R_t, \tag{27}$$

$$R/R = AR/RISK. \tag{28}$$

Among them, R/R is the most important measure for a portfolio strategy. We also evaluate the maximum draw-down (MaxDD), which is another widely used risk measure [44] for the portfolio strategy. In particular, MaxDD is the largest drop from a peak defined as

$$\text{MaxDD} = \min_{t \in [1,T]} \left(0, \frac{W_t}{\max_{\tau \in [1,t]} W_\tau} - 1 \right), \quad (29)$$

where W_k is the cumulative return of the portfolio until time k; that is, $W_t = \prod_{t'=1}^{t}(1 + R_{t'})$.

The turnover (TO) indicates the volumes of rebalancing [18]. Since a high TO inevitably generates high explicit and implicit trading costs, the portfolio return tends to be reduced. The TO is a proxy for the transaction costs of the portfolio. The one-way annualized turnover is calculated as an average absolute value of the rebalancing trades over all the trading periods:

$$\text{TO} = \frac{12}{2(T-1)} \sum_{t=1}^{T-1} ||w_t - w_t^-||_1 \quad (30)$$

where $T-1$ indicates the total number of the rebalancing periods and $w_t^- = \frac{w_{t-1} \otimes (1+r_t)}{1+w_{t-1}^\top r_t}$ is the re-normalized portfolio weight vector before rebalance. Here, r_t is the return vector of the assets at time t, w_{t-1} is the weight vector at time $t-1$, and the operator $\otimes$ denotes the Hadamard (element-wise) product.

5.4. Experimental Results

Tables 1–3 reports the overall performance measures of RM-WCVaR Portfolio, our proposed portfolio, and the 11 compared portfolios introduced in the Experimental Settings section for FF25, FF48, and FF100 dataset. The out-of-sample period is from January 2005 to June 2020. Among the comparisons of the various portfolios, the best performance is highlighted in **bold**.

Table 1 shows that the RM-WCVaR Portfolio outperformed all the compared portfolios in all performance measures. It achieved the highest AR and R/R and the lowest RISK, MaxDD and TO.

Table 1. The out-of-sample performance of each portfolio for FF25 dataset.

FF25		AR[%] ↑	RISK[%] ↓	R/R ↑	MaxDD[%] ↓	TO[%] ↓
EW		8.92	18.60	0.48	−54.12	12.36
MV		9.75	14.34	0.68	−50.69	33.10
DRP		9.74	14.35	0.68	−50.72	9.35
EGO		8.64	19.59	0.44	−57.26	76.52
RMCVaR		9.65	15.50	0.62	−49.59	34.96
AWCVaR		9.14	16.03	0.57	−55.82	23.11
WCVaR	95%	9.12	16.56	0.55	−54.23	18.19
	96%	9.01	15.82	0.56	−53.29	20.82
	97%	9.01	15.94	0.56	−57.11	26.00
	98%	9.41	16.04	0.58	−55.91	22.41
	99%	9.08	16.15	0.56	−58.43	31.22
RM-WCVaR		**10.44**	**14.26**	**0.73**	**−45.26**	**8.12**

Performance measures are the annualized return (AR), annualized risk (RISK), annualized return–risk ratio (R/R), maximum drawdown (MaxDD) and turnover rate (TO). The out-of-sample period is from January 2005 to June 2020. Among the comparisons of the various portfolios, the best performance is highlighted in **bold**.

In Table 2, we can see the RM-WCVaR Portfolio had the best AR, R/R, MaxDD and TO. Only the RISK was the best for the DRP portfolio.

Table 2. The out-of-sample performance of each portfolio for FF48 dataset.

FF48		AR[%] ↑	RISK[%] ↓	R/R ↑	MaxDD[%] ↓	TO[%] ↓
EW		9.36	17.12	0.55	−52.90	22.03
MV		8.86	12.77	0.69	−43.84	28.48
DRP		8.78	**12.20**	0.72	−38.92	17.15
EGO		11.11	20.61	0.54	−57.39	79.60
RMCVaR		8.27	12.82	0.65	−38.28	129.31
AWCVaR		11.70	13.01	0.90	−42.60	39.44
WCVaR	95%	11.43	13.29	0.85	−42.65	43.98
	96%	10.95	13.25	0.83	−43.56	41.38
	97%	11.28	13.14	0.86	−41.58	37.66
	98%	12.12	13.15	0.92	−44.35	44.27
	99%	12.77	13.21	0.97	−40.91	40.84
RM-WCVaR		**14.48**	14.63	**0.99**	**−36.66**	**7.87**

Performance measures are the annualized return (AR), annualized risk (RISK), annualized return–risk ratio (R/R), maximum drawdown (MaxDD) and turnover rate (TO). The out-of-sample period is from January 2005 to June 2020. Among the comparisons of the various portfolios, the best performance is highlighted in **bold**.

In Table 3, the RM-WCVaR Portfolio had the best AR, R/R, and MaxDD. The TO for the RM-WCVaR portfolio was the second lowest after the EW portfolio.

Table 3. The out-of-sample performance of each portfolio for FF100 dataset.

FF100		AR[%] ↑	RISK[%] ↓	R/R ↑	MaxDD[%] ↓	TO[%] ↓
EW		8.86	18.87	0.47	−54.53	**16.18**
MV		9.47	**14.13**	0.67	−50.69	39.10
DRP		9.92	14.42	0.69	−51.23	19.20
EGO		8.66	20.12	0.43	−57.79	78.65
RMCVaR		9.87	15.42	0.64	−49.97	35.20
AWCVaR		8.74	16.33	0.54	−43.02	23.27
WCVaR	95%	7.82	16.59	0.47	−40.19	18.31
	96%	9.09	16.44	0.55	−37.12	20.97
	97%	9.10	16.55	0.55	−40.74	26.18
	98%	9.63	16.14	0.60	−43.89	22.57
	99%	8.04	16.59	0.48	−52.50	31.44
RM-WCVaR		**14.26**	20.67	**0.69**	**−37.10**	18.00

Performance measures are the annualized return (AR), annualized risk (RISK), annualized return–risk ratio (R/R), maximum drawdown (MaxDD) and turnover rate (TO). The out-of-sample period is from January 2005 to June 2020. Among the comparisons of the various portfolios, the best performance is highlighted in **bold**.

In all datasets, the proposed RM-WCVaR Portfolio achieved the highest AR and R/R, and the lowest MaxDD.

Unsurprisingly, the RM-WCVaR Portfolio was different from ACVaR, which is the simple average of five probability levels' WCVaR portfolios. RM-WCVaR Portfolio also exceeded the individual β levels of WCVaR portfolios in terms of AR, R/R, MaxDD and TO. This is because the RM procedure implies a minimization of the maximum margin among multiple WCVaR levels, which enables more efficient portfolio construction. Analyzing the relationship between the margin level and performance of RM-WCVaR is an important future task.

Therefore, we can confirm that the RM-WCVaR Portfolio has high R/R and avoids a large drawdown despite the lower turnover rate. Since the TO is the lowest of all compared portfolios, the results do not change when transaction costs are taken into account. We consider the RM-WCVaR portfolio to have had a good R/R because it reduced tail risk, resulting in lower drawdowns and higher returns.

6. Conclusions

Our study makes the following contributions. We propose a Regularized Multiple β WCVaR Portfolio, which solves three challenges in the minimum CVaR portfolio. We prove that the optimization problem reduces to a linear programming problem. We perform experiments on well-known benchmarks in finance to evaluate our proposed portfolio. Our portfolio shows superior performance in terms of having both higher risk-adjusted returns and lower maximum drawdown despite the lower turnover rate.

Directions of promising future work include (1) constructing a more sophisticated mixture distribution by assuming a probability distribution as in [15], rather than a simple empirical distribution in this study, (2) directly using a semi-nonparametric distribution capturing true CVaR as in [25,26] instead of WCVaR, and (3) obtaining a higher R/R by incorporating the expected return into our proposed portfolio.

Author Contributions: Conceptualization, K.N.; methodology, K.N.; software, K.I.; validation, K.N. and K.I.; formal analysis, K.N. and K.I.; writing—original draft preparation, K.N.; writing—review and editing, K.N. and K.I. All authors have read and agreed to the published version of the manuscript.

Funding: This research received no external funding.

Data Availability Statement: The data that support the findings of this study are openly available in https://mba.tuck.dartmouth.edu/pages/faculty/ken.french/data_library.html.

Acknowledgments: The authors would like to thank the referees for their valuable comments and suggestions. Discussions with Masaya Abe, Senior Quants Analyst of Nomura Asset Management and Shuhei Noma, Nomura Asset Management have been insightful.

Conflicts of Interest: The authors declare no conflict of interest.

References

1. Markowitz, H. Portfolio selection. *J. Financ.* **1952**, *7*, 77–91.
2. Morgan, J.; Spencer, M. *Riskmetrics Technical Document*; Morgan Guaranty Trust Company of New York: New York, NY, USA, 1996.
3. Herring, R.J. The Basel 2 approach to bank operational risk: Regulation on the wrong track. *J. Risk Financ.* **2002**, *4*, 42–45. [CrossRef]
4. Artzner, P.; Delbaen, F.; Eber, J.M.; Heath, D. Coherent measures of risk. *Math. Financ.* **1999**, *9*, 203–228. [CrossRef]
5. Wang, D.; Chen, Y.; Wang, H.; Huang, M. Formulation of theNon-Parametric Value at Risk Portfolio Selection Problem Considering Symmetry. *Symmetry* **2020**, *12*, 1639. [CrossRef]
6. McNeil, A.J.; Frey, R.; Embrechts, P. *Quantitative Risk Management: Concepts, Techniques and Tools—Revised Edition*; Princeton University Press: Princeton, NJ, USA, 2015.
7. Pflug, G.C. Some remarks on the value-at-risk and the conditional value-at-risk. In *Probabilistic Constrained Optimization*; Springer: Berlin/Heidelberg, Germany, 2000; pp. 272–281.
8. Rockafellar, R.T.; Uryasev, S. Optimization of conditional value-at-risk. *J. Risk* **2000**, *2*, 21–42. [CrossRef]
9. Rockafellar, R.T.; Uryasev, S. Conditional value-at-risk for general loss distributions. *J. Bank. Financ.* **2002**, *26*, 1443–1471. [CrossRef]
10. Goel, A.; Sharma, A.; Mehra, A. Index tracking and enhanced indexing using mixed conditional value-at-risk. *J. Comput. Appl. Math.* **2018**, *335*, 361–380. [CrossRef]
11. Karmakar, M.; Paul, S. Intraday portfolio risk management using VaR and CVaR: A CGARCH-EVT-Copula approach. *Int. J. Forecast.* **2019**, *35*, 699–709. [CrossRef]
12. Guastaroba, G.; Mansini, R.; Ogryczak, W.; Speranza, M.G. Enhanced index tracking with CVaR-based ratio measures. *Ann. Oper. Res.* **2020**, *292*, 883–931. [CrossRef]
13. Ghaoui, L.E.; Oks, M.; Oustry, F. Worst-case value-at-risk and robust portfolio optimization: A conic programming approach. *Oper. Res.* **2003**, *51*, 543–556. [CrossRef]

14. Čerbáková, J. Worst-case var and cvar. In *Operations Research Proceedings 2005*; Springer: Berlin/Heidelberg, Germany, 2006; pp. 817–822.
15. Zhu, S.; Fukushima, M. Worst-case conditional value-at-risk with application to robust portfolio management. *Oper. Res.* **2009**, *57*, 1155–1168. [CrossRef]
16. Nakagawa, K.; Noma, S.; Abe, M. RM-CVaR: Regularized Multiple β-CVaR Portfolio. *IJCAI* **2020**, 4562–4568. [CrossRef]
17. Michaud, R.O. The Markowitz optimization enigma: Is 'optimized'optimal? *Financ. Anal. J.* **1989**, *45*, 31–42. [CrossRef]
18. Shen, W.; Wang, J.; Ma, S. Doubly regularized portfolio with risk minimization. In Proceedings of the Twenty-Eighth AAAI Conference on Artificial Intelligence, Québec City, QC, Canada, 27–31 July 2014.
19. Mansini, R.; Ogryczak, W.; Speranza, M.G. Portfolio Optimization with Transaction Costs. In *Linear and Mixed Integer Programming for Portfolio Optimization*; Springer: Berlin/Heidelberg, Germany, 2015; pp. 47–62.
20. DeMiguel, V.; Garlappi, L.; Nogales, F.J.; Uppal, R. A generalized approach to portfolio optimization: Improving performance by constraining portfolio norms. *Manag. Sci.* **2009**, *55*, 798–812. [CrossRef]
21. Merton, R.C. *On Estimating the Expected Return on the Market: An Exploratory Investigation*; Technical report; National Bureau of Economic Research: Cambridge, MA, USA, 1980.
22. Gotoh, J.y.; Takeda, A. On the role of norm constraints in portfolio selection. *Comput. Manag. Sci.* **2011**, *8*, 323. [CrossRef]
23. Tütüncü, R.H.; Koenig, M. Robust asset allocation. *Ann. Oper. Res.* **2004**, *132*, 157–187. [CrossRef]
24. Qiu, H.; Han, F.; Liu, H.; Caffo, B. Robust portfolio optimization. *Adv. Neural Inf. Process. Syst.* **2015**, *28*, 46–54.
25. Del Brio, E.B.; Mora-Valencia, A.; Perote, J. Expected shortfall assessment in commodity (L) ETF portfolios with semi-nonparametric specifications. *Eur. J. Financ.* **2019**, *25*, 1746–1764. [CrossRef]
26. Molina-Muñoz, E.; Mora-Valencia, A.; Perote, J. Backtesting expected shortfall for world stock index ETFs with extreme value theory and Gram–Charlier mixtures. *Int. J. Financ. Econ.* **2020**. [CrossRef]
27. Clarke, R.; De Silva, H.; Thorley, S. Minimum-variance portfolio composition. *J. Portf. Manag.* **2011**, *37*, 31–45. [CrossRef]
28. Qian, E. Risk Parity Portfolios: Efficient Portfolios Through true Diversification. 2005. Available online: https://www.panagora.com/assets/PanAgora-Risk-Parity-Portfolios-Efficient-Portfolios-Through-True-Diversification.pdf (accessed on 12 March 2021).
29. Maillard, S.; Roncalli, T.; Teïletche, J. The properties of equally weighted risk contribution portfolios. *J. Portf. Manag.* **2010**, *36*, 60–70. [CrossRef]
30. Choueifaty, Y.; Coignard, Y. Toward maximum diversification. *J. Portf. Manag.* **2008**, *35*, 40–51. [CrossRef]
31. Nakagawa, K.; Imamura, M.; Yoshida, K. Risk-based portfolios with large dynamic covariance matrices. *Int. J. Financ. Stud.* **2018**, *6*, 52. [CrossRef]
32. Du Plessis, H.; van Rensburg, P. Risk-based portfolio sensitivity to covariance estimation. *Invest Anal. J.* **2020**, *49*, 243–268. [CrossRef]
33. Bodnar, T.; Schmid, W.; Zabolotskyy, T. Minimum VaR and Minimum CVaR optimal portfolios: estimators, confidence regions, and tests. *Stat. Risk Model.* **2012**, *29*, 281–314. [CrossRef]
34. Meucci, A. Managing diversification. *Risk* **2009**, 74–79.
35. Uchiyama, Y.; Kadoya, T.; Nakagawa, K. Complex valued risk diversification. *Entropy* **2019**, *21*, 119. [CrossRef]
36. Nakagawa, K.; Uchiyama, Y. GO-GJRSK Model with Application to Higher Order Risk-Based Portfolio. *Mathematics* **2020**, *8*, 1990. [CrossRef]
37. Poddig, T.; Unger, A. On the robustness of risk-based asset allocations. *Financ. Mark. Portf. Manag.* **2012**, *26*, 369–401. [CrossRef]
38. Zou, H.; Yuan, M. Regularized simultaneous model selection in multiple quantiles regression. *Comput. Stat. Data Anal.* **2008**, *52*, 5296–5304. [CrossRef]
39. Fama, E.F.; French, K.R. The cross-section of expected stock returns. *J. Financ.* **1992**, *47*, 427–465. [CrossRef]
40. DeMiguel, V.; Garlappi, L.; Uppal, R. Optimal versus naive diversification: How inefficient is the 1/N portfolio strategy? *Rev. Financ. Stud.* **2007**, *22*, 1915–1953. [CrossRef]
41. Clarke, R.G.; De Silva, H.; Thorley, S. Minimum-variance portfolios in the US equity market. *J. Portf. Manag.* **2006**, *33*, 10–24. [CrossRef]
42. Shen, W.; Wang, B.; Pu, J.; Wang, J. The Kelly Growth Optimal Portfolio with Ensemble Learning. In Proceedings of the AAAI Conference on Artificial Intelligence, Honolulu, HI, USA, January 27–1 February 2019; Volume 33, pp. 1134–1141.
43. Brandt, M.W. Portfolio choice problems. In *Handbook of Financial Econometrics: Tools and Techniques*; Elsevier: Amsterdam, The Netherlands, 2010; pp. 269–336.
44. Magdon-Ismail, M.; Atiya, A.F. Maximum drawdown. *Risk Mag.* **2004**, *17*, 99–102.

Article

Inventory Models for Non-Instantaneous Deteriorating Items with Expiration Dates and Imperfect Quality under Hybrid Payment Policy in the Three-Level Supply Chain

Jui-Jung Liao [1], Hari Mohan Srivastava [2,3,4,5,*], Kun-Jen Chung [6,7], Shih-Fang Lee [8], Kuo-Nan Huang [9] and Shy-Der Lin [10]

[1] Department of Business Administration, Chihlee University of Technology, Banqiao District, New Taipei City 22050, Taiwan; liaojj@mail.chihlee.edu.tw
[2] Department of Mathematics and Statistics, University of Victoria, Victoria, BC V8W 3R4, Canada
[3] Department of Medical Research, China Medical University Hospital, China Medical University, Taichung 40402, Taiwan
[4] Department of Mathematics and Informatics, Azerbaijan University, 71 Jeyhun Hajibeyli Street, Baku AZ1007, Azerbaijan
[5] Section of Mathematics, International Telematic University Uninettuno, I-00186 Rome, Italy
[6] College of Business, Chung Yuan Christian University, Chung Li 320314, Taiwan; kjchung@cycu.edu.tw
[7] Department of Industrial Management, National Taiwan University of Science and Technology, Taipei 10607, Taiwan
[8] Department of Applied Mathematics, Chung Yuan Christian University, Chung Li 320314, Taiwan; g10601101@cycu.edu.tw
[9] Department of Industrial Management and Business Administration, St. John's University, Tamsui District, New Taipei City 25135, Taiwan; hsiaosa@mail.sju.edu.tw
[10] Department of Applied Mathematics and Business Administration, Chung Yuan Christian University, Chung Li 320314, Taiwan; shyder@cycu.edu.tw
* Correspondence: harimsri@math.uvic.ca

Abstract: This article considers an inventory model for non-instantaneous deteriorating items with expiration dates, such as seasonal items, first-hand vegetables, and fruits. Interestingly, an inspection will be performed to manage the quality of the items during the state of no deterioration because it is difficult to purchase items with 100% perfection. Additionally, we assume that the upstream member has the power of controlling or influencing downstream members' decisions. That is, the supplier asks the retailer for a partial advance payment to avoid cancellation of orders and offers them a credit payment to stimulate sales; in turn, the customer must pay some cash when placing an order and pay the remainder in credit for the retailer. The goal of this article is to determine an optimal replenishment cycle and the total annual cost function, so we explore the functional properties of the total annual cost function and show that the total annual cost function is convex. Theoretical analysis of the optimal properties shows the existence and uniqueness of the optimal solution. Then, we obtain simple and easy solution procedures for the inventory system. Moreover, numerical analysis of the inventory model is conducted, and the corresponding examples are considered with a view to illustrating the application of the supply chain model that we have investigated in this article. Finally, in the concluding section, we have not only provided the motivation and the need for our usages of mathematical analytic solution procedures based upon the convexity, monotonicity (increasing and decreasing) and differentiability properties of the object function (that is, the total annual cost function), which involve some symmetry aspects of the object function, but we have also indicated the limitations and shortcomings in our investigation, which will naturally lead to some potential directions for further research on the supply chain model, which we have considered and mathematically analyzed in this article.

Keywords: inventory modeling; mathematical analytic solution procedures; economic order quantity (EOQ) model; deteriorating products; imperfect quality; hybrid payment policy; non-instantaneous deterioration; expiration date; trade credit financing; permissible delay in payments; object function (that is total annual cost function); supply chain management

1. Introduction

In today's competitive business environment, more than 80% of businesses offer their products on various short-term, interest-free credit terms (that is, a credit payment) with a view to stimulate sales and to reduce inventory in the United Kingdom and the United States of America. Likewise, trade credit financing is used by approximately 60% of international trade transactions, rendering it to be the second after that of banks and other financial institutions in the United States of America. Additionally, in order to avoid the risk of order cancellation and non-payment risks, the business frequently offers a partial credit period to the downstream members, who must pay a portion of the procurement amount at the time of placing an order and then receive a permissible delay on the rest of the outstanding amount (that is, a cash-credit payment). On the other hand, granting trade credit increases not only the opportunity loss, but also the default risk from the viewpoint of the business, so the powerful businesses may ask the downstream members to prepay the entire or a fraction of the procurement amount before the delivery to mitigate interest loss and default risks (that is, an advance payment). For example, insurance companies generally require an advance payment in order to extend coverage to the insured party.

In existing literatures, Zhang [1] proposed an advance payment plan because it may save time and money for a customer to prepay, for example 80.00 USD for 4 months of water bills, instead of paying 20.00 USD each month for 4 months. All the above mentioned payment types can be combined such that, for example, the supplier demands the retailer to prepay 5 to 10% of the total procurement cost as a good-faith deposit when both sign a contract of agreement to install some item(s). Upon delivery of the item(s), a cash-on-delivery payment to cover the supplier's cost of the item(s) is then required. In this contractual arrangement, the retailer will pay the remainder of the total cost after the work is completed.

In reality, the deteriorating items have a maximum lifetime due to their physical nature and must be disposed of after the expiration date, due to the fact that consumers evaluate the freshness of a deteriorating item by checking its expiration date before making a purchase, and the willingness to purchase a deteriorating item decreases throughout its shelf-life. Furthermore, the expiration date is the most important factor that is time-bound and plays an important role in developing the inventory model. In practice, most of the products maintain their quality or original situation over a span; that is, during this span, deterioration does not occur, and then they begin to deteriorate in the next period. It is observed that foodstuffs, first-hand vegetables, and fruits have a short span during which fresh quality is maintained and there is almost no spoilage. These processes are defined as the non-instantaneous deterioration of the product.

The quality of the products is considered to be another direct factor to affect a consumer's purchase decision as well. Furthermore, this article assumes that the retailer receives the items with a time-varying deterioration rate depending on its expiration date, such as seasonal products, and that an inspection will occur during the state of no deterioration in order to manage the quality of the products. By performing the screening process, the retailer detects the imperfect items and throws them out.

In this article, we first establish an inventory model for non-instantaneous deteriorating items with expiration dates and imperfect quality in which we assume a 100% screening process to identify imperfect items. We then consider that the supplier asks the retailer to prepay a fraction of the procurement cost when signing a contract to buy products, to pay another fraction of the procurement cost in cash upon receiving the ordered quantity, and to receive a short-term interest-free credit term on the remaining procurement cost (that is, an advance-cash-credit payment). Likewise, the retailer gives the customer the opportunity to pay a fraction of the procurement cost after delivery of the ordered items and then to pay the remaining procurement cost at a later date without any additional charges to reduce the risk of cancellations of the order from customers (that is, a cash-credit payment). It is worth mentioning that, by the usage of the mathematical analytic solution procedures, the present article shows that the total annual cost function is convex by exploring the functional properties of the total annual cost function such as, for example, the continuity, convexity, monotonicity (increasing and decreasing), and differentiability properties, whereby one can also see the symmetry aspects of the total annual const function. Furthermore, by applying the mathematical analytic solution procedures again, we prove that the retailer's optimal replenishment cycle not only exists, but it also is unique. With a view to illustrating and validating the proposed inventory model, we have considered numerical examples involving different fixed markup rates. Finally, in the concluding section of this article (Section 6), we have briefly discussed the limitations and shortcomings of this investigation in that we have concentrated upon the inventory system without shortage and that it can affect the supply chain from the producer to the retailer. Furthermore, this model has the potential to be extended to incorporate inflation and quantity discount effects, different demand forms such as credit-linked promotion-dependent demand and other issues under the system with shortages. Additionally, this article has considered the deterministic situation, so considering the stochastic situation, such as stochastic demand, can be another future research direction on the subject of this article.

Literature Review

There is a large volume of published studies concerning the inventory models with cash payments, credit payments, or advance payments, such as those that we have reviewed or cited below.

In these literatures, Taleizadeh et al. [2] established an economic order quantity (EOQ) model with partial backordering in which the supplier asks the retailer to pay a fraction of the purchasing cost in advance and allows them to divide the prepayment into multiple equal installments during a lead time. Taleizadeh [3] extended the inventory model of Taleizadeh et al. [2] to the cases of deteriorating items with and without shortages. Taleizadeh [4] used an advance-cash-payment plan to develop an EOQ model for an evaporating item with partial backordering for a real case study of a gasoline station. Zhang et al. [5] developed an inventory model under advance payment, which includes all payments in advance and partially advanced-partially delayed payment plans. Eck et al. [6] explored the role of cash-in-advance financing for export decisions in firms. Lashgari et al. [7] considered an EOQ model with hybrid partial payment, such as upstream partial prepayment and downstream partial delayed payment without shortage, with full backordering, or with partial backordering. Tavakoli and Taleizadeh [8] gave a lot-sizing model for decaying item for the retailer to pay all the purchasing cost in advance with no shortage or with full backordering shortage or partial lost sale. Heydari et al. [9] assumed the demand is stochastic and credit-dependent under the two-level trade credit, then they found the optimal ordering quantity and the length of the credit period. Feng and Chan [10] expanded the two-level trade credit to include joint pricing and production decisions for new products with pronounced learning-by-doing phenomenon. Much of the current research attention has been directed towards trade-credit inventory models for deteriorating items with its own expiration date. For example, Chen and Teng [11] established an inventory model for deteriorating items under two-level trade credit by discounted cash flow analysis in which the deterioration rate is non-decreasing over time and near 100 percent particularly close to its expiration date. Then, they demonstrated that the retailer's optimal credit period and cycle time not only exist, but are also unique. Mahata [12] discussed an EOQ model for deteriorating items having fixed lifetime under two-level trade credit. He showed that the retailer's optimal replenishment cycle time not only exists but is also unique. Wu et al. [13] examined an inventory model with expiration date dependent deterioration under an advance-cash-credit payment scheme to find the optimal replenishment cycle time and the fraction of no shortages such that the total profit is maximized. Moreover, some related recent articles are those by, for example, Zia and Taleizadeh [14], Wu et al. [15], Chen et al. [16], Teng et al. [17], Diabat et al. [18], Feng et al. [19], Mahata and De [20], Tiwari et al. [21], Taleizadeh et al. [22], Li et al. [23,24], Taleizadeh [25], Krommyda et al. [26], Tsao et al. [27], Mashud et al. ([28,29]), AlArjani et al. [30], and Hou et al. [31].

There is a large volume of published studies describing the inventory models for non-instantaneous deteriorating items. Udayakumar and Geetha [32] considered time, value of money, and the effect of inflation to develop an economic-ordering policy for non-instantaneous deteriorating items over a finite time horizon in which the demand is a deterministic function of selling price and advertisement cost. They found the optimal length of replenishment and the optimal order quantity. Lashgari et al. [33] presented an EOQ model for non-instantaneous deteriorating items under an advance-delay payment when shortages are allowed in a partial form. They found the optimal order and shortage quantities to minimize the retailer's total inventory cost function. Udayakumar and Geetha [34] developed an EOQ model for non-instantaneous deteriorating items with capacity constraint under a trade credit policy. They found the optimal replenishment cycle time and order quantity to minimize the total inventory cost. Babangida and Baraya [35] showed an inventory model for non-instantaneous deteriorating items with two-phase demand rates, capacity constraint and complete backlogged under trade credit policy. They provided the necessary and sufficient conditions for the existence and uniqueness of solutions. Soni and Suthar [36] revealed an inventory model for non-instantaneous deteriorating items with partial backlogging; they considered that the demand rate has a negative and positive exponential effect of price and promotional effort, respectively, while the item is not in a state of deterioration and then found the joint optimal pricing and replenishment policy for the non-instantaneous deteriorating items. Cenk Çalışkan [37] deals with the inventory model for deteriorating items in which the opportunity cost is based on compound interest, and backorders are allowed. The article determines a near-optimal and intuitive closed-form solution, which is simple to the practitioners. Under a variety of practical conditions, some researchers have considered the above items, such as Tiwari et al. [38], Tsao [39], Geetha and Udayakumar [40], Jaggi et al. [41], Maihami et al. [42], Mashud et al. [43], Bounkhel et al. [44], and Udayakumar et al. [45].

Given that it is worthwhile studying the effect of defective items on inventory problems, numerous researchers, such as Khanna et al. [46], have developed inventory models for deteriorating imperfect quality items with allowable shortages and permissible delays in payments. Zhou et al. [47] found a synergy economic order quantity model, in which the concepts of imperfect quality, inspection error, and shortages with trade credit are considered. They found the annual profit function is concave and obtained the closed form optimal solution to the model. Datta [48] proposed a production-inventory model with defective items. The model incorporates additional investment opportunity on quality improvement for reducing the proportion of defective products. Taleizadeh et al. [49] developed an imperfect EPQ model with upstream trade credit periods linked to raw material order quantity and downstream trade credit periods. Pal and Mahapatra [50] developed an inventory model with imperfect products for a three-level supply chain, and three different ways of dealing with defective products were investigated in their model. Khakzad and Gholamian [51] investigated the effect of inspection time on the deterioration rate; they showed the convexity of the model and illustrated the uniqueness of the solution. Taleizadeh et al. [52] revealed an EOQ inventory model with imperfect items and partial backordering. They assumed a percent of the products in a lot is imperfect and the imperfect items are replenished by perfect ones at a higher cost. The objective is to obtain the optimal value of the length period and the percent of period duration in which the inventory level is positive. Some imperfect production models with trade credit have been studied, in recent years, by (among others) Wang et al. [53], Alamri et al. [54], Palanivel and Uthayakumar [55], Aghili and Hoseinabadi [56], Tsao et al. [57,58], Khanna et al. [59], Liao et al. [60], Kazemi et al. [61], Liao et al. [62], Mashud et al. [63], and Srivastava et al. [64].

We remark, in passing to the next section, that the mathematical analytic solution procedures, which we have used in the mathematical analysis and discussions of the inventory and supply chain models considered in this article, are full of elaborate usages of the intricate techniques of calculus in determining the continuity, convexity, monotonicity (increasing or decreasing), and differentiability properties of the object functions (that is, the total optimal cost functions). We have stated our main results of this investigation in the form of five theorems (Theorems 1 to 5), which we have proved by appealing also to two Lemmas (Lemma 1 and Lemma 2). For the sake of brevity and compact presentation, the proof of Lemma 2 has been given in the Appendix A instead of the main text. It is quite natural to expect such a format and style in a mathematically oriented article. Furthermore, as we have already mentioned, for the accuracy, completeness, and safe applicability of the results and discussions presented in this article, the usage of the mathematical analytic solution procedures, which are based upon the elaborate and intricate techniques of calculus, is essential here.

2. Mathematical Formulation of the Supply Chain Model and Its Analysis

Based on the above assumptions, the inventory level drops at the demand rate and the defective rate during the time interval $[0, t_d]$. Then, the inventory level drops to zero due to the demand and the deterioration with the expiration dates during the time interval $[t_d, T]$. Furthermore, the variations in the inventory level with respect to time t can be expressed below.

The differential equation representing the inventory status during the time interval $t \in [0, t_s]$, $t_s = \frac{y}{x}$, is given by

$$\frac{dI_1(t)}{dt} = -D \tag{1}$$

where t is restricted, as in Equation (2). Under the condition $I_1(0) = y$, by solving Equation (1), we obtain

$$I_1(t) = y - Dt, 0 < t \leq t_s \tag{2}$$

In the second interval $[t_s, t_d]$, the differential equation represents the inventory status:

$$\frac{dI_2(t)}{dt} = -D, t_s \leq t \leq t_d \tag{3}$$

Under the condition $I_2(t_d) = (1-p)y - Dt_d$, Equation (3) yields

$$I_2(t) = (1-p)y - Dt, t_s \leq t \leq t_d \tag{4}$$

During the third interval $[t_d, T]$, the change in the inventory level is represented by the following differential equation:

$$\frac{dI_3(t)}{dt} + \theta(t) \cdot I_3(t) = -D, t_d \leq t \leq T \tag{5}$$

Under the condition $I_3(T) = 0$, the solution of Equation (5) is given by

$$I_3(t) = D(1 + m - t) \cdot \ln(\frac{1 + m - t}{1 + m - T}), t_d \leq t \leq T \tag{6}$$

Making use of the continuity property of $I_2(t_d) = I_3(t_d)$, it follows from Equations (4) and (6) that

$$(1-p)y - Dt_d = D(1 + m - t_d) \ln(\frac{1 + m - t_d}{1 + m - T}) \tag{7}$$

which implies that the order quantity is given by

$$y = \frac{D}{(1-p)}[t_d + (1+m-t_d) \cdot \ln(\frac{1+m-t_d}{1+m-T})] \tag{8}$$

Substituting Equation (8) into Equations (2) and (4), we get

$$I_1(t) = \frac{D}{(1-p)}[t_d + (1+m-t_d) \cdot \ln(\frac{1+m-t_d}{1+m-T}) - (1-p)t] \tag{9}$$

and

$$I_2(t) = D[t_d + (1+m-t_d) \cdot \ln(\frac{1+m-t_d}{1+m-T}) - t] \tag{10}$$

Additionally, this article focuses on $t_s \leq t_d$, so we have $T \leq R^*$ if and only if $t_s \leq t_d$. Here,

$$R^* = (1+m) - (1+m-t_d) \cdot e^{-\frac{[(1-p)x-D]t_d}{D(1+m-t_d)}} \tag{11}$$

We now calculate the annual total relevant cost which results from the following components:

1. Order cost $= \frac{o}{T}$
2. The holding cost (excluding interest charges) after receiving y units at time 0 is given below:
   Case 1. When $0 < T < t_d$,
   The holding cost
   $= \frac{h}{T}[\int_0^{\frac{y}{x}}(y - Dt)dt + \int_{\frac{y}{x}}^T D(T-t)dt] = \frac{hD}{(1-p)}[\frac{(1-p)T}{2} + \frac{pDT}{x(1-p)}]$
   Case 2. When $t_d \leq T$
   The holding cost $= \frac{h}{T}\left\{\int_0^{\frac{y}{x}} I_1(t)dt + \int_{\frac{y}{x}}^{t_d} I_2(t)dt + \int_{t_d}^T I_3(t)dt\right\}$

$$= \frac{h}{T}\left\{\frac{D}{2}t_d^2 + D(1+m-t_d) \cdot t_d \ln(\frac{1+m-t_d}{1+m-T}) + \frac{pD^2}{x(1-p)^2}\right.$$
$$\times [t_d + (1+m-t_d) \cdot \ln(\frac{1+m-t_d}{1+m-T})]^2 + \frac{D}{2}(1+m-t_d)^2 \cdot \ln(\frac{1+m-t_d}{1+m-T})$$
$$\left. + \frac{D}{4}(1+m-T)^2 - \frac{D}{4}(1+m-t_d)^2 \right\}$$

3. The procurement cost per replenishment cycle is:
   Case 1. When $0 < T < t_d$
   The procurement cost $= \frac{cy}{T} = \frac{cD}{(1-p)}$
   Case 2. When $t_d \leq T$
   The procurement cost $= \frac{cy}{T} = \frac{cD}{(1-p)T}[t_d + (1+m-t_d) \cdot \ln(\frac{1+m-t_d}{1+m-T})]$
4. The screening cost per replenishment cycle is
   Case 1. When $0 < T < t_d$
   The screening cost $= \frac{sy}{T} = \frac{sD}{(1-p)}$
   Case 2. When $t_d \leq T$
   The screening cost $= \frac{sy}{T} = \frac{sD}{(1-p)T}[t_d + (1+m-t_d) \cdot \ln(\frac{1+m-t_d}{1+m-T})]$
5. The cost of deteriorated units
   Case 1. When $0 < T < t_d$
   The cost of deteriorated units is zero.
   Case 2. When $t_d \leq T$
   The cost of deteriorated units $= \frac{c}{T}[(1-p)y - DT]$

$$= \frac{cD}{T}[t_d + (1+m-t_d) \cdot \ln(\frac{1+m-t_d}{1+m-T}) - T]$$

6. The interest charged for advance payment per replenishment cycle is

$$\frac{cI_kDT}{T}(\int_{-L}^{N} \alpha dt) + \frac{cI_kD}{T}\int_{N}^{T+N} \alpha(T+N-t)t$$
$$= \frac{\alpha cI_kDT}{T}(N+L) + \frac{\alpha cI_kDT^2}{2T}$$

7. The interest charged for cash payment per replenishment cycle is

$$\frac{cI_kDT}{T}(\int_{0}^{N} \beta dt) + \frac{cI_kD}{T}\int_{N}^{T+N} \beta(T+N-t)dt = \frac{\beta cI_kDTN}{T} + \frac{\beta cI_kDT^2}{2T}$$

8. The interest charged for credit payment per replenishment is
   Case 1. When $N \leq M$ and $M \leq T \leq T+N$
   The interest charged for credit payment

$$= \frac{\tau cDI_k}{T}\left\{\rho[\int_{M}^{T+N}(T+N-t)dt]+(1-\rho)[\int_{M}^{T}(T-t)dt\right\}$$

$$= \frac{\tau cDI_k}{2T}\left\{\rho(T+N-M)^2+(1-\rho)(T-M)^2\right\}$$

Case 2. When $N \leq M$ and $T \leq M \leq T+N$
The interest charged for credit payment

$$= \frac{\tau cDI_k}{T}\left[\rho\int_{M}^{T+N}(T+N-t)dt\right] = \frac{\tau cDI_k}{2T}\left[\rho(T+N-M)^2\right]$$

Case 3. When $N \leq M$ and $T+N \leq M$
The interest charged for credit payment is zero.
Case 4. When $N > M$ and $M \leq T$
The interest charged for credit payment

$$= \frac{\tau cDI_k}{T}\left\{\rho[\int_{M}^{N} Tdt + \int_{N}^{T+N}(T+N-t)dt]+(1-\rho)[\int_{M}^{T}(T-t)dt\right\}$$

$$= \frac{\tau cDI_k}{2T}\left\{\rho[T^2 + 2(N-M)T] + (1-\rho)(T-M)^2\right\}$$

Case 5. When $N > M$ and $M \geq T$
The interest charged for credit payment

$$= \frac{\tau cDI_k}{T}\left\{\rho\left[\int_{M}^{N} Tdt + \int_{N}^{T+N}(T+N-t)dt\right]\right\}$$
$$= \frac{\tau cDI_k}{2T}\left\{\rho[T^2 + 2T(N-M)]\right\}$$

9. The interest earned for credit payment per replenishment is
   Case 1. When $N \leq M$ and $M \leq T \leq T+N$
   The interest earned for credit payment

$$= \frac{\tau vDI_e}{T}\left\{\rho\int_{N}^{M}(t-N)dt+(1-\rho)\int_{0}^{M}tdt\right\} = \frac{\tau vDI_e}{2T}\left[\rho(M-N)^2+(1-\rho)M^2\right]$$

Case 2. When $N \leq M$ and $T \leq M \leq T+N$
The interest earned for credit payment

$$= \frac{\tau vDI_e}{T}\left\{\rho\int_{N}^{M}(t-N)dt + (1-\rho)[\int_{0}^{T}tdt + \int_{T}^{M}Tdt]\right\}$$

$$= \frac{\tau v DI_e}{2T} \{\rho (M-N)^2 + (1-\rho)[T^2 + 2T(M-T)]\}$$

Case 3. When $N \leq M$ and $T + N \leq M$
The interest earned for credit payment

$$= \frac{\tau v DI_e}{T} \{\rho [\int_N^{T+N}(t-N)dt + \int_{T+N}^M Tdt] + (1-\rho)[\int_0^T tdt + \int_T^M Tdt]\}$$

$$= \frac{\tau v DI_e}{2T} \{\rho [T^2 + 2T(M-T-N)] + (1-\rho)[T^2 + 2T(M-T)]\}$$

Case 4. When $N > M$ and $M \leq T$
$$= \frac{\tau v DI_e}{T}[(1-\rho)\int_0^M tdt] = \frac{\tau v DI_e}{2T}[(1-\rho)M^2]$$

Case 5. When $N > M$ and $N \geq T$
$$= \frac{\tau v DI_e}{T}\{(1-\rho)[\int_0^T tdt + \int_T^M Tdt]\} = \frac{\tau v DI_e}{T}\{(1-\rho)[T^2 + 2T(M-T)]\}$$

Finally, the total annual relevant cost $TC(T)$ is obtained as follows:
$TC(T)$ = ordering cost + stock holding cost (excluding interest charges) + procurement cost + screening cost + deterioration cost + interest charged – interest earned.
Furthermore, we obtain the following cases:
Case I. Suppose that $N \leq M$
Case (I-1). Suppose that $t_d < M - N < M$

$$TC(T) = \begin{cases} TC_1(T) & \text{if} & 0 < T < t_d \\ TC_2(T) & \text{if} & t_d \leq T < M-N \\ TC_3(T) & \text{if} & M-N \leq T < M \\ TC_4(T) & \text{if} & M \leq T \leq R^* \end{cases} \quad (12)$$

where

$$TC_1(T) = \frac{o}{T} + \frac{hD}{(1-p)}[\frac{(1-p)T}{2} + \frac{pDT}{x(1-p)}] + \frac{(c+s)D}{1-p} + \frac{c I_k DT}{T}[\alpha(N+L) + \beta N] \quad (13)$$
$$+ \frac{c I_k DT^2}{2T}(\alpha + \beta) - \frac{\tau v DI_e}{2T}\{\rho [T^2 + 2T(M-T-N)] + (1-\rho)[T^2 + 2T(M-T)]\}$$

$$TC_2(T) = \frac{o}{T} + \frac{h}{T}\{\frac{D}{2}t_d^2 + D(1+m-t_d)\cdot t_d \cdot >\ln(\frac{1+m-t_d}{1+m-T}) + \frac{pD^2}{x(1-p)^2}[t_d + (1+m-t_d)$$
$$\times \ln(\frac{1+m-t_d}{1+m-T})]^2 + \frac{D}{2}(1+m-t_d)^2 \cdot \ln(\frac{1+m-t_d}{1+m-T}) + \frac{D}{4}(1+m-T)^2 - \frac{D}{4}(1+m-t_d)^2\} \quad (14)$$
$$+ \frac{(c+s)D}{(1-p)T}[t_d + (1+m-t_d)\cdot \ln(\frac{1+m-t_d}{1+m-T})] + \frac{cD}{T}[t_d + (1+m-t_d)\cdot \ln(\frac{1+m-t_d}{1+m-T}) - T]$$
$$+ \frac{c I_k DT}{T}[\alpha(N+L) + \beta N] + \frac{c I_k DT^2}{2T}(\alpha + \beta) - \frac{\tau v DI_e}{2T}\{\rho [T^2 + 2T(M-T-N)]$$
$$+ (1-\rho)[T^2 + 2T(M-T)]\}$$

$$TC_3(T) = \frac{o}{T} + \frac{h}{T}\{\frac{D}{2}t_d^2 + D(1+m-t_d)\cdot t_d \cdot \ln(\frac{1+m-t_d}{1+m-T}) + \frac{pD^2}{x(1-p)^2}[t_d + (1+m-t_d)$$
$$\times \ln(\frac{1+m-t_d}{1+m-T})]^2 + \frac{D}{2}(1+m-t_d)^2 \cdot \ln(\frac{1+m-t_d}{1+m-T}) + \frac{D}{4}(1+m-T)^2 - \frac{D}{4}(1+m-t_d)^2\}$$
$$+ \frac{(c+s)D}{(1-p)T}[t_d + (1+m-t_d)\cdot \ln(\frac{1+m-t_d}{1+m-T})] + \frac{cD}{T}[t_d + (1+m-t_d)\cdot \ln(\frac{1+m-t_d}{1+m-T}) - T] \quad (15)$$
$$+ \frac{c I_k DT}{T}[\alpha(N+L) + \beta N] + \frac{c I_k DT^2}{2T}(\alpha + \beta) + \frac{\tau c DI_k}{2T}[\rho(T+N-M)^2]$$
$$- \frac{\tau v DI_e}{2T}\{\rho(M-N)^2 + (1-\rho)[T^2 + 2T(M-T)]\}$$

$$TC_4(T) = \frac{o}{T} + \frac{h}{T}\{\frac{D}{2}t_d^2 + D(1+m-t_d)\cdot t_d \cdot \ln(\frac{1+m-t_d}{1+m-T}) + \frac{pD^2}{x(1-p)^2}[t_d + (1+m-t_d)$$
$$\times \ln(\frac{1+m-t_d}{1+m-T})]^2 + \frac{D}{2}(1+m-t_d)^2 \cdot \ln(\frac{1+m-t_d}{1+m-T}) + \frac{D}{4}(1+m-T)^2 - \frac{D}{4}(1+m-t_d)^2\}$$
$$+ \frac{(c+s)D}{(1-p)T}[t_d + (1+m-t_d)\cdot \ln(\frac{1+m-t_d}{1+m-T})] + \frac{cD}{T}[t_d + (1+m-t_d)\cdot \ln(\frac{1+m-t_d}{1+m-T}) - T] \quad (16)$$
$$+ \frac{c I_k DT}{T}[\alpha(N+L) + \beta N] + \frac{c I_k DT^2}{2T}(\alpha + \beta) + \frac{\tau c DI_k}{2T}[\rho(T+N-M)^2$$
$$+ (1-\rho)(T-M)^2] - \frac{\tau v DI_e}{2T}[\rho(M-N)^2 + (1-\rho)M^2]$$

Since $TC_1(t_d) = TC_2(t_d)$, $TC_2(M-N) = TC_3(M-N)$ and $TC_3(M) = TC_4(M)$, $TC(T)$ is continuous and well-defined on $T > 0$.

Case (I-2). Suppose that $M - N < t_d < M$

$$TC(T) = \begin{cases} TC_1(T) & \text{if } 0 < T < M - N \\ TC_5(T) & \text{if } M - N \leq T < t_d \\ TC_3(T) & \text{if } t_d \leq T < M \\ TC_4(T) & \text{if } M \leq T \leq R^* \end{cases} \quad (17)$$

where

$$\begin{aligned}
TC_5(T) &= \tfrac{o}{T} + \tfrac{hD}{(1-p)}\left[\tfrac{(1-p)T}{2} + \tfrac{pDT}{x(1-p)}\right] + \tfrac{(c+s)D}{1-p} + \tfrac{cI_kDT}{T}[\alpha(N+L) + \beta N] \\
&\quad + \tfrac{cI_kDT^2}{2T}(\alpha + \beta) + \tfrac{TcDI_k}{2T}[\rho(T+N-M)^2] - \tfrac{TvDI_e}{2T}\big\{\rho(M-N)^2 \\
&\quad + (1-\rho)[T^2 + 2T(M-T)]\big\}
\end{aligned} \quad (18)$$

Since $TC_1(M - N) = TC_5(M - N)$, $TC_5(t_d) = TC_3(t_d)$ and $TC_3(M) = TC_4(M)$, $TC(T)$ is continuous and well-defined on $T > 0$.

Case (I-3). Suppose that $M - N < M < t_d$

$$TC(T) = \begin{cases} TC_1(T) & \text{if } 0 < T < M - N \\ TC_5(T) & \text{if } M - N \leq T < M \\ TC_6(T) & \text{if } M \leq T < t_d \\ TC_4(T) & \text{if } t_d \leq T \leq R^* \end{cases} \quad (19)$$

where

$$\begin{aligned}
TC_6(T) &= \tfrac{o}{T} + \tfrac{hD}{(1-p)}\left[\tfrac{(1-p)T}{2} + \tfrac{pDT}{x(1-p)}\right] + \tfrac{(c+s)D}{1-p} + \tfrac{cI_kDT}{T}[\alpha(N+L) + \beta N] \\
&\quad + \tfrac{cI_kDT^2}{2T}(\alpha + \beta) + \tfrac{TcDI_k}{2T}\left[\rho(T+N-M)^2 + (1-\rho)(T-M)^2\right] \\
&\quad - \tfrac{TvDI_e}{2T}[\rho(M-N)^2 + (1-\rho)M^2]
\end{aligned} \quad (20)$$

Since $TC_1(M - N) = TC_5(M - N)$, $TC_5(M) = TC_6(M)$ and $TC_6(t_d) = TC_4(t_d)$, $TC(T)$ is continuous and well-defined on $T > 0$.

Case II. Suppose that $N > M$
Case (II-1). Suppose that $t_d < M$

$$TC(T) = \begin{cases} TC_7(T) & \text{if } 0 < T < t_d \\ TC_8(T) & \text{if } t_d \leq T < M \\ TC_9(T) & \text{if } M \leq T \leq R^* \end{cases} \quad (21)$$

where

$$\begin{aligned}
TC_7(T) &= \tfrac{o}{T} + \tfrac{hD}{(1-p)}\left[\tfrac{(1-p)T}{2} + \tfrac{pDT}{x(1-p)}\right] + \tfrac{(c+s)D}{1-p} + \tfrac{cI_kDT}{T}[\alpha(N+L) + \beta N] \\
&\quad + \tfrac{cI_kDT^2}{2T}(\alpha + \beta) + \tfrac{TcDI_k}{2T}\{\rho[T^2 + 2T(N-M)]\} \\
&\quad - \tfrac{TvDI_e}{2T}\{(1-\rho)[T^2 + 2T(M-T)]\}
\end{aligned} \quad (22)$$

$$\begin{aligned}
TC_8(T) &= \tfrac{o}{T} + \tfrac{h}{T}\Big\{\tfrac{D}{2}t_d^2 + D(1+m-t_d)\cdot t_d \cdot \ln(\tfrac{1+m-t_d}{1+m-T}) + \tfrac{pD^2}{x(1-p)^2}[t_d + (1+m-t_d) \\
&\quad \times \ln(\tfrac{1+m-t_d}{1+m-T})]^2 + \tfrac{D}{2}(1+m-t_d)^2 \cdot \ln(\tfrac{1+m-t_d}{1+m-T}) + \tfrac{D}{4}(1+m-T)^2 - \tfrac{D}{4}(1+m-t_d)^2\Big\} \\
&\quad + \tfrac{(c+s)D}{(1-p)T}[t_d + (1+m-t_d)\cdot \ln(\tfrac{1+m-t_d}{1+m-T})] + \tfrac{cD}{T}[t_d + (1+m-t_d)\cdot \ln(\tfrac{1+m-t_d}{1+m-T}) - T] \\
&\quad + \tfrac{cI_kDT}{T}[\alpha(N+L) + \beta N] + \tfrac{cI_kDT^2}{2T}(\alpha + \beta) + \tfrac{TcDI_k}{2T}\{\rho[T^2 + 2T(N-M)]\} \\
&\quad - \tfrac{TvDI_e}{2T}\{(1-\rho)[T^2 + 2T(M-T)]\}
\end{aligned} \quad (23)$$

$$
\begin{aligned}
TC_9(T) &= \tfrac{o}{T} + \tfrac{h}{T}\Big\{\tfrac{D}{2}t_d^2 + D(1+m-t_d)\cdot t_d \cdot \ln(\tfrac{1+m-t_d}{1+m-T}) + \tfrac{pD^2}{x(1-p)^2}[t_d + (1+m-t_d) \\
&\quad \times \ln(\tfrac{1+m-t_d}{1+m-T})]^2 + \tfrac{D}{2}(1+m-t_d)^2 \cdot \ln(\tfrac{1+m-t_d}{1+m-T}) + \tfrac{D}{4}(1+m-T)^2 - \tfrac{D}{4}(1+m-t_d)^2\Big\} \\
&\quad + \tfrac{(c+s)D}{(1-p)T}[t_d + (1+m-t_d)\cdot \ln(\tfrac{1+m-t_d}{1+m-T})] + \tfrac{cD}{T}[t_d + (1+m-t_d)\cdot \ln(\tfrac{1+m-t_d}{1+m-T}) - T] \\
&\quad + \tfrac{cI_kDT}{T}[\alpha(N+L) + \beta N] + \tfrac{cI_kDT^2}{2T}(\alpha+\beta) + \tfrac{\tau cDI_k}{2T}\{\rho[T^2 + 2T(N-M)] \\
&\quad + (1-\rho)(T-M)^2\} - \tfrac{\tau v DI_e}{2T}(1-\rho)M^2
\end{aligned}
\tag{24}
$$

Since $TC_7(t_d) = TC_8(t_d)$ and $TC_8(M) = TC_9(M)$, $TC(T)$ are continuous and well-defined on $T > 0$.

Case (II-2). Suppose that $t_d \geq M$

$$
TC(T) = \begin{cases} TC_7(T) & \text{if } 0 < T < M \\ TC_{10}(T) & \text{if } M \leq T < t_d \\ TC_9(T) & \text{if } t_d \leq T \leq R^* \end{cases}
\tag{25}
$$

where

$$
\begin{aligned}
TC_{10}(T) &= \tfrac{o}{T} + \tfrac{hD}{(1-p)}[\tfrac{(1-p)T}{2} + \tfrac{pDT}{x(1-p)}] + \tfrac{(c+s)D}{1-p} + \tfrac{cI_kDT}{T}[\alpha(N+L)+\beta N] \\
&\quad + \tfrac{cI_kDT^2}{2T}(\alpha+\beta) + \tfrac{\tau cDI_k}{2T}\{\rho[T^2+2T(N-M)] + (1-\rho)(T-M)^2\} \\
&\quad - \tfrac{\tau v DI_e}{2T}(1-\rho)M^2
\end{aligned}
\tag{26}
$$

Since $TC_7(M) = TC_{10}(M)$ and $TC_{10}(t_d) = TC_9(t_d)$, $TC(T)$ is continuous and well-defined on $T > 0$.

3. The Convexity and Monotonicity Properties of $TC_i(T)$ ($i = 1, 2, 3, 4, 5, 6, 7, 8, 9, 10$)

In this section, we continue the derivations described in above section and adopt Equations (13)–(16), (18), (20), (22)–(24) and (26) to find the first-order and the second-order derivatives of the annual total relevant costs $TC_i(T)$ with respect to T in order to obtain the convexity properties as follows:

$$
TC'_1(T) = \tfrac{1}{T^2}\Big\{-o + \tfrac{hD}{2}[1 + \tfrac{2pD}{x(1-p)^2}]T^2 + \tfrac{cI_kD}{2}(\alpha+\beta)T^2 + \tfrac{\tau v DI_e}{2}T^2\Big\}
\tag{27}
$$

$$
TC''_1(T) = \tfrac{2o}{T^3} > 0
\tag{28}
$$

$$
\begin{aligned}
TC'_2(T) &= \tfrac{1}{T^2}\Big\{-o + h\cdot G(T) + [\tfrac{(2-p)c+s}{1-p}]\cdot[D(1+m-t_d)\cdot \tfrac{T}{1+m-T} - Dt_d \\
&\quad - D(1+m-t_d)\cdot \ln(\tfrac{1+m-t_d}{1+m-T})] + \tfrac{cI_kD}{2}(\alpha+\beta)T^2 + \tfrac{\tau v DI_e}{2}T^2\Big\}
\end{aligned}
\tag{29}
$$

$$
\begin{aligned}
TC''_2(T) &= \tfrac{1}{T^3}\Big\{2o + h\cdot H(T) + [\tfrac{(2-p)c+s}{1-p}]\cdot[D(1+m-t_d)\cdot \tfrac{(1+m)T}{(1+m-T)^2} \\
&\quad - 3D(1+m-t_d)\tfrac{T}{1+m-T} + 2Dt_d + 2D(1+m-t_d)\cdot \ln(\tfrac{1+m-t_d}{1+m-T})]\Big\}
\end{aligned}
\tag{30}
$$

$$
\begin{aligned}
TC'_3(T) &= \tfrac{1}{T^2}\Big\{-o + h\cdot G(T) + [\tfrac{(2-p)c+s}{1-p}]\cdot[D(1+m-t_d)\cdot \tfrac{T}{1+m-T} - Dt_d \\
&\quad - D(1+m-t_d)\cdot \ln(\tfrac{1+m-t_d}{1+m-T})] + \tfrac{cI_kD}{2}(\alpha+\beta)T^2 + \tfrac{\tau cDI_k}{2}\{\rho[T^2-(N-M)^2]\} \\
&\quad + \tfrac{\tau v DI_e}{2}[\rho(M-N)^2 + (1-\rho)T^2]\Big\}
\end{aligned}
\tag{31}
$$

$$
\begin{aligned}
TC''_3(T) &= \tfrac{1}{T^3}\Big\{2o + h\cdot H(T) + [\tfrac{(2-p)c+s}{1-p}]\cdot[D(1+m-t_d)\cdot \tfrac{(1+m)T}{(1+m-T)^2} \\
&\quad - 3D(1+m-t_d)\tfrac{T}{1+m-T} + 2Dt_d + 2D(1+m-t_d)\cdot \ln(\tfrac{1+m-t_d}{1+m-T})] \\
&\quad + \tau cDI_k\rho(N-M)^2 - \tau v DI_e\rho(M-N)^2\Big\}
\end{aligned}
\tag{32}
$$

$$TC'_4(T) = \tfrac{1}{T^2}\Big\{-o + h\cdot G(T) + [\tfrac{(2-p)c+s}{1-p}]\cdot[D(1+m-t_d)\cdot\tfrac{T}{1+m-T} - Dt_d \\ -D(1+m-t_d)\cdot\ln(\tfrac{1+m-t_d}{1+m-T})] + \tfrac{cI_kD}{2}(\alpha+\beta)T^2 + \tfrac{\tau cDI_k}{2}\{\rho[T^2-(N-M)^2] \\ +(1-\rho)(T^2-M^2)\} + \tfrac{\tau vDI_e}{2}[\rho(M-N)^2+(1-\rho)M^2]\Big\} \quad (33)$$

$$TC''_4(T) = \tfrac{1}{T^3}\Big\{2o + h\cdot H(T) + [\tfrac{(2-p)c+s}{1-p}]\cdot[D(1+m-t_d)\cdot\tfrac{(1+m)T}{(1+m-T)^2} \\ -3D(1+m-t_d)\tfrac{T}{1+m-T} + 2Dt_d + 2D(1+m-t_d)\cdot\ln(\tfrac{1+m-t_d}{1+m-T})] \\ + \tau cDI_k[\rho(N-M)^2+(1-\rho)M^2] - \tau vDI_e[\rho(M-N)^2+(1-\rho)M^2]\Big\} \quad (34)$$

$$TC'_5(T) = \tfrac{1}{T^2}\Big\{-o + \tfrac{hD}{2}[1+\tfrac{2pD}{x(1-p)^2}]T^2 + \tfrac{cI_kD}{2}(\alpha+\beta)T^2 + \tfrac{\tau cDI_k}{2}\{\rho[T^2-(N-M)^2]\} \\ + \tfrac{\tau vDI_e}{2}[\rho(M-N)^2+(1-\rho)T^2]\Big\} \quad (35)$$

$$TC''_5(T) = \tfrac{1}{T^3}\Big\{2o + \tau cDI_k\rho(N-M)^2 - \tau vDI_e\rho(M-N)^2\Big\} \quad (36)$$

$$TC'_6(T) = \tfrac{1}{T^2}\Big\{-o + \tfrac{hD}{2}[1+\tfrac{2pD}{x(1-p)^2}]T^2 + \tfrac{cI_kD}{2}(\alpha+\beta)T^2 + \tfrac{\tau cDI_k}{2}\{\rho[T^2-(N-M)^2] \\ +(1-\rho)(T^2-M^2)\} + \tfrac{\tau vDI_e}{2}[\rho(M-N)^2+(1-\rho)M^2]\Big\} \quad (37)$$

$$TC''_6(T) = \tfrac{1}{T^3}\Big\{2o + \tau cDI_k[\rho(N-M)^2+(1-\rho)M^2] - \tau vDI_e[\rho(M-N)^2+(1-\rho)M^2]\Big\} \quad (38)$$

$$TC'_7(T) = \tfrac{1}{T^2}\Big\{-o + \tfrac{hD}{2}[1+\tfrac{2pD}{x(1-p)^2}]T^2 + \tfrac{cI_kD}{2}(\alpha+\beta)T^2 + \tfrac{\tau cDI_k}{2}\rho T^2 \\ + \tfrac{\tau vDI_e}{2}(1-\rho)T^2\Big\} \quad (39)$$

$$TC''_7(T) = \tfrac{2o}{T^3} > 0 \quad (40)$$

$$TC'_8(T) = \tfrac{1}{T^2}\Big\{-o + h\cdot G(T) + [\tfrac{(2-p)c+s}{1-p}][D(1+m-t_d)\tfrac{T}{1+m-T} \\ -Dt_d - D(1+m-t_d)\cdot\ln(\tfrac{1+m-t_d}{1+m-T})] + \tfrac{cI_kD}{2}(\alpha+\beta)T^2 + \tfrac{\tau cDI_k}{2}\rho T^2 \\ + \tfrac{\tau vDI_e}{2}(1-\rho)T^2\Big\} \quad (41)$$

$$TC''_8(T) = \tfrac{1}{T^3}\Big\{2o + h\cdot H(T) + [\tfrac{(2-p)c+s}{1-p}][D(1+m-t_d)\tfrac{(1+m)T}{(1+m-T)^2} \\ -3D(1+m-t_d)\tfrac{T}{1+m-T} + 2Dt_d + 2D(1+m-t_d)\cdot\ln(\tfrac{1+m-t_d}{1+m-T})]\Big\} \quad (42)$$

$$TC'_9(T) = \tfrac{1}{T^2}\Big\{-o + h\cdot G(T) + [\tfrac{(2-p)c+s}{1-p}][D(1+m-t_d)\tfrac{T}{1+m-T} \\ -Dt_d - D(1+m-t_d)\cdot\ln(\tfrac{1+m-t_d}{1+m-T})] + \tfrac{cI_kD}{2}(\alpha+\beta)T^2 + \tfrac{\tau cDI_k}{2}[T^2-(1-\rho)M^2] \\ + \tfrac{\tau vDI_e}{2}(1-\rho)M^2\Big\} \quad (43)$$

$$TC''_9(T) = \tfrac{1}{T^3}\Big\{2o + h\cdot H(T) + [\tfrac{(2-p)c+s}{1-p}][D(1+m-t_d)\tfrac{(1+m)T}{(1+m-T)^2} \\ -3D(1+m-t_d)\tfrac{T}{1+m-T} + 2Dt_d + 2D(1+m-t_d)\cdot\ln(\tfrac{1+m-t_d}{1+m-T})] \\ + \tau cDI_k(1-\rho)M^2 - \tau vDI_e(1-\rho)M^2\Big\} \quad (44)$$

$$TC'_{10}(T) = \tfrac{1}{T^2}\Big\{-o + \tfrac{hD}{2}[1+\tfrac{2pD}{x(1-p)^2}]T^2 + \tfrac{cI_kD}{2}(\alpha+\beta)T^2 + \tfrac{\tau cDI_k}{2}[T^2-(1-\rho)M^2] \\ + \tfrac{\tau vDI_e}{2}(1-\rho)M^2\Big\} \quad (45)$$

and

$$TC''_{10}(T) = \tfrac{1}{T^3}\Big\{2o + \tau cDI_k(1-\rho)M^2 - \tau vDI_e(1-\rho)M^2\Big\} \quad (46)$$

where

$$G(T) = D(1+m-t_d)\cdot t_d\tfrac{T}{1+m-T} + \tfrac{2pD^2}{x(1-p)^2}(1+m-t_d)[t_d+(1+m-t_d) \\ \times \ln(\tfrac{1+m-t_d}{1+m-T})]\cdot\tfrac{T}{1+m-T} + \tfrac{D}{2}(1+m-t_d)^2\cdot\tfrac{T}{1+m-T} - \tfrac{D}{2}(1+m-T)T \\ -\tfrac{D}{2}t_d^2 - D(1+m-t_d)\cdot t_d\cdot\ln(\tfrac{1+m-t_d}{1+m-T}) - \tfrac{pD^2}{x(1-p)^2}[t_d+(1+m-t_d)\cdot\ln(\tfrac{1+m-t_d}{1+m-T})]^2 \\ -\tfrac{D}{2}(1+m-t_d)^2\cdot\ln(\tfrac{1+m-t_d}{1+m-T}) - \tfrac{D}{4}(1+m-T)^2 + \tfrac{D}{4}(1+m-t_d)^2 \quad (47)$$

and

$$\begin{aligned}H(T) &= D(1+m-t_d)t_d\frac{T^2}{(1+m-T)^2} + \frac{D}{2}(1+m-t_d)^2\frac{T^2}{(1+m-T)^2} + \frac{D}{2}T^2 \\ &\quad -2D(1+m-t_d)\cdot t_d\frac{T}{1+m-T} - D(1+m-t_d)^2\frac{T}{1+m-T} + D(1+m-T)T \\ &\quad +Dt_d^2 + 2D(1+m-t_d)t_d\cdot\ln(\frac{1+m-t_d}{1+m-T}) + D(1+m-t_d)^2\ln(\frac{1+m-t_d}{1+m-T}) \\ &\quad +\frac{D}{2}(1+m-T)^2 - \frac{D}{2}(1+m-t_d)^2 + \frac{2pD^2}{x(1-p)^2}(1+m-t_d)^2\frac{T^2}{(1+m-T)^2} \\ &\quad +\frac{2pD^2}{x(1-p)^2}(1+m-t_d)[t_d+(1+m-t_d)\cdot\ln(\frac{1+m-t_d}{1+m-T})]\frac{T^2}{(1+m-T)^2} \\ &\quad -\frac{4pD^2}{x(1-p)^2}(1+m-t_d)[t_d+(1+m-t_d)\cdot\ln(\frac{1+m-t_d}{1+m-T})]\frac{T}{1+m-T} \\ &\quad +\frac{2pD^2}{x(1-p)^2}[t_d+(1+m-t_d)\cdot\ln(\frac{1+m-t_d}{1+m-T})]^2\end{aligned} \quad (48)$$

Obviously, it is shown that $TC_1(T)$ and $TC_7(T)$ are convex functions on $(0,\infty)$, respectively.

Now, we let

$$W_1 = 2o - \tau v I_e D\rho(M-N)^2 \quad (49)$$

$$W_2 = 2o - \tau v I_e D[\rho(M-N)^2 + (1-\rho)M^2] \quad (50)$$

and

$$W_3 = 2o - \tau v I_e D(1-\rho)M^2 \quad (51)$$

Then, we have the following convexity results.

Lemma 1. *Each of the following assertions holds true:*

(A) $TC_r(T)$ $(r = 2, 8)$ is convex on $[t_d, \infty)$.
(B) If $W_2 \geq 0$, then $TC_l(T)$ $(l = 3, 4, 5, 6, 9, 10)$ is convex on $[t_d, \infty)$.
(C) If $W_1 < 0$, then $TC_i(T)$ $(i = 3, 5)$ is increasing on $[t_d, \infty)$.
(D) If $W_2 < 0$, then $TC_j(T)$ $(j = 4, 6)$ is increasing on $[t_d, \infty)$.
(E) If $W_3 < 0$, then $TC_k(T)$ $(k = 9, 10)$ is increasing on $[t_d, \infty)$.

Remark 1. *In our proof of Lemma 1, we need the assertions of Lemma 2.*

Lemma 2. *Each of the following assertions holds true:*

(A) $G(T) > 0$ if $T \geq t_d$
(B) $D(1+m-t_d)\frac{T}{1+m-T} - Dt_d - D(1+m-t_d)\cdot\ln(\frac{1+m-t_d}{1+m-T}) > 0$ if $T \geq t_d$
(C) $H(T) > 0$ if $T \geq t_d$
(D) $D(1+m-t_d)\frac{(1+m)T}{(1+m-T)^2} - 3D(1+m-t_d)\frac{T}{1+m-T}$
$\quad +2Dt_d + 2D(1+m-t_d)\cdot\ln(\frac{1+m-t_d}{1+m-T}) > 0$ if $T \geq t_d$

Remark 2. *The proof of Lemma 2 is given in the Appendix A.*

Proof of Lemma 1.

(A) Lemma 2(C) and 2(D) reveal that $TC''_r(T) > 0$ $(r = 2, 8)$ for $T \geq t_d$. Furthermore, $TC_r(T)$ $(r = 2, 8)$ is convex on $[t_d, \infty)$.
(B) If $W_2 > 0$, then $W_1 > 0$ and $W_3 > 0$. Moreover, Equations (32), (34), (36), (38), (44) and (46), together with Lemma 2(C) and 2(D), yield

$$TC''_i(T) > \frac{1}{T^3}\left\{2o - \tau v DI_e\rho(M-N)^2\right\} > 0, \quad i = 3 \text{ and } 5$$

$$TC''_j(T) > \frac{1}{T^3}\left\{2o - \tau v DI_e[\rho(M-N) + (1-\rho)M^2]\right\} > 0, \quad j = 4 \text{ and } 6$$

and

$$TC''_k(T) > \frac{1}{T^3}\left\{2o - \tau v DI_e[(1-\rho)M^2]\right\} > 0, \quad k = 9 \text{ and } 10 \qquad (52)$$

The above results imply that $TC_l(T)$ $(l = 3, 4, 5, 6, 9, 10)$ is convex on $[t_d, \infty)$.

(C) When $W_1 < 0$, from Equations (31) and (33) and Lemma 2(A) and 2(B), we have the following results:

$$TC'_i(T) > \frac{1}{2T^2}\left\{-2o + \tau v DI_e\rho(M-N)^2\right\} > 0, \quad i = 3 \text{ and } 5$$

Furthermore, $TC_i(T)$ $(i = 3, 5)$ is increasing on $[T_d, \infty)$.

(D) When $W_2 < 0$, from Equations (35) and (37) and Lemma 2(A) and 2(B), we have the following results:

$$TC'_j(T) > \frac{1}{2T^2}\left\{-2o + \tau v DI_e[\rho(M-N)^2 + (1-\rho)M^2]\right\} > 0, \quad j = 4 \text{ and } 6$$

Furthermore, $TC_j(T)$ $(j = 4, 6)$ is increasing on $[t_d, \infty)$.

(E) When $W_3 < 0$, from Equations (43) and (45) and Lemma 2(A) and 2(B), we have the following results:

$$TC'_k(T) > \frac{1}{2T^2}\left\{-2o + \tau v DI_e(1-\rho)M^2\right\} > 0, \quad k = 9 \text{ and } 10$$

Furthermore, $TC_k(T)$ $(k = 9, 10)$ is increasing on $[t_d, \infty)$. This completes the proof of Lemma 1. □

4. The Main Theorems for Optimal Replenishment Cycle Time T^* of $TC(T)$

In this section, we apply the convexity and monotonicity properties in order to develop efficient decision rules for the optimal replenishment cycle time T^* of $TC(T)$.

4.1. Decision Rule of the Optimal Replenishment Cycle Time T^* When $N \leq M$

4.1.1. Decision Rule of the Optimal Replenishment Cycle Time T^* When $t_d < M - N < M$

From Equation (12), we have

$$TC(T) = \begin{cases} TC_1(T) & \text{if} & 0 < T < t_d \\ TC_2(T) & \text{if} & t_d \leq T < M - N \\ TC_3(T) & \text{if} & M - N \leq T < M \\ TC_4(T) & \text{if} & M \leq T < R^* \end{cases}$$

All $TC_i(T)$ $(i = 1, 2, 3, 4)$ and $TC(T)$ are defined on $T > 0$. From Equations (27), (29), (31) and (33), we have

$$TC'_1(t_d) = TC'_2(t_d) = \frac{\Delta_1}{t_d^2}$$

$$TC'_2(M-N) = TC'_3(M-N) = \frac{\Delta_2}{(M-N)^2}$$

$$TC'_3(M) = TC'_4(M) = \frac{\Delta_3}{M^2}$$

and

$$TC'_4(R^*) = \frac{\Delta^*}{R^{*2}}$$

where

$$\Delta_1 = -o + \frac{hD}{2}[1 + \frac{2pD}{x(1-p)^2}]t_d^2 + \frac{cI_kD}{2}(\alpha+\beta)t_d^2 + \frac{\tau v DI_e}{2}t_d^2 \qquad (53)$$

$$\Delta_2 = -o + h \cdot G(M-N) + [\tfrac{(2-p)c+s}{1-p}] \cdot [D(1+m-t_d) \cdot \tfrac{(M-N)}{1+m-(M-N)} - Dt_d$$
$$- D(1+m-t_d) \cdot \ln(\tfrac{1+m-t_d}{1+m-(M-N)})] + \tfrac{c l_k D}{2}(\alpha+\beta)(M-N)^2 + \tfrac{\tau v D I_e}{2}(M-N)^2 \quad (54)$$

$$\Delta_3 = -o + h \cdot G(M) + [\tfrac{(2-p)c+s}{1-p}] \cdot [D(1+m-t_d) \cdot \tfrac{M}{1+m-M} - Dt_d$$
$$- D(1+m-t_d) \cdot \ln(\tfrac{1+m-t_d}{1+m-M})] + \tfrac{c l_k D}{2}(\alpha+\beta)M^2 + \tfrac{\tau c D I_k}{2}\{\rho\,[M^2 - (N-M)^2]\}$$
$$+ \tfrac{\tau v D I_e}{2}[\rho(M-N)^2 + (1-\rho)M^2] \quad (55)$$

and

$$\Delta^* = -o + h \cdot G(R^*) + [\tfrac{(2-p)c+s}{1-p}] \cdot [D(1+m-t_d) \cdot \tfrac{R^*}{1+m-R^*} - Dt_d$$
$$- D(1+m-t_d) \cdot \ln(\tfrac{1+m-t_d}{1+m-R^*})] + \tfrac{c l_k D}{2}(\alpha+\beta)R^{*2} + \tfrac{\tau c D I_k}{2}\{\rho\,[R^{*2} - (N-M)^2]$$
$$+ (1-\rho)(R^{*2} - M^2)\} + \tfrac{\tau v D I_e}{2}[\rho(M-N)^2 + (1-\rho)M^2] \quad (56)$$

From the above results, we have $\Delta_1 < \Delta_2$. In addition, if $W_1 \geq 0$, then $\Delta_1 < \Delta_2 < \Delta_3 < \Delta^*$. Otherwise, if $W_1 < 0$, we obtain $0 < \Delta_2 < \Delta_3 < \Delta^*$. From the above discussions, the following results are achieved.

Theorem 1. *Suppose that $t_d < M - N < M$. Then, each of the following results holds true:*

(I) If $W_1 \geq 0$, then
  (A) If $\Delta_1 < 0, \Delta_2 < 0, \Delta_3 < 0$ and $\Delta^* < 0$, then $TC(T^*) = TC_4(R^*)$.
  (B) If $\Delta_1 < 0, \Delta_2 < 0, \Delta_3 < 0$ and $\Delta^* \geq 0$, then $TC(T^*) = TC_4(T_4^*)$.
  (C) If $\Delta_1 < 0, \Delta_2 < 0, \Delta_3 \geq 0$ and $\Delta^* \geq 0$, then $TC(T^*) = TC_3(T_3^*)$.
  (D) If $\Delta_1 < 0, \Delta_2 \geq 0, \Delta_3 \geq 0$ and $\Delta^* \geq 0$, then $TC(T^*) = TC_2(T_2^*)$.
  (E) If $\Delta_1 \geq 0, \Delta_2 \geq 0, \Delta_3 \geq 0$ and $\Delta^* \geq 0$, then $TC(T^*) = TC_1(T_1^*)$.

(II) If $W_1 < 0$, then
  (A) If $\Delta_1 < 0, \Delta_2 \geq 0, \Delta_3 \geq 0$ and $\Delta^* \geq 0$, then $TC(T^*) = TC_2(T_2^*)$.
  (B) If $\Delta_1 \geq 0, \Delta_2 \geq 0, \Delta_3 \geq 0$ and $\Delta^* \geq 0$, then $TC(T^*) = TC_1(T_1^*)$.

Proof. The proof of Theorem 1 follows immediately from the above discussions. □

4.1.2. Decision Rule of the Optimal Replenishment Cycle Time T^* When $M - N < t_d < M$

From Equation (17), we have

$$TC(T) = \begin{cases} TC_1(T) & \text{if } 0 < T < M - N \\ TC_5(T) & \text{if } M - N \leq T < t_d \\ TC_3(T) & \text{if } t_d \leq T < M \\ TC_4(T) & \text{if } M \leq T \leq R^* \end{cases}$$

Herein, $TC_5(T)$ is defined on $T > 0$ as well. Equations (27), (31) and (35) imply that

$$TC'_1(M-N) = TC'_5(M-N) = \frac{\Delta_4}{(M-N)^2}$$

and

$$TC'_5(t_d) = TC'_3(t_d) = \frac{\Delta_5}{t_d^2}$$

where

$$\Delta_4 = -o + \tfrac{hD}{2}[1 + \tfrac{2pD}{x(1-p)^2}](M-N)^2 + \tfrac{c l_k D}{2}(\alpha+\beta)(M-N)^2 + \tfrac{\tau v D I_e}{2}(M-N)^2 \quad (57)$$

and

$$\Delta_5 = -o + \tfrac{hD}{2}[1 + \tfrac{2pD}{x(1-p)^2}]t_d^2 + \tfrac{c l_k D}{2}(\alpha+\beta)t_d^2 + \tfrac{\tau c D I_k}{2}\{\rho\,[t_d^2 - (N-M)^2]\}$$
$$+ \tfrac{\tau v D I_e}{2}\{\rho(M-N)^2 + (1-\rho)t_d^2\} \quad (58)$$

From the above results, we have these three situations: one is $\Delta_4 < \Delta_5 < \Delta_3 < \Delta^*$ if $W_2 \geq 0$, another is $\Delta_4 < \Delta_5 < \Delta_3 < \Delta^*$ and $0 < \Delta_3 < \Delta^*$ if $W_2 < 0$ and $W_1 \geq 0$, and the other is $0 < \Delta_4 < \Delta_5 < \Delta_3 < \Delta^*$ if $W_1 < 0$. Furthermore, we have the following results.

Theorem 2. *Suppose that $M - N < t_d < M$ Then, each of the following results holds true:*

(I) *If $W_2 \geq 0$, then*

  (A) *If $\Delta_4 < 0, \Delta_5 < 0, \Delta_3 < 0$ and $\Delta^* < 0$, then $TC(T^*) = TC_4(R^*)$.*
  (B) *If $\Delta_4 < 0, \Delta_5 < 0, \Delta_3 < 0$ and $\Delta^* \geq 0$, then $TC(T^*) = TC_4(T_4^*)$.*
  (C) *If $\Delta_4 < 0, \Delta_5 < 0, \Delta_3 \geq 0$ and $\Delta^* \geq 0$, then $TC(T^*) = TC_3(T_3^*)$.*
  (D) *If $\Delta_4 < 0, \Delta_5 \geq 0, \Delta_3 \geq 0$ and $\Delta^* \geq 0$, then $TC(T^*) = TC_5(T_5^*)$.*
  (E) *If $\Delta_4 \geq 0, \Delta_5 \geq 0, \Delta_3 \geq 0$ and $\Delta^* \geq 0$, then $TC(T^*) = TC_1(T_1^*)$.*

(II) *If $W_2 < 0$ and $W_1 \geq 0$, then*

  (A) *If $\Delta_4 < 0, \Delta_5 < 0$ and $\Delta_3 \geq 0$, then $TC(T^*) = TC_3(T_3^*)$.*
  (B) *If $\Delta_4 < 0, \Delta_5 \geq 0$ and $\Delta_3 \geq 0$, then $TC(T^*) = TC_5(T_5^*)$.*
  (C) *If $\Delta_4 \geq 0, \Delta_5 \geq 0$ and $\Delta_3 \geq 0$, then $TC(T^*) = TC_1(T_1^*)$.*

(III) *If $W_1 < 0$, then*

  (A) *If $\Delta_4 \geq 0, \Delta_5 \geq 0$ and $\Delta_3 \geq 0$, then $TC(T^*) = TC_1(T_1^*)$.*

Proof. The proof of Theorem 2 follows immediately from the above discussions. □

4.1.3. The Decision Rule of the Optimal Replenishment Cycle Time T^* When $M - N < M < t_d$

$$TC(T) = \begin{cases} TC_1(T) & \text{if } 0 < T < M - N \\ TC_5(T) & \text{if } M - N \leq T < M \\ TC_6(T) & \text{if } M \leq T < t_d \\ TC_4(T) & \text{if } t_d \leq T \leq R^* \end{cases}$$

Likewise, $TC_6(T)$ is defined on $T > 0$, Equations (33), (35) and (37) imply that

$$TC'_5(M) = TC'_6(M) = \frac{\Delta_6}{M^2}$$

and

$$TC'_6(t_d) = TC'_4(t_d) = \frac{\Delta_7}{t_d^2}$$

where

$$\Delta_6 = -o + \frac{hD}{2}[1 + \frac{2pD}{x(1-p)^2}]M^2 + \frac{cI_kD}{2}(\alpha + \beta)M^2 + \frac{\tau c DI_k}{2}\{\rho [M^2 - (N-M)^2]\} + \frac{\tau v DI_k}{2}[\rho(M-N)^2 + (1-\rho)M^2] \quad (59)$$

and

$$\Delta_7 = -o + \frac{hD}{2}[1 + \frac{2pD}{x(1-p)^2}]t_d^2 + \frac{cI_kD}{2}(\alpha + \beta)t_d^2 + \frac{\tau c DI_k}{2}\{\rho [t_d^2 - (N-M)^2] + (1-\rho)(t_d^2 - M^2)\} + \frac{\tau v DI_k}{2}[\rho(M-N)^2 + (1-\rho)M^2] \quad (60)$$

In addition, there are three situations to occur here: one is $\Delta_4 < \Delta_6 < \Delta_7 < \Delta^*$ when $W_2 \geq 0$, another is $\Delta_4 < \Delta_6$ and $0 < \Delta_6 < \Delta_7 < \Delta^*$ when $W_2 < 0$ and $W_1 \geq 0$, and the other is $0 < \Delta_4 < \Delta_6 < \Delta_7 < \Delta^*$ when $W_1 < 0$. Furthermore, we have the following results.

Theorem 3. *Suppose that $M - N < M < t_d$. Then, each of the the following results holds true:*

(I) *If $W_2 \geq 0$, then*

  (A) *If $\Delta_4 < 0, \Delta_6 < 0, \Delta_7 < 0$ and $\Delta^* < 0$, then $TC(T^*) = TC_4(R^*)$.*

(B) If $\Delta_4 < 0$, $\Delta_6 < 0$, $\Delta_7 < 0$ and $\Delta^* \geq 0$, then $TC(T^*) = TC_4(T_4^*)$.
(C) If $\Delta_4 < 0$, $\Delta_6 < 0$, $\Delta_7 \geq 0$ and $\Delta^* \geq 0$, then $TC(T^*) = TC_6(T_6^*)$.
(D) If $\Delta_4 < 0$, $\Delta_6 \geq 0$, $\Delta_7 \geq 0$ and $\Delta^* \geq 0$, then $TC(T^*) = TC_5(T_5^*)$.
(E) If $\Delta_4 \geq 0$, $\Delta_6 \geq 0$, $\Delta_7 \geq 0$ and $\Delta^* \geq 0$, then $TC(T^*) = TC_1(T_1^*)$.

(II) If $W_2 < 0$ and $W_1 \geq 0$, then

(A) If $\Delta_4 < 0$, $\Delta_6 \geq 0$, $\Delta_7 \geq 0$ and $\Delta^* \geq 0$, then $TC(T^*) = TC_5(T_5^*)$.
(B) If $\Delta_4 \geq 0$, $\Delta_6 \geq 0$, $\Delta_7 \geq 0$ and $\Delta^* \geq 0$, then $TC(T^*) = TC_1(T_1^*)$.

(III) If $W_1 < 0$, then $\Delta_4 > 0$ and $TC(T^*) = TC_1(T_1^*)$.

Proof. The proof of Theorem 3 follows immediately from the above discussions. □

4.2. The Decision Rule of the Optimal Replenishment Cycle Time T^* When $N > M$
4.2.1. The Decision Rule of the Optimal Replenishment Cycle Time T^* When $t_d < M$

From Equation (21), we have

$$TC(T) = \begin{cases} TC_7(T) & if \quad 0 < T < t_d \\ TC_8(T) & if \quad t_d \leq T < M \\ TC_9(T) & if \quad M \leq T \leq R^* \end{cases}$$

All $TC_v(T)$ ($v = 7, 8, 9$) are defined on $T > 0$. From Equations (39), (41), and (43), we have

$$TC'_7(t_d) = TC'_8(t_d) = \frac{\Delta_8}{t_d^2}$$

$$TC'_8(M) = TC'_9(M) = \frac{\Delta_9}{M^2}$$

and

$$TC'_9(R^*) = \frac{\Delta^{**}}{R^{*2}}$$

where

$$\Delta_8 = -o + \frac{hD}{2}[1 + \frac{2pD}{x(1-p)^2}]t_d^2 + \frac{cI_kD}{2}(\alpha + \beta)t_d^2 + \frac{\tau cDI_k}{2}\rho t_d^2 + \frac{\tau v DI_e}{2}(1-\rho)t_d^2 \quad (61)$$

$$\begin{aligned}\Delta_9 &= -o + h \cdot G(M) + [\tfrac{(2-p)c+s}{1-p}][D(1+m-t_d)\tfrac{M}{1+m-M} - Dt_d \\ &\quad -D(1+m-t_d)\cdot \ln(\tfrac{1+m-t_d}{1+m-M})] + \tfrac{cI_kD}{2}(\alpha+\beta)M^2 + \tfrac{\tau cDI_k}{2}\rho M^2 \\ &\quad + \tfrac{\tau v DI_e}{2}(1-\rho)M^2 \end{aligned} \quad (62)$$

and

$$\begin{aligned}\Delta^{**} &= -o + h \cdot G(R^*) + [\tfrac{(2-p)c+s}{1-p}][D(1+m-t_d)\tfrac{R^*}{1+m-R^*} - Dt_d \\ &\quad -D(1+m-t_d)\cdot \ln(\tfrac{1+m-t_d}{1+m-R^*})] + \tfrac{cI_kD}{2}(\alpha+\beta)R^{*2} + \tfrac{\tau cDI_k}{2}[R^{*2} - (1-\rho)M^2] \\ &\quad + \tfrac{\tau v DI_e}{2}(1-\rho)M^2\} \end{aligned} \quad (63)$$

Additionally, if $W_3 \geq 0$, then $\Delta_8 < \Delta_9 < \Delta^{**}$. Otherwise, if $W_3 < 0$, we have $\Delta_8 < \Delta_9$ and $0 < \Delta_9 < \Delta^{**}$. Furthermore, we have the following Theorem.

Theorem 4. *Suppose that $t_d < M$ Then, each of the following results holds true:*

(I) If $W_3 \geq 0$, then

(A) If $\Delta_8 < 0$, $\Delta_9 < 0$ and $\Delta^{**} < 0$, then $TC(T^*) = TC_9(R^*)$.
(B) If $\Delta_8 < 0$, $\Delta_9 < 0$ and $\Delta^{**} \geq 0$, then $TC(T^*) = TC_9(T_9^*)$.
(C) If $\Delta_8 < 0$, $\Delta_9 \geq 0$ and $\Delta^{**} \geq 0$, then $TC(T^*) = TC_8(T_8^*)$.
(D) If $\Delta_8 \geq 0$, $\Delta_9 \geq 0$ and $\Delta^{**} \geq 0$, then $TC(T^*) = TC_7(T_7^*)$.

(II) If $W_3 < 0$, then

(A) If $\Delta_8 < 0$, $\Delta_9 \geq 0$ and $\Delta^{**} \geq 0$, then $TC(T^*) = TC_8(T_8^*)$.
(B) If $\Delta_8 \geq 0$, $\Delta_9 \geq 0$ and $\Delta^{**} \geq 0$, then $TC(T^*) = TC_7(T_7^*)$.

Proof. The proof of Theorem 4 follows immediately from the above discussions. □

4.2.2. Decision Rule of the Optimal Replenishment Cycle Time T^* When $t_d \geq M$

From Equations (25), we have

$$TC(T) = \begin{cases} TC_7(T) & \text{if } 0 < T < M \\ TC_{10}(T) & \text{if } M \leq T < t_d \\ TC_9(T) & \text{if } t_d \leq T \leq R^* \end{cases}$$

Herein, $TC_{10}(T)$ is defined on $T > 0$. From Equations (39), (43), and (45), we have

$$TC'_7(M) = TC'_{10}(M) = \frac{\Delta_{10}}{M^2}$$

and

$$TC'_{10}(t_d) = TC'_9(t_d) = \frac{\Delta_{11}}{t_d^2}$$

where

$$\Delta_{10} = -o + \frac{hD}{2}[1 + \frac{2pD}{x(1-p)^2}]M^2 + \frac{cI_kD}{2}(\alpha+\beta)M^2 + \frac{\tau c DI_k}{2}\rho M^2 + \frac{\tau v DI_e}{2}(1-\rho)M^2 \bigg\} \quad (64)$$

and

$$\Delta_{11} = -o + \frac{hD}{2}[1 + \frac{2pD}{x(1-p)^2}]t_d^2 + \frac{cI_kD}{2}(\alpha+\beta)t_d^2 + \frac{\tau c DI_k}{2}[t_d^2 - (1-\rho)M^2]$$
$$+ \frac{\tau v DI_e}{2}(1-\rho)M^2 \bigg\} \quad (65)$$

Likewise, if $W_3 \geq 0$, then $\Delta_{10} < \Delta_{11} < \Delta^{**}$. Otherwise, if $W_3 < 0$, we have $0 < \Delta_{10} < \Delta_{11} < \Delta^{**}$. From above arguments, we have the following theorem.

Theorem 5. *Suppose that $t_d \geq M$ Then, each of the following results holds true:*

(I) If $W_3 \geq 0$, then

  (A) If $\Delta_{10} < 0$, $\Delta_{11} < 0$ and $\Delta^{**} < 0$, then $TC(T^*) = TC_9(R^*)$.
  (B) If $\Delta_{10} < 0$, $\Delta_{11} < 0$ and $\Delta^{**} \geq 0$, then $TC(T^*) = TC_9(T_9^*)$.
  (C) If $\Delta_{10} < 0$, $\Delta_{11} \geq 0$ and $\Delta^{**} \geq 0$, then $TC(T^*) = TC_{10}(T_{10}^*)$.
  (D) If $\Delta_{10} \geq 0$, $\Delta_{11} \geq 0$ and $\Delta^{**} \geq 0$, then $TC(T^*) = TC_7(T_7^*)$.

(II) If $W_3 < 0$, then $\Delta_{10} \geq 0$ and $TC(T^*) = TC_7(T_7^*)$.

Proof: The proof follows immediately from the above discussions. □

5. Illustrative Numerical Examples

In this section, we will provide numerical examples to illustrate the theoretical results. We assume that the maximum lifetime of the deteriorating items is 2 years ($m = 2$). The computed results are shown in Tables 1–9.

Table 1. The optimal replenishment policy used Theorem 1(I).

				Theorem 1(I) If $W_1 \geq 0$					
				$t_d = 0.008, N = 0.01$					
	Δ_1	Δ_2	Δ_3	Δ^*	o	h	M	R^*	T^*	$TC(T^*)$
(A)	<0	<0	<0	<0	0.200	1.5	0.02	0.0237	$R^* = 0.0237$	1329.5
(B)	<0	<0	<0	≥ 0	0.150	1.5	0.02	0.0237	$T_4^* = 0.0218$	1327.4
(C)	<0	<0	≥ 0	≥ 0	0.080	1.5	0.02	0.0237	$T_3^* = 0.0166$	1323.7
(D)	<0	≥ 0	≥ 0	≥ 0	0.010	1.5	0.02	0.0237	$T_2^* = 0.0086$	1317.9
(E)	≥ 0	≥ 0	≥ 0	≥ 0	0.005	1.5	0.02	0.0237	$T_1^* = 0.0072$	1317.2

Table 2. The optimal replenishment policy used Theorem 1(II).

				Theorem 1(II) If $W_1 < 0$							
				$o = 0.002, N = 0.01, M = 0.02$							
	Δ_1	Δ_2	Δ_3	Δ^*	h	D	x	p	I_k	t_d	R^*	T^*	$TC(T^*)$
(A)	<0	≥ 0	≥ 0	≥ 0	0.01	95	1000	0.001	0.13	0.002	0.0210	$T_2^* = 0.0021$	1238.6
(B)	≥ 0	≥ 0	≥ 0	≥ 0	1.50	100	300	0.010	0.15	0.008	0.0237	$T_1^* = 0.0014$	1316.1

Table 3. The optimal replenishment policy used Theorem 2(I).

				Theorem 2(I) If $W_2 \geq 0$					
				$t_d = 0.012, R^* = 0.1240$					
	Δ_4	Δ_5	Δ_3	Δ^*	o	h	N	M	T^*	$TC(T^*)$
(A)	<0	<0	<0	<0	6.00	0.01	0.01	0.02	$R^* = 0.1240$	1315.4
(B)	<0	<0	<0	≥ 0	4.00	0.01	0.01	0.02	$T_4^* = 0.1190$	1299.2
(C)	<0	<0	<0	≥ 0	0.01	0.01	0.01	0.02	$T_3^* = 0.0131$	1239.5
(D)	<0	≥ 0	≥ 0	≥ 0	0.01	1.50	0.01	0.02	$T_2^* = 0.0106$	1240.3
(E)	≥ 0	≥ 0	≥ 0	≥ 0	0.01	2.00	0.01	0.02	$T_1^* = 0.0094$	1240.6

Table 4. The optimal replenishment policy used Theorem 2(II) and (III).

	Theorem 2(II) If $W_2 < 0$ and $W_1 \geq 0$											
	Δ_4	Δ_5	Δ_3	Δ^*	o	h	D	c	v	x	I_k	I_e	t_d
(A)	<0	<0	≥ 0	≥ 0	0.0005	0.0001	94	0.005	3	100	0.14	0.10	0.0125
(B)	<0	≥ 0	≥ 0	≥ 0	0.0020	0.0100	95	3.000	4	1000	0.13	0.12	0.0120
(C)	≥ 0	≥ 0	≥ 0	≥ 0	0.0020	0.1000	95	3.000	4	1000	0.13	0.12	0.0120
	Theorem 2(II) If $W_2 < 0$ and $W_1 \geq 0$											
	Δ_4	Δ_5	Δ_3	Δ^*	N	M	R^*	T^*	$TC(T^*)$				
(A)	<0	<0	≥ 0	≥ 0	0.012	0.013	0.0133	$T_3^* = 0.0125$	941.4161				
(B)	<0	≥ 0	≥ 0	≥ 0	0.010	0.020	0.1240	$T_5^* = 0.0104$	1238.82				
(C)	≥ 0	≥ 0	≥ 0	≥ 0	0.010	0.020	0.1240	$T_1^* = 0.0094$	1238.9				
	Theorem 2(III) If $W_1 < 0$												
	Δ_4	Δ_5	Δ_3	Δ^*	o	h	D	c	v	x	I_k	I_e	t_d	N
(A)	≥ 0	≥ 0	≥ 0	≥ 0	0.0002	0.01	95	3	4	100	0.13	0.12	0.012	0.01
	Theorem 2(III) If $W_1 < 0$												
	Δ_4	Δ_5	Δ_3	Δ^*	M	R^*	T^*	$TC(T^*)$					
(A)	≥ 0	≥ 0	≥ 0	≥ 0	0.02	0.1240	$T_1^* = 0.0033$	1238.6					

Table 5. The optimal replenishment policy used Theorem 3(I).

							Theorem 3(I) If $W_2 \geq 0$				
	Δ_4	Δ_6	Δ_7	Δ^*	o	h	t_d	N	M	R^*	T^*	$TC(T^*)$
(A)	<0	<0	<0	<0	8	1	0.025	0.01	0.02	0.0827	$R^* = 0.0827$	4057.5
(B)	<0	<0	<0	≥0	6	1	0.025	0.01	0.02	0.0827	$T_4^* = 0.0795$	4033.2
(C)	<0	<0	≥0	≥0	0.1	1	0.025	0.01	0.02	0.0827	$T_6^* = 0.0225$	3919.9
(D)	<0	≥0	≥0	≥0	0.1	2	0.025	0.01	0.02	0.0827	$T_5^* = 0.0168$	3922.8
(E)	≥0	≥0	≥0	≥0	0.1	8	0.025	0.01	0.02	0.0827	$T_1^* = 0.0089$	3933.3

Table 6. The optimal replenishment policy used Theorem 3(II) and (III).

						Theorem 3(II) If $W_2 < 0$ and $W_1 \geq 0$					
						$t_d = 0.025$					
	Δ_4	Δ_6	Δ_7	Δ^*	o	h	D	N	M	R^*	T^*	$TC(T^*)$
(A)	<0	≥0	≥0	≥0	0.004	0.01	200	0.010	0.020	0.1232	$T_5^* = 0.0102$	2608.0
(B)	≥0	≥0	≥0	≥0	0.001	0.10	300	0.010	0.020	0.0827	$T_1^* = 0.0037$	3911.4
						Theorem 3(III) If $W_1 < 0$					
(A)	≥0	≥0	≥0	≥0	0.001	0.01	300	0.025	0.003	0.020	0.0827	$T_1^* = 0.0042$	3910.8

Table 7. The optimal replenishment policy used Theorem 4(I).

						Theorem 4(I) If $W_3 \geq 0$					
	Δ_8	Δ_9	Δ^{**}	o	h	D	t_d	N	M	R^*	T^*	$TC(T^*)$
(A)	<0	<0	<0	2.00	1.0	200	0.01	0.03	0.02	0.0497	$R^* = 0.0497$	2672.5
(B)	<0	<0	≥0	1.00	0.5	100	0.01	0.03	0.02	0.0986	$T_9^* = 0.0570$	1334.7
(C)	<0	≥0	≥0	0.10	1.0	200	0.01	0.03	0.02	0.0497	$T_8^* = 0.0151$	2618.0
(D)	≥0	≥0	≥0	0.01	2.0	100	0.01	0.03	0.02	0.0986	$T_7^* = 0.0092$	1306.4

Table 8. The optimal replenishment policy used Theorem 4(II).

						Theorem 4(II) If $W_3 < 0$					
	Δ_8	Δ_9	Δ^{**}	o	h	D	t_d	N	M	R^*	T^*	$TC(T^*)$
(A)	<0	≥0	≥0	0.01	0.10	250	0.01	0.04	0.03	0.0398	$T_8^* = 0.0103$	3262.4
(B)	≥0	≥0	≥0	0.01	2.00	250	0.01	0.04	0.03	0.0398	$T_7^* = 0.0058$	3264.2

Table 9. The optimal replenishment policy used Theorem 5(I) and 5(II).

						Theorem 5(I) If $W_3 \geq 0$					
	Δ_{10}	Δ_{11}	Δ^{**}	o	h	D	t_d	N	M	R^*	T^*	$TC(T^*)$
(A)	<0	<0	<0	10	1.0	300	0.03	0.04	0.02	0.0991	$R^* = 0.0991$	4074.2
(B)	<0	<0	≥0	0.2	1.0	100	0.03	0.04	0.02	0.2878	$T_9^* = 0.0362$	1312.7
(C)	<0	≥0	≥0	0.05	1.0	100	0.03	0.04	0.02	0.2878	$T_{10}^* = 0.0279$	1308.0
(D)	≥0	≥0	≥0	0.01	1.0	100	0.03	0.04	0.02	0.2878	$T_7^* = 0.0121$	1306.1
						Theorem 5(II) If $W_3 < 0$					
(A)	≥0	≥0	≥0	0.005	1.0	300	0.03	0.04	0.02	0.0991	$T_7^* = 0.0049$	3915.4

Example 1. $h = 1.5$, $c = 3$, $v = 4$, $D = 100$, $x = 300$, $p = 0.01$, $s = 10$, $t_d = 0.008$, $N = 0.01$ year, $M = 0.02$ year, $L = 0.3$, $I_k = \$0.15/\$/\text{year}$, $I_e = \$0.12/\$/\text{year}$, $\tau = 0.3$, $\alpha = 0.3$,

$\theta(t)$	the time-varying deterioration rare at time t, where $0 \leq \theta(t) \leq 1$;
t_d	the fresh product time;
t_s	the screening time per cycle;
M	the upstream credit period by the supplier to the retailer;
N	the downstream credit period by the retailer to customers;
I_e	the interest earned per dollar per year;
I_k	the interest charged by the supplier per dollar per year;
L	the length of time in years during which the prepayments are paid;
α	the fraction of procurement cost to be prepaid before the time of delivery, $0 \leq \alpha \leq 1$;
β	the fraction of procurement cost to be paid at the time of delivery, $0 \leq \beta \leq 1$;
τ	the fraction of procurement cost granted a credit period from the supplier to the retailer, $0 \leq \tau \leq 1$ and $\alpha + \beta + \tau = 1$;
ρ	the fraction of the sales revenue offered a credit period by the retailer to the customers, $0 \leq \rho \leq 1$;
$TC(T)$	the total annual relevant cost in dollars;
T	the length of inventory cycle time in years, $T \leq m$;
T^*	the (fixed) optimal cycle time of $TC(T)$;
$I_1(t)$	the inventory level at time $t \in [0, t_s]$ in which the product has no deterioration;
$I_2(t)$	the inventory level at time $t \in [t_s, t_d]$ in which the product has no deterioration;
$I_3(t)$	the inventory level at time $t \in [t_d, T]$ in which the product has deterioration;

Assumptions

1. All deteriorating items continuously deteriorate with time and cannot be sold when time exceeds the expiration date m. To make the problem tractable, we assume the same as in Wang et al. [65] and Chen et al. [16], that the deterioration rate is $\theta(t) = \frac{1}{1+m-t}$, $0 \leq t \leq T \leq m$.
2. There is no replacement or repair of deteriorated items during the replenishment cycle time $(0, T]$.
3. The demand rate is known and constant.
4. Shortages are not allowed.
5. The replenishment rate is infinite.
6. The time horizon is infinite.
7. There exists an inspection process that is 100% effective.
8. The screening rate is faster than the demand rate.
9. The supplier imposes a prepayment policy to the retailer, in which the retailer should prepay a fraction of procurement cost (α percent) at the moment they place an order to the supplier (at time L), they pay another β percentage of procurement cost at time 0 upon the receipt of all items, and receive an upstream credit period of M years on the remaining τ portion of procurement cost.
10. During the selling period, the retailer offers the partial trade credit to his customers, in which their customers must immediately make a partial payment (at the rate $1 - \rho$) to the retailer in cash at the time of purchasing items and then receive credit period N on the outstanding amount.
11. If $M \geq N$, then the retailer deposits the sales revenue into an interest bearing account. If $M \geq T + N$ (i.e., the permissible delay period is longer than the time at which the retailer receives the last payment from its customers), then the retailer receives all revenue and pays off the entire purchase cost at the end of the permissible delay M. Otherwise, (if $M \leq T + N$), the retailer pays the supplier the sum of all units sold by $M - N$ and the collateral deposit received from N to M, keeps the profit for the use of the other activities, and starts paying for the interest charges on the items sold after $M - N$.

12. If $N \geq M$, then the retailer finances and pays its supplier the entire amount of the delayed payment $(1 - \rho)cDT$ at the end of the trade credit M, and then pays down the loan after time N at which the retailer starts to receive sales revenue from its customers. For the collateral deposit the retailer deposits the sales revenue into an interest bearing account until the end of the permissible delay M. If $T \geq M$, then the retailer pays the supplier all units sold by M, keeps the profit for the use of the other activities, and starts paying for the interest charges on the items sold after M.

Appendix A

Proof of Lemma 2. In proving Lemma 2, we consider the assertions of Lemma 2 item-wise.

(A) Taking the first-order derivative of $G(T)$ with respect to T, we obtain

$$G'(T) = \frac{D(1+m-t_d)t_dT}{(1+m-T)^2} + \frac{2pD^2}{x(1-p)^2}\{[t_d + (1+m-t_d) \cdot \ln(\frac{1+m-t_d}{1+m-T})] \cdot \frac{(1+m-t_d)T}{(1+m-T)^2} + \frac{(1+m-t_d)^2T}{(1+m-T)^2}\}$$
$$+ \frac{D}{2}(1+m-t_d)^2 \cdot \frac{T}{(1+m-T)^2} + \frac{DT}{2}$$
$$> 0$$

and

$$G(t_d) = \frac{pD^2}{x(1-p)^2} > 0$$

Furthermore, we see that $G(T) > 0$ if $T \geq t_d$.

(B) We define $g(T)$ as follows:

$$g(T) = D(1+m-t_d)\frac{T}{1+m-T} - Dt_d - D(1+m-t_d) \cdot \ln(\frac{1+m-t_d}{1+m-T})$$

Taking the first-order derivative of $g(T)$ with respect to T, we derive

$$g'(T) = \frac{D(1+m-t_d)T}{(1+m-T)^2} > 0$$

and

$$g(t_d) = 0$$

Furthermore, we have

$$D(1+m-t_d)\frac{T}{1+m-T} - Dt_d - D(1+m-t_d)\ln(\frac{1+m-t_d}{1+m-T}) > 0 \text{ if } T \geq t_d$$

(C) Taking the first-order derivative of $H(T)$ with respect to T, we obtain

$$H'(T) = \frac{4pD^2}{x(1-p)^2}(1+m-t_d)[t_d + (1+m-t_d) \cdot \ln(\frac{1+m-t_d}{1+m-T})]\frac{T^2}{(1+m-T)^3}$$
$$+ \frac{6pD^2}{x(1-p)^2}(1+m-t_d)^2\frac{T^2}{(1+m-T)^3}$$

and

$$H(t_d) = \frac{Dt_d^3}{(1+m-t_d)} + \frac{2pD^2}{x(1-p)^2} \cdot \frac{t_d^3}{(1+m-t_d)} > 0$$

Furthermore, we have $H(T) > 0$ if $T \geq t_d$.

(D) We define $h(T)$ by

$$h(T) = D(1+m-t_d)\frac{(1+m)T}{(1+m-T)^2} - 3D(1+m-t_d)\frac{T}{1+m-T} + 2Dt_d$$
$$+ 2D(1+m-t_d) \cdot \ln(\frac{1+m-t_d}{1+m-T})$$

Taking the first-order derivative of $h(T)$ with respect to T, we find that

$$h'(T) = D(1 + m - t_d) \frac{2T^2}{(1 + m - T)^3} > 0$$

and

$$h(t_d) = \frac{Dt_d^2}{(1 + m - t_d)} > 0$$

So, we finally have

$$D(1 + m - t_d) \frac{(1+m)T}{(1+m-T)^2} - 3D(1 + m - t_d) \frac{T}{1+m-T} \\ + 2Dt_d + 2D(1 + m - t_d) \cdot \ln(\frac{1+m-t_d}{1+m-T}) > 0 \quad \text{(A1)}$$

if $T \geq t_d$.

We thus have completed the proof of Lemma 2. □

References

1. Zhang, A.X. Optimal advance payment scheme involving fixed per-payment costs. *Omega* **1996**, *24*, 577–582. [CrossRef]
2. Taleizadeh, A.A.; Pentico, D.W.; Jabalameli, M.S.; Aryanezhad, M. An economic order quantity model with multiple partial prepayments and partial backordering. *Math. Comput. Model.* **2013**, *57*, 311–323. [CrossRef]
3. Taleizadeh, A.A. An economic order quantity model for deteriorating item in a purchasing system with multiple prepayments. *Appl. Math. Model.* **2014**, *38*, 5357–5366. [CrossRef]
4. Taleizadeh, A.A. An EOQ model with partial backordering and advance payments for an evaporating item. *Int. J. Prod. Econ.* **2014**, *155*, 185–193. [CrossRef]
5. Zhang, Q.; Tsao, Y.-C.; Chen, T.-H. Economic order quantity under advance payment. *Appl. Math. Model.* **2014**, *38*, 5910–5921. [CrossRef]
6. Eck, K.; Engemann, M.; Schnitzer, M. How trade credits foster exporting. *Rev. World Econ.* **2014**, *151*, 73–101. [CrossRef]
7. Lashgari, M.; Taleizadeh, A.A.; Ahmadi, A. Partial up-stream advanced payment and partial down-stream delayed payment in a three-level supply chain. *Ann. Oper. Res.* **2016**, *238*, 329–354. [CrossRef]
8. Tavakoli, S.; Taleizadeh, A.A. An EOQ model for decaying item with full advanced payment and conditional dis-count. *Ann. Oper. Res.* **2017**, *259*, 415–436. [CrossRef]
9. Heydari, J.; Rastegar, M.; Glock, C. A two-level delay in payments contract for supply chain coordination: The case of credit-dependent demand. *Int. J. Prod. Econ.* **2017**, *191*, 26–36. [CrossRef]
10. Feng, L.; Chan, Y.-L. Joint pricing and production decisions for new products with learning curve effects under up-stream and downstream trade credits. *Eur. J. Oper. Res.* **2019**, *272*, 905–913. [CrossRef]
11. Chen, S.-C.; Teng, J.-T. Inventory and credit decisions for time-varying deteriorating items with up-stream and down-stream trade credit financing by discounted cash flow analysis. *Eur. J. Oper. Res.* **2015**, *243*, 566–575. [CrossRef]
12. Mahata, G.C. Optimal ordering policy with trade credit and variable deterioration for fixed life time products. *Int. J. Oper. Res.* **2016**, *25*, 307–326. [CrossRef]
13. Wu, J.; Teng, J.-T.; Chan, Y.-L. Inventory policies for perishable products with expiration dates and ad-vance-cash-credit payment schemes. *Int. J. Syst. Sci. Oper. Logist.* **2018**, *5*, 310–326.
14. Zia, N.P.; Taleizadeh, A.A. A lot-sizing model with backordering under hybrid linked-to-order multiple advance payments and delayed payment. *Transp. Res. Part E Logist. Transp. Rev.* **2015**, *82*, 19–37. [CrossRef]
15. Wu, J.; Al-Khateeb, F.B.; Teng, J.-T.; Cárdenas-Barrón, L.E. Inventory models for deteriorating items with maximum lifetime under downstream partial trade credits to credit-risk customers by discounted cash-flow analysis. *Int. J. Prod. Econ.* **2016**, *171*, 105–115. [CrossRef]
16. Chen, S.-C.; Min, J.; Teng, J.-T.; Li, F. Inventory and shelf-space management for fresh produce with fresh-ness-and-stock dependent demand and expiration date. *J. Oper. Res. Soc.* **2016**, *67*, 884–896. [CrossRef]
17. Teng, J.-T.; Cárdenas-Barrón, L.E.; Chang, H.-J.; Wu, J.; Hu, Y. Inventory lot-size policies for deteriorating items with expiration dates and advance payments. *Appl. Math. Model.* **2016**, *40*, 8605–8616. [CrossRef]
18. Diabat, A.; Taleizadeh, A.A.; Lashgari, M. A lot sizing model with partial downstream delayed payment, partial upstream advance payment, and partial backordering for deteriorating items. *J. Manuf. Syst.* **2017**, *45*, 322–342. [CrossRef]
19. Feng, L.; Chan, Y.-L.; Cárdenas-Barrón, L.E. Pricing and lot-sizing polices for perishable goods when the demand depends on selling price, displayed stocks, and expiration date. *Int. J. Prod. Econ.* **2017**, *185*, 11–20. [CrossRef]
20. Mahata, G.C.; De, S.K. Supply chain inventory model for deteriorating items with maximum lifetime and partial trade credit to credit-risk customers. *Int. J. Manag. Sci. Eng. Manag.* **2017**, *12*, 21–32. [CrossRef]
21. Tiwari, S.; Cárdenas-Barrón, L.E.; Goh, M.; Shaikh, A.A. Joint pricing and inventory model for deteriorating items with expiration dates and partial backlogging under two-level partial trade credits in supply chain. *Int. J. Prod. Econ.* **2018**, *200*, 16–36. [CrossRef]

22. Taleizadeh, A.A.; Akram, R.; Lashgari, M.; Heydari, J. A three-level supply chain with up-stream and down-stream trade credit Periods linked to ordered quantity. *Appl. Math. Model.* **2017**, *40*, 8777–8793. [CrossRef]
23. Li, R.; Chan, Y.-L.; Chang, C.-T.; Cárdenas-Barrón, L.E. Pricing and lot-sizing policies for perishable products with advance-cash-credit payments by a discounted cash-flow analysis. *Int. J. Prod. Econ.* **2017**, *193*, 578–589. [CrossRef]
24. Li, R.; Liu, Y.; Teng, J.-T.; Tsao, Y.-C. Optimal pricing, lot-sizing and backordering decisions when a seller demands an advance-cash-credit payment scheme. *Eur. J. Oper. Res.* **2019**, *278*, 283–295. [CrossRef]
25. Taleizadeh, A.A. Lot-sizing model with advance payment pricing and disruption in supply under planned partial backordering. *Int. Trans. Oper. Res.* **2017**, *24*, 783–800. [CrossRef]
26. Krommyda, I.-P.; Skouri, K.; Lagodimos, A. A unified EOQ model with financial constraints and market tolerance. *Appl. Math. Model.* **2019**, *65*, 89–105. [CrossRef]
27. Tsao, Y.-C.; Putri, R.P.F.R.; Zhang, C.; Linh, V.T. Optimal pricing and ordering policies for perishable products under advance-cash-credit payment scheme. *J. Ind. Eng. Int.* **2019**, *15*, 131–146. [CrossRef]
28. Mashud, A.H.M.; Roy, D.; Daryanto, Y.; Wee, H.-M. A Joint pricing deteriorating inventory model considering the product life cycle and advance payment. *RAIRO-Oper. Res.* **2021**, *55*, S1069–S1088. [CrossRef]
29. Mashud, A.H.M.; Roy, D.; Daryanto, Y.; Chakraborty, R.K.; Tseng, M.-L. A controllable carbon emission and deteri-oration inventory model with advance payments scheme. *J. Clean. Prod.* **2021**, *296*, 126608. [CrossRef]
30. Arjani, A.; Miah, M.M.; Uddin, M.S.; Mashud, A.H.M.; Wee, H.-M.; Sana, S.S.; Srivastava, H.M. A sustainable economic recycle quantity model for imperfect production system with shortages. *J. Risk Financ. Manag.* **2021**, *14*, 173. [CrossRef]
31. Hou, K.-L.; Srivastava, H.M.; Lin, L.-C.; Lee, S.-F. The impact of system deterioration and product warranty on optimal lot sizing with maintenance and shortages backordered. *Rev. Real Acad. Cienc. Exactas Físicas Nat. Ser. A Mat.* **2021**, *115*, 1–18. [CrossRef]
32. Udayakumar, R.; Geetha, K.V. Economic ordering policy of single item inventory mode over finite time horizon. *Int. J. Syst. Assur. Eng. Manag.* **2017**, *8*, 734–757. [CrossRef]
33. Lashgari, M.; Taleizadeh, A.A.; Sadjadi, S.J. Ordering policies for non-instantaneous deteriorating items under hybrid partial prepayment, partial trade credit and partial backordering. *J. Oper. Res. Soc.* **2017**, *69*, 1167–1196. [CrossRef]
34. Udayakumar, R.; Geetha, K.V. An EOQ model for non-instantaneous deteriorating items with two levels of storage under trade credit policy. *J. Ind. Eng. Int.* **2018**, *14*, 343–365. [CrossRef]
35. Babangida, B.; Baraya, Y. An inventory model for non-instantaneous deteriorating items with time dependent quadratic demand, two storage facilities and shortages under trade credit policy. *Int. J. Model. Oper. Manag.* **2020**, *8*, 1–44. [CrossRef]
36. Soni, N.H.; Suthar, D.N. Optimal pricing and replenishment policy for non-instantaneous deteriorating items with varying rate of demand and partial backlogging. *Opsearch* **2020**, *57*, 986–1021. [CrossRef]
37. Çalışkan, C. An Inventory Ordering Model for Deteriorating Items with Compounding and Backordering. *Symmetry* **2021**, *13*, 1078. [CrossRef]
38. Tiwari, S.; Cárdenas-Barrón, L.E.; Khanna, A.; Jaggi, C.K. Impact of trade credit and inflation on retailer's ordering policies for non-instantaneous deteriorating items in a two-warehouse environment. *Int. J. Prod. Econ.* **2016**, *176*, 154–169. [CrossRef]
39. Tsao, Y.-C.; Zhang, Q.; Chang, F.-C.; Vu-Thuy, L. An imperfect production model under Radio Frequency Identification adoption and trade credit. *Appl. Math. Model.* **2016**, *42*, 493–508. [CrossRef]
40. Geetha, K.V.; Udayakumar, R. Optimal lot sizing policy for non-instantaneous deteriorating items with price and ad-vertisement dependent demand under partial backlogging. *Int. J. Appl. Comput. Math.* **2016**, *2*, 171–193. [CrossRef]
41. Jaggi, C.K.; Tiwari, S.; Goel, S.K. Credit financing in economic ordering policies for non-instantaneous deteriorating items with price dependent demand and two storage facilities. *Ann. Oper. Res.* **2017**, *248*, 253–280. [CrossRef]
42. Maihami, R.; Karimi, B.; Ghomi, S.F. Effect of two-echelon trade credit on pricing-inventory policy of non-instantaneous deteriorating products with probabilistic demand and deterioration functions. *Ann. Oper. Res.* **2017**, *257*, 237–273. [CrossRef]
43. Mashud, A.; Khan, M.; Uddin, M.; Islam, M. A non-instantaneous inventory model having different deterioration rates with stock and price dependent demand under partially backlogged shortages. *Uncertain Supply Chain. Manag.* **2018**, *6*, 49–64. [CrossRef]
44. Bounkhel, M.; Tadj, L.; Benhadid, Y.; Hedjar, R. Optimal Control of Nonsmooth Production Systems with Deteriorating Items, Stock-Dependent Demand, with or without Backorders. *Symmetry* **2019**, *11*, 183. [CrossRef]
45. Udayakumar, R.; Geetha, K.; Sana, S.S. Economic ordering policy for non-instantaneous deteriorating items with price and advertisement dependent demand and permissible delay in payment under inflation. *Math. Methods Appl. Sci.* **2021**, *44*, 7697–7721. [CrossRef]
46. Khanna, A.; Kishore, A.; Jaggi, C.K. Strategic production modeling for defective items with imperfect inspection pro-cess, rework, and sales return under two-level trade credit. *Int. J. Ind. Eng. Comput.* **2016**, *8*, 85–118.
47. Zhou, Y.; Chen, C.; Li, C.; Zhong, Y. A synergic economic order quantity model with trade credit, shortages, imperfect quality and inspection errors. *Appl. Math. Model.* **2016**, *40*, 1012–1028. [CrossRef]
48. Datta, T.K. Inventory system with defective products and investment opportunity for reducing defective proportion. *Oper. Res.* **2017**, *17*, 297–312. [CrossRef]
49. Taleizadeh, A.A.; Lashgari, M.; Akram, R.; Heydari, J. Imperfect economic production quantity model with upstream trade credit periods linked to raw material order quantity and downstream trade credit periods. *Appl. Math. Model.* **2016**, *40*, 8777–8793. [CrossRef]

50. Pal, S.; Mahapatra, G.S. A manufacturing-oriented supply chain model for imperfect quality with inspection errors, stochastic demand under rework and shortages. *Comput. Ind. Eng.* **2017**, *106*, 299–314. [CrossRef]
51. Khakzad, A.; Gholamian, M.R. The effect of inspection on deterioration rate: An inventory model for deteriorating items with advanced payment. *J. Clean. Prod.* **2020**, *254*, 120117. [CrossRef]
52. Taleizadeh, A.A.; Khanbaglo, M.P.S.; Cárdenas-Barrón, L.E. Replenishment of imperfect items in an EOQ inventory model with partial backordering. *RAIRO-Oper. Res.* **2020**, *54*, 413–434. [CrossRef]
53. Wang, W.T.; Wee, H.M.; Cheng, Y.L.; Wen, C.L.; Cárdenas-Barrón, L.E. EOQ model for imperfect quality items with partial backorders and screening constraint. *Eur. J. Ind. Eng.* **2015**, *9*, 744. [CrossRef]
54. Alamri, A.A.; Irina, H.; Aris, A.S. Efficient inventory control for imperfect quality items. *Eur. J. Oper. Res.* **2016**, *254*, 92–104. [CrossRef]
55. Palanivel, M.; Uthayakumar, R. Inventory model with imperfect items, stock dependent demand and permissible delay in payments under inflation. *RAIRO-Oper. Res.* **2016**, *50*, 473–489. [CrossRef]
56. Aghili, S.J.; Hoseinabadi, H.H. Reliability evaluation of repairable systems using various fuzzy-based methods-a sub-station automation case study. *Int. J. Electr. Power Energy Syst.* **2017**, *85*, 130–142. [CrossRef]
57. Tsao, Y.-C. Joint location, inventory, and preservation decisions for non-instantaneous deterioration items under delay in payments. *Int. J. Syst. Sci.* **2014**, *47*, 572–585. [CrossRef]
58. Tsao, Y.-C.; Lee, P.-L.; Liao, L.-W.; Zhang, Q.; Vu, T.-L.; Tsai, J. Imperfect economic production quantity models under predictive maintenance and reworking. *Int. J. Syst. Sci. Oper. Logist.* **2020**, *7*, 347–360. [CrossRef]
59. Khanna, A.; Mittal, M.; Gautam, P.; Jaggi, C.K. Credit financing for deteriorating imperfect quality items with allowable shortages. *Decis. Sci. Lett.* **2016**, *5*, 45–60. [CrossRef]
60. Liao, J.-J.; Huang, K.; Chung, K.; Lin, S.; Ting, P.; Srivastava, H.M. Retailer's optimal ordering policy in the EOQ model with imperfect-quality items under limited storage capacity and permissible delay. *Math. Methods Appl. Sci.* **2018**, *41*, 7624–7640. [CrossRef]
61. Kazemi, N.; Abdul-Rashid, S.H.; Ghazilla, R.A.R.; Shekarian, E.; Zanoni, S. Economic order quantity models for items with imperfect quality and emission considerations. *Int. J. Syst. Sci. Oper. Logist.* **2018**, *5*, 99–115. [CrossRef]
62. Liao, J.-J.; Huang, K.-N.; Chung, K.-J.; Lin, S.-D.; Chuang, S.-T.; Srivastava, H.M. Optimal ordering policy in an economic order quantity (EOQ) model for non-instantaneous deteriorating items with defective quality and permissible delay in payments. *Rev. Real Acad. Cienc. Exactas Físicas Nat. Ser. A Mat.* **2020**, *114*, 41. [CrossRef]
63. Mashud, A.H.M.; Roy, D.; Daryanto, Y.; Ali, M.H. A Sustainable Inventory Model with Imperfect Products, Deterioration, and Controllable Emissions. *Mathematics* **2020**, *8*, 2049. [CrossRef]
64. Srivastava, H.M.; Chung, K.-J.; Liao, J.-J.; Lin, S.-D.; Lee, S.-F. An accurate and reliable mathematical analytic solution procedure for the EOQ model with non-instantaneous receipt under supplier credits. *Rev. Real Acad. Cienc. Exactas Físicas Nat. Ser. A Mat.* **2020**, *115*, 1–22. [CrossRef]
65. Wang, W.-C.; Teng, J.-T.; Lou, K.-R. Seller's optimal credit period and cycle time in a supply chain for deteriorating items with maximum lifetime. *Eur. J. Oper. Res.* **2014**, *232*, 315–321. [CrossRef]

Article

An Alternate Generalized Odd Generalized Exponential Family with Applications to Premium Data

Sadaf Khan [1,*], Oluwafemi Samson Balogun [2,*], Muhammad Hussain Tahir [1], Waleed Almutiry [3] and Amani Abdullah Alahmadi [4]

1. Department of Statistics, The Islamia University of Bahawalpur, Bahawalpur 63100, Pakistan; mht@iub.edu.pk
2. School of Computing, University of Eastern Finland, 70211 Kuopio, Northern Europe, Finland
3. Department of Mathematics, College of Science and Arts in Ar Rass, Qassim University, Buryadah 52571, Saudi Arabia; wkmtierie@qu.edu.sa
4. College of Science and Humanities, Shaqra University, Shaqra 15572, Saudi Arabia; aalahmadi@su.edu.sa
* Correspondence: drsmkhan22@gmail.com (S.K.); samson.balogun@uef.fi (O.S.B.)

Abstract: In this article, we use Lehmann alternative-II to extend the odd generalized exponential family. The uniqueness of this family lies in the fact that this transformation has resulted in a multitude of inverted distribution families with important applications in actuarial field. We can characterize the density of the new family as a linear combination of generalised exponential distributions, which is useful for studying some of the family's properties. Among the structural characteristics of this family that are being identified are explicit expressions for numerous types of moments, the quantile function, stress-strength reliability, generating function, Rényi entropy, stochastic ordering, and order statistics. The maximum likelihood methodology is often used to compute the new family's parameters. To confirm that our results are converging with reduced mean square error and biases, we perform a simulation analysis of one of the special model, namely OGE2-Fréchet. Furthermore, its application using two actuarial data sets is achieved, favoring its superiority over other competitive models, especially in risk theory.

Keywords: generalized exponential distribution; generalized exponential distribution; OGE-G family; Rényi entropy; order statistic

1. Introduction

In recent years, there has been a dramatic growth in the number of generalisations of well-known probability distributions. Most notable generalizations are achieved by (i) inducting power parameters in well established parent distributions, (ii) extending the classical distribution by modification in their functions, (iii) introducing special functions such as W[K(x)] as generators and (iv) by compounding of distributions. This heaped surge of generalized families is due to the flexibility in modelling phenomenons related to the changing scenarios of contemporary scientific field including demography, actuarial, survival, biological, ecological, communication theory, epidemiology and environmental sciences. However, a clear understanding of the applicability of these models in most applied areas is necessary if one is to gain insights into systems that can be modeled as random processes. The model, thus obtained, acquires improved empirical results to the real data that is collected adaptively.

Although there exist many functions which act as generators to produce flexible classes of distributions, in this project, we will emphasize generalizations in which a ratio of survival function (sf) has been used in some form, commonly known as the odd ratio. In the reference [1], a proportional odd family viz. a viz. the Marshall Olkin-G (MO-G) was generalized by sf $\overline{K}(x) = 1 - K(x)$, where $K(x)$ is the distribution function (cdf) of parent distribution, with the induction of a tilt parameter. Gleaton and Lynch, in the reference [2], used the odd function as generator when they defined a log odd family (OLL-G). In the reference [3], defined the odd Weibull family, as an asymptotically equivalent log-logistic model for larger values of θ, the scale parameter. The reference [4] used the Transformed-Transformer (TX) family, due to the reference [5], to define odd Weibul-G families of distribution. Since then, a myriad of distributions has been generalized using odd function. Some of the important families include [6–31], among others.

Focussing on the origins and motivations of our proposed scheme, the authors in [32] proposed the odd generalized exponential family (which we refer to OGE-G) as a better alternative to generalized exponential (GE) family using Lehmann Alternative-I (LA-I). The cdf of the two parameter OGE-G family is mentioned below:

$$F_{OGE-G}(x;\alpha,\lambda,\psi) = \left(1 - e^{-\lambda \frac{K(x;\psi)}{\overline{K}(x;\psi)}}\right)^{\alpha}, \quad x>0, \alpha>0, \lambda>0.$$

In the reference [33], an odd family of GE was proposed so-called generalized odd generalized exponential family (which we refer to OGE1-G). The cdf of OGE1-G family is presented as:

$$F_{OGE1-G}(x;\alpha,\beta,\psi) = \left(1 - e^{-\frac{K^{\alpha}(x;\psi)}{1-K^{\alpha}(x;\psi)}}\right)^{\beta}, \quad x>0, \alpha>0, \beta>0.$$

Because of its capacity to simulate variable hazard rate function (hrf) forms of all traditional types in lifetime data analysis, we believe OGE-G offers a sensible combination of simplicity and flexibility. However, the relevance of OGE1-G to lifespan modelling in domains such as reliability, actuarial sciences, informatics, telecommunications, and computational social sciences (just to highlight a few) is still debatable. According to the reference [34], the Lehmann Alternative-II (LA2) approach has received less attention. This motivated us to use LA2 approach to develop the exponentiated odd generalized exponential (OGE2-G), in the same vein as OGE-G and OGE1-G. Adhering to the framework defined in the reference [5], if T follows GE random variable (rv), then the cdf of OGE2-G family is mentioned below:

$$F_{OGE2-G}(x;\alpha,\beta,\psi) = \left[1 - e^{-\frac{1-\overline{K}(x;\psi)^{\alpha}}{\overline{K}(x;\psi)^{\alpha}}}\right]^{\beta}, \quad x>0, \alpha,\beta>0 \quad (1)$$

where α and β are shape parameter and ψ is the vector of baseline parameter.

Consider the following points to emphasise the model's distinctiveness; (i) In the literature, the proposed model in its current form has not been studied to the best of our knowledge, (ii) From an analytical standpoint, the OGE2-G family has a significantly better configuration and practicality than OGE-G and OGE1-G for inverted models with minimal chance to counter non-identifiability issues, (iii) The OGE2-G has several curious connections to other families. When α approaches 0, $F(x;\alpha,\beta,\psi)$ tends to GE with $\lambda = 1$, when $\alpha = 1$ $F(x;\alpha,\beta,\psi)$ tends to OGE-G, if $\alpha \to 0$ and $\beta = 1$ then $F(x;\alpha,\beta,\psi)$ tends to odd exponential (OE) (iv) This new dimension allowed us to explore models which are naturally constituted by LA2. The generalizations, thus attained, produced skewed distributions with much heavier tails enabling its practicality in risk evaluation theory with far better results, (v) The successful application of OGE2-G family motivates future research, as it outperforms nine well-established existing models, (vi) We present a physical explanation for X when α and β are integers. Consider there be a parallel system consisting of β identically independent components. Suppose that the lifetime of a rv Y with a specific $K(x;\psi)$ with α components in a series system such that the risk of failing at time x is represented by the odd function as $\frac{1-\overline{K}(x;\psi)^\alpha}{\overline{K}(x;\psi)^\alpha}$. Consider that the randomness of this risk is represented by the rv X, then we can assume the following relation holds

$$Pr(Y \leq x) = Pr(X \leq \frac{1-\overline{K}(x;\psi)^\alpha}{\overline{K}(x;\psi)^\alpha}) = F(x;\alpha,\beta,\psi),$$

explicitly given in Equation (1). The OGE2-G family is offered and explored in this research, emphasising its diversity and scope for application to real life phenomenons. The major features of the OGE2-G family, including the pdf, hrf, qf, and ten unique models from OGE2-G family presented in Table 1, are provided in the first half. Then, certain mathematical properties of the OGE2-G such as series expansion of the exponentiated pdf, moments, parameter estimation, order statistics, Rényi entropy, stress-strength analysis and stochastic dominance results are investigated. Furthermore, Fréchet is specified as baseline model termed as OGE2-Fréchet (denoted as OGE2Fr) and the maximum likelihood (ML) technique is then used to construct statistical applications of the special model. We choose to study OGE2Fr specifically as its nested model include inverse-Rayleigh (IR) and inverse exponential (IE), favoring its suitability over sub-models as well. It is applied to fit two sets of premium data from actuarial field. Using key performance indicators, we reveal that OGE2Fr outperforms nine competing models. A portion pertinent to specific risk measures, with an emphasis on the value at risk (VaR) and the expected shortfall (ES), is presented. Eventually, the estimation of risk measures for the examined data sets is then discussed, with the proposed methodology yielding a rather satisfying result. Equation (1) can be useful in modelling real life survival data with different shapes of hrf. Table 1 lists $\frac{1-\overline{K}(x;\psi)^\alpha}{\overline{K}(x;\psi)^\alpha}$ and the corresponding parameters for some special distributions which are considered to be the potential sub-models of OGE2-G family.

Table 1. Distributions and corresponding $\frac{1-\overline{K}(x;\psi)^\alpha}{\overline{K}(x;\psi)^\alpha}$ functions.

Distribution	$\frac{1-\overline{K}(x;\psi)^\alpha}{\overline{K}(x;\psi)^\alpha}$	ψ
Fréchet ($x > 0$)	$\left[1 - e^{(a/x)^b}\right]^{-\alpha} - 1$	(a,b)
Generalized exponential ($x > 0$)	$\left[1 - (1 - e^{-\lambda x})^\theta\right]^{-\alpha} - 1$	(λ, θ)
Power function ($0 < x < a$)	$\left[1 - (x/a)^b\right]^{-\alpha} - 1$	(a,b)
Burr III ($x > 0$)	$\left[1 - (1 + x^{-c})^{-k}\right]^{-\alpha} - 1$	(c,k)
Half-logistic ($x > 0$)	$\left[2(e^x + 1)^{-1}\right]^{-\alpha} - 1$	(α)
Log-logistic ($x > 0$)	$\left[1 + (x/a)^b\right]^{\alpha} - 1$	(a,b)
Inverse Rayleigh ($x > 0$)	$\left[1 - e^{\gamma/x^2}\right]^{-\alpha} - 1$	(γ)
Inverse Exponential ($x > 0$)	$\left[1 - e^{\gamma/x}\right]^{-\alpha} - 1$	(γ)
Normal ($-\infty < x < \infty$)	$\left[1 - \phi(\frac{x-\mu}{\sigma})\right]^{-\alpha} - 1$	(μ, σ)
Gumbel ($-\infty < x < \infty$)	$\left[1 - e^{-e^{\frac{x-\mu}{\sigma}}}\right]^{-\alpha} - 1$	(μ, σ)

The following is a breakdown of how the paper is constructed. In Section 2, we acquaint the readers to the new family with basic properties and ten potential baseline models which can become members of OGE2-G family. Section 3 is comprised of the mathematical properties of the OGE2-G family. Section 4 progresses by taking Fréchet (Fr) as sub-model to propose OGE2Fr and related statistical and inferential properties. Section 5 specifies two applications of actuarial data sets with emphasis on risk evaluation (premium returns) and the proposed model's veracity is established. Furthermore, the model is applied to compute some actuarial measures. Section 6 is the final section, with some annotations and useful insights.

2. The OGE2G Family

In this segment, basic statistical properties of the newly proposed family characterized by the cdf, in Equation (1) are presented. Functional forms of ten sub models are also defined.

2.1. Definition of pdf and hrf

The pdf in agreement with Equation (1) is given as (2).

$$f_{OGE2-G}(x; \alpha, \beta, \psi) = \alpha \beta k(x; \psi) \overline{K}(x; \psi)^{-\alpha-1} e^{-\left\{\frac{1-\overline{K}(x;\psi)^{\alpha}}{\overline{K}(x;\psi)^{\alpha}}\right\}} \left[1 - e^{-\left\{\frac{1-\overline{K}(x;\psi)^{\alpha}}{\overline{K}(x;\psi)^{\alpha}}\right\}}\right]^{\beta-1} \quad (2)$$

Using the results defined in Equations (1) and (2), the hrf is defined as

$$\tau(x; \alpha, \beta, \psi) = \frac{f_{OGE2-G}(x; \alpha, \beta, \psi)}{1 - F_{OGE2-G}(x; \alpha, \beta, \psi)}$$

$$= \alpha \beta k(x; \psi) \overline{K}(x; \psi)^{-\alpha-1} e^{-\left\{\frac{1-\overline{K}(x;\psi)^{\alpha}}{\overline{K}(x;\psi)^{\alpha}}\right\}} \left[1 - e^{-\left\{\frac{1-\overline{K}(x;\psi)^{\alpha}}{\overline{K}(x;\psi)^{\alpha}}\right\}}\right]^{\beta-1}$$

$$\times \left[1 - \left(1 - e^{-\left\{\frac{1-\overline{K}(x;\psi)^{\alpha}}{\overline{K}(x;\psi)^{\alpha}}\right\}}\right)^{\beta-1}\right] \quad (3)$$

The hazard rate is just a calculation of the change in survivor rate per unit of time. Hence, its importance in reliability and survival analysis is crucial. The hrf has some characteristic shapes which include monotonic (increasing, decreasing), non-monotonic (bathtub or upside down bathtub) or constant. Standard statistical distribution yield maximum three shapes, but OGE2-G family can yield a diverse range of shapes (including increasing-decreasing-increasing) depending upon the choice of special model. For further details on hrf, see [35].

2.2. Quantile Function and Potential Sub-Models

The OGE2-G family may be readily approximated by reversing Equation (1) as shown below: If indeed the distribution of u is uniform $u(0,1)$, therefore

$$x = Q_K \left[1 - \left\{1 - \log\left(1 - u^{1/\beta}\right)\right\}^{-1/\alpha}\right]. \quad (4)$$

Equation (4) can be useful to define statistical measures such as median, skewness, and kurtosis based on quartiles, deciles, or percentiles. These measures facilitates to concisely define the skewness and kurtosis measures which are significant tool to comprehend the shape(s) of the distribution.

Theorem 1 shows how the OGE2 family is related to other distributions.

Theorem 1. *Let $X \sim OGE2\text{-}G(\alpha, \beta; \psi)$, then*

(a) If $Y = 1 - \overline{K}(x; \psi)^{\alpha}$, then $F_Y(y) = \left(1 - e^{-\frac{Y}{1-Y}}\right)^{\beta}$, $0 < y < 1$, and

(b) If $Y = \frac{1-\overline{K}(x;\psi)^{\alpha}}{\overline{K}(x;\psi)^{\alpha}}$, then $Y \sim GE(1, \beta)$.

3. Mathematical Properties of OGE2-G Family

To capture the family's modelling capacity, numerous mathematical features of the OGE2-G are examined in this section. Some of the key results established in this section are then applied in Section 5.

3.1. Linear Expansion of cdf

We provide a useful expansion for (1) in terms of linear combinations of exp-G density functions using the following series expansion as

$$(1-z)^{\eta-1} = \sum_{i=0}^{\infty} \frac{(-1)^i \Gamma(\eta)}{i! \Gamma(\eta-i)} z^i,$$

whereas the expansion holds for all $|z| < 1$ and $\eta > 0$ a non-integer value. Then, the cdf of OGE2-G class in (1) can indeed be phrased with

$$F(x) = \sum_{i=0}^{\infty} \frac{(-1)^i \Gamma(\beta+1)}{i! \Gamma(\beta+1-i)} e^{-i\left(\frac{1-\overline{K}^{ff}}{\overline{K}^{ff}}\right)}. \quad (5)$$

Using series expansion and power series expansion in Equation (5), will yield the following cdf

$$F(x) = F(x:\alpha,\beta,\psi) = \sum_{\ell=0}^{\infty} \xi_\ell H_\ell(x), \quad (6)$$

where $H_\ell(x) = K(x;\psi)^\ell$ (for $\ell \geq 1$) denotes the cdf of exp-G distribution with power parameter ℓ and

$$\xi_\ell = (-1)^\ell \sum_{i,j=1}^{\infty} \sum_{k=0}^{j} (-1)^{i+j+k} \frac{\Gamma(\beta+1)}{i!j!\Gamma(\beta+1-i)} \binom{j}{k} \binom{\alpha(k-i)}{\ell}.$$

Through differentiating Equation (6) the OGE2-G family density, we may express it as a combination of exp-G densities.

$$f(x:\alpha,\beta,\psi) = \sum_{i,j=1}^{\infty} \xi_\ell h_\ell(x), \quad (7)$$

where $h_\ell(x) = \ell K^{\ell-1}(x;\psi) k(x;\psi)$ is the exp-G pdf with power parameter ℓ. As a result, numerous features of the proposed model may be deduced from the exp-G distribution's attributes. Most modern computation frameworks, such as MathCad, Maple, Mathematica, and Matlab, can efficiently handle the formulas derived throughout the article, which can currently operate using the use of analytic formulations of enormous size and complexity.

3.2. Numerous Types of Moments

The fundamental formula for the pth moment of X is supplied by (7) as

$$\mu'_p = \sum_{i,j=0}^{\infty} \xi_\ell E(X_\ell^p). \quad (8)$$

where $\mathbb{E}(X_\ell^p) = \int_0^\infty x^p h_\ell(x) dx$. Setting $p = 1$ in (8) can provide explicit expression for the mean of several parent distributions.

A another expression for μ'_p is taken from (8) as far as the baseline qf is concerned

$$\mu'_p = \sum_{i,j=0}^{\infty} \xi_\ell \, \tau(p, \ell-1). \qquad (9)$$

where $\tau(p, \ell-1) = \int_0^1 Q_G(u)^p \, u^\ell du$.

The central moments (μ_p) and cumulants (κ_p) of X can follow from Equation (8) as $\mu_p = \sum_{k=0}^{p} \binom{p}{k} (-1)^k \mu_1'^k \mu'_{p-k}$ and $\kappa_s = \mu'_s - \sum_{k=1}^{s-1} \binom{s-1}{k-1} \kappa_k \mu'_{s-k}$, respectively, where $\kappa_1 = \mu'_1$.

The rth lower incomplete moment of X can be determined from Equation (7) as

$$m_r(y) = \sum_{i,j=0}^{\infty} \xi_\ell \int_0^{G(y)} Q_G(u)^r \, u^{l-1} du. \qquad (10)$$

For most G distributions, the final integral may be calculated.

3.3. Inference Related to OGE2 Family

The strategy of maximum likelihood (MLL) approach is used to estimate the unknown parameters of the new class. Let $x_1, \ldots, x_n$ be n observations from the OGE2-G density class (2) with parameter vector $\Theta = (\alpha, \beta, \psi)^\top$. Then the likelihood function $\mathcal{L}(\alpha, \beta, \delta)$ on the domain Θ is defined as

$$\begin{aligned}\mathcal{L} =\ & n \log(\alpha) + n \log(\beta) + \sum_{i=1}^{n} \log k(x_i; \psi) - (\alpha+1) \log \overline{K}(x_i; \psi) \\ & -V(x_i; \alpha, \psi) + (\beta-1) \sum_{i=1}^{n} \log\left[1 - e^{-V(x_i; \alpha, \psi)}\right], \end{aligned} \qquad (11)$$

where $V(x_i; \alpha, \psi) = \frac{1 - \overline{K}(x_i; \psi)^\alpha}{\overline{K}(x_i; \psi)^\alpha}$.

The elements of the score vector $U(\Theta)$ are as described in the following:

$$U_\alpha = \frac{n}{\alpha} - \sum_{i=1}^{n} \log \overline{K}(x_i; \psi) - V'^{(\alpha)}(x_i; \alpha, \psi)$$

$$+ \sum_{i=1}^{n} \frac{(\beta-1) e^{-V(x_i; \alpha, \psi)} V'^{(\alpha)}(x_i; \alpha, \psi)}{(1 - e^{-V(x_i; \alpha, \psi)})},$$

$$U_\beta = \frac{n}{\beta} + \sum_{i=1}^{n} \log\left[1 - e^{-V(x_i; \alpha, \psi)}\right],$$

$$U_\psi = \sum_{i=1}^{n} \left[\frac{k'(x_i; \psi)}{k(x_i; \psi)}\right] + (\alpha+1) \sum_{i=1}^{n} \left[\frac{k(x_i; \psi) k'(x_i; \psi)}{\overline{K}(x_i; \psi)}\right] - V'^{(\xi_k)}(x_i; \alpha, \psi)$$

$$+ (\beta-1) \sum_{i=1}^{n} \left[\frac{e^{-V(x_i; \alpha, \psi)} \left\{V'^{(\xi_k)}(x_i; \alpha, \psi)\right\}}{1 - e^{-V(x_i; \alpha, \psi)}}\right],$$

where $V'^{(\alpha)}(.)$ and $V'^{(\psi_k)}(.)$ means the derivative of the function V with respect to α and ψ, respectively.

The next elements are produced by the components of the score vector $J(\Theta)$.

$$J_{\alpha\alpha} = -\frac{n}{\alpha^2} + \sum_{i=1}^{n} \frac{k(x_i;\alpha,\beta,\psi_k)V'^{(\psi_k)}}{\bar{K}(x_i;\alpha,\beta,\psi_k)} - V''^{(\alpha\alpha)} + (\beta-1)$$

$$\times \sum_{i=1}^{n} \frac{e^{-V(x_i;\alpha,\psi)}V'(x_i;\alpha,\alpha) + e^{-V(x_i;\alpha,\psi)}(V'(x_i;\alpha))^2}{(1-e^{-V(x_i;\alpha,\psi)})^2},$$

$$J_{\alpha\beta} = \sum_{i=1}^{n} \frac{e^{-V(x_i;\alpha,\psi)}V'^{\alpha}(x_i;\alpha,\psi)}{[1-e^{-V(x_i;\alpha,\psi)}]^2},$$

$$J_{\alpha\psi} = \sum_{i=1}^{n} \frac{k(x_i;\alpha,\beta,\psi)k'(x_i;\alpha,\beta,\psi)}{\bar{K}(x_i;\alpha,\beta,\psi)} - V''^{(\alpha\psi)}(x_i;\alpha,\psi) + (\beta-1)$$

$$\times \sum_{i=1}^{n} \frac{[e^{-V(x_i;\alpha,\psi)}]^2 V'^{(\alpha)}(x_i;\alpha,\psi)V'^{(\psi)}(x_i;\alpha,\psi) - e^{-V(x_i;\alpha,\psi)}V'''^{(\alpha\psi)}(x_i;\alpha,\psi)}{(1-e^{-V(x_i;\alpha,\psi)})^2}$$

$$-(\beta-1)\sum_{i=1}^{n} \frac{e^{-V(x_i;\alpha,\beta,\psi)}V'^{(\alpha)}(x_i;\alpha,\psi)V'^{(\psi)}(x_i;\alpha,\psi)}{(1-e^{-V(x_i;\alpha,\psi)})^2}$$

$$+(\beta-1)\sum_{i=1}^{n} \frac{[e^{-V(x_i;\alpha,\psi)}]^2 V'^{(\alpha)}(x_i;\alpha,\psi)V'^{(\psi)}(x_i;\alpha,\psi)}{(1-e^{-V(x_i;\alpha,\psi)})^2},$$

$$J_{\beta\beta} = -\frac{n}{\beta^2},$$

$$J_{\beta\psi} = \sum_{i=1}^{n} \frac{e^{-V(x_i;\alpha,\psi)}V'^{(\psi)}(x_i;\alpha,\psi)}{1-e^{-V(x_i;\alpha,\psi)}},$$

$$J_{\psi\psi} = \sum_{i=1}^{n} \frac{k(x_{i;\psi})k''(x_{i;\psi}) - [k'(x_{i;\psi})]^2}{[k(x_{i;\psi})]^2} + (\alpha+1)\sum_{i=1}^{n}\left[\frac{k(x_{i;\psi})k'(x_{i;\psi})\{-k'(x_{i;\psi})\}^2}{\bar{K}^2((x_{i;\psi}))}\right]$$

$$-V''^{(\psi\psi)}(x_{i;\psi}) - (\beta-1)\sum_{i=1}^{n} \frac{[e^{-V(x_i;\alpha,\psi)}V'^{(\psi)}(x_i;\alpha,\psi)]^2}{(1-e^{-V(x_i;\alpha,\psi)})^2}$$

$$-(\beta-1)\sum_{i=1}^{n} \frac{e^{-V(x_i;\alpha,\psi)}V''^{(\psi\psi)}(x_i;\alpha,\psi) + e^{-V(x_i;\alpha,\psi)}[V'^{(\psi)}(x_i;\alpha,\psi)]^2}{(1-e^{-V(x_i;\alpha,\psi)})^2}$$

$$+(\beta-1)\sum_{i=1}^{n} \frac{[e^{-V(x_i;\alpha,\psi)}]^2 V''^{(\psi\psi)}(x_i;\alpha,\psi) + [e^{-V(x_i;\alpha,\psi)}V'^{(\psi)}(x_i;\alpha,\psi)]^2}{(1-e^{-V(x_i;\alpha,\psi)})^2},$$

where $V''^{(\alpha\alpha)}(.)$ is the derivative of $V'^{(\alpha)}(.)$ with respect to α, $V''^{(\alpha\psi)}(.)$ is the derivative of $V'^{\alpha}(.)$ with respect to ψ_k and $V''^{\psi\psi}(.)$ is the derivative of $V'^{(\psi)}(.)$ with respect to ψ.

3.4. Entropy

The Rényi entropy due to [36], is characterized as

$$I_R(\gamma) = \frac{1}{1-\gamma}\log\left(\int_0^\infty f^\gamma(x)dx\right),$$

Let us consider

$$f^\gamma(x) = (\alpha\beta)^\gamma k^\gamma(x;\psi)\bar{K}(x;\psi)^{\gamma(-\alpha-1)} e^{-\gamma\left[\frac{1-\bar{K}(x;\psi)^\alpha}{\bar{K}(x;\psi)^\alpha}\right]}$$

$$\times \left\{1 - e^{-\frac{1-\bar{K}(x;\psi)^\alpha}{\bar{K}(x;\psi)^\alpha}}\right\}^{\gamma(\beta-1)}. \qquad (12)$$

Expanding Equation (12) as in Section 3.1, the Rényi entropy reduces to

$$I_R(\gamma) = \frac{1}{1-\gamma} \log\left\{\sum_{i=0}^{\infty}\sum_{l=0}^{i} \zeta_{i,l}^* \int_0^{\infty} k^\gamma(x) \overline{K}^{-\{\alpha(\gamma+i-l)-\gamma\}} dx\right\}, \quad (13)$$

where $\zeta_{i,l}^* = \frac{(-1)^{i+l}}{i!}(\alpha\beta)^\gamma \binom{i}{l} \sum_{j=0}^{i}(-1)^j(j+i)^i \binom{\gamma(\beta-1)}{j}$.

3.5. Order Statistics

Assume that $X_1,\ldots,X_n$ is a random sample (RS) from the OGE2-G. Furthermore, assume that $X_{i:n}$ denote the ith order statistic (OS). Consequently, pdf of $X_{i:n}$ may be interpreted as

$$f_{i:n}(x) = \frac{1}{\beta(i,n-i+1)} f(x) F(x)^{i-1} \{1-F(x)\}^{n-i}.$$

$$= \frac{1}{\beta(i,n-i+1)} \sum_{j=0}^{n-i}(-1)^j \binom{n-i}{j} f(x) F(x)^{j+i-1}.$$

Inserting Equations (1) and (2) in the last equation, and expanding it as in Section 3.1, we get

$$f_{i:n}(x) = \sum_{j=0}^{n-i} \eta_j h_m(x), \quad (14)$$

where

$$\eta_j = \frac{(-1)^j}{\beta(i,n-i+1)} \binom{n-i}{j} \sum_{m=0}^{\infty} \zeta_m^*$$

and

$$\zeta_m^* = (-1)^m \sum_{i,k=0}^{\infty}\sum_{l=0}^{i} \frac{(-1)^{i+k+l}(k+1)^i \Gamma\{\beta(i+j)\}}{i!k!\Gamma\{\beta(i+j)-k\}} \binom{i}{l}\binom{-\alpha(i+l+1)-1}{m}.$$

3.6. Stress-Strength Reliability

Supp $X_1 \sim$ OGE2-G$(\alpha,\beta_1;\psi)$ and $X_2 \sim$ OGE2-G$(\alpha,\beta_2;\psi)$ are two continuous rvs with pdfs $f_1(x)$ and $f_2(x)$ and cdfs $F_1(x)$ and $F_2(x)$, therefore the reliability R is supplied via

$$R = \mathbb{P}(X_1 > X_2) = \int_0^{\infty} f_1(x) F_2(x) dx. \quad (15)$$

Theorem 2. *Assume that X_1 and X_2 are two independent rvs established previously with constant parameters β_1 and β_2. Eventually,*

$$R = \beta_1 \sum_{i=0}^{\infty}\binom{\beta_1-1}{i}(-1)^i \Gamma(i+1) - \beta_1 \sum_{i=0}^{\infty}\binom{\beta_1-1}{i}\binom{\beta_2}{j}(-1)^{i+j}\Gamma(i+j+1). \quad (16)$$

Proof. Using Equations (1) and (2) in Equation (15), we have

$$\int_0^{\infty} f_1(x) F_2(x) dx = \int_0^{\infty} \alpha\beta_1 k(x;\psi) \overline{K}(x;\psi)^{-(\alpha+1)} e^{-\left\{\frac{1-\overline{K}(x;\psi)^\alpha}{\overline{K}(x;\psi)^\alpha}\right\}}$$

$$\times \sum_{i=0}^{\infty}\binom{\beta_1-1}{i}(-1)^i \left\{\frac{1-\overline{K}(x;\psi)^\alpha}{\overline{K}(x;\psi)^\alpha}\right\}^i$$

$$\times \left[1 - \sum_{j=0}^{\infty}\binom{\beta_2}{j}(-1)^j\left\{\frac{1-\overline{K}(x;\psi)^\alpha}{\overline{K}(x;\psi)^\alpha}\right\}^j\right] dx.$$

Equation (16) follows immediately after solving the integral with any mathematical software. □

3.7. Stochastic Ordering

Stochastic ordering has indeed been acknowledged as an essential tool for assessing comparative behavior in reliability theory and other disciplines. Assume X and Y be two rvs via cdfs, sfs and pdfs $F_1(x)$ and $F_2(x)$, $\bar{F}_1(x) = 1 - F_1(x)$ and $\bar{F}_2(x) = 1 - F_2(x)$, and $f_1(x)$ and $f_2(x)$, respectively. In the specific planning, the rv X_1 is considered to be lower than X_2:

1. Stochastic order (symbolized via $X_1 \leq_{st} X_2$) if $\bar{F}_1(x) \leq \bar{F}_2(x)$ for all x;
2. LL ratio order (symbolized via $X_1 \leq_{lr} X_1$) if $f_1(x)/f_2(x)$ is decreasing in $x \geq 0$;
3. Hazard rate order (symbolized via $X_1 \leq_{hr} X_2$) if $\bar{F}_1(x)/\bar{F}_2(x)$ is decreasing in $x \geq 0$;
4. Reversed hazard rate order (symbolized via $X_1 \leq_{rhr} X_2$) if $F_1(x)/F_2(x)$ is decreasing in $x \geq 0$.

All these four stochastic orders studied in (1)–(4) are connected to one another as a result of [37] and the accompanying ramifications apply:

$$(X_1 \leq_{rhr} X_2) \Leftarrow (X_1 \leq_{lr} X_2) \Rightarrow (X_1 \leq_{hr} X_2) \Rightarrow (X_1 \leq_{st} X_2).$$

when sufficient conditions are met, the OGE2-G distributions are ordered with regard to the strongest LL ratio ordering, as shown by the next theorem.

Theorem 3. *Assume $X_1 \sim OGE2(\alpha_1, \beta; \psi)$ and $X_2 \sim OGE2(\alpha_2, \beta; \psi)$. If $\alpha_1 < \alpha_2$, then $X_1 \leq_{lr} X_2$.*

Proof. First, we have the ratio

$$\frac{f_1(x)}{f_2(x)} = \frac{\alpha_1 \beta k(x) \bar{K}^{-\alpha_1 - 1} e^{-\left\{\frac{1-\bar{K}^{\alpha_1}}{\bar{K}^{\alpha_1}}\right\}} \left[1 - e^{-\left\{\frac{1-\bar{K}^{\alpha_1}}{\bar{K}^{\alpha_1}}\right\}}\right]^{\beta-1}}{\alpha_2 \beta k(x) \bar{K}^{-\alpha_2 - 1} e^{-\left\{\frac{1-\bar{K}^{\alpha_2}}{\bar{K}^{\alpha_2}}\right\}} \left[1 - e^{-\left\{\frac{1-\bar{K}^{\alpha_2}}{\bar{K}^{\alpha_2}}\right\}}\right]^{\beta-1}}.$$

After simplification, we obtain

$$\frac{f_1(x)}{f_2(x)} = \frac{\alpha_1 \bar{K}^{(\alpha_2 - \alpha_1)} e^{-\left\{\frac{1-\bar{K}^{\alpha_1}}{\bar{K}^{\alpha_1}}\right\} + \left\{\frac{1-\bar{K}^{\alpha_2}}{\bar{K}^{\alpha_2}}\right\}} \left[1 - e^{-\left\{\frac{1-\bar{K}^{\alpha_1}}{\bar{K}^{\alpha_1}}\right\}}\right]^{\beta-1}}{\alpha_2 \left[1 - e^{-\left\{\frac{1-\bar{K}^{\alpha_1}}{\bar{K}^{\alpha_1}}\right\}}\right]^{\beta-1}}.$$

Next,

$$\log\left[\frac{f_1(x)}{f_2(x)}\right] = -\log(\alpha_2 - \alpha_1) + (\alpha_2 - \alpha_1)\log(\bar{K}) - \left\{\frac{1-\bar{K}^{\alpha_1}}{\bar{K}^{\alpha_1}}\right\} + \left\{\frac{1-\bar{K}^{\alpha_2}}{\bar{K}^{\alpha_2}}\right\}$$
$$+ (\beta - 1)\log\left[1 - e^{-\left\{\frac{1-\bar{K}^{\alpha_1}}{\bar{K}^{\alpha_1}}\right\}}\right]$$
$$- (\beta - 1)\log\left[1 - e^{-\left\{\frac{1-\bar{K}^{\alpha_2}}{\bar{K}^{\alpha_2}}\right\}}\right].$$

If $a_1 < a_2$, we obtain

$$\frac{d}{dx}\log\left[\frac{f_1(x)}{f_2(x)}\right] = (\alpha_2 - \alpha_1)\, k(x)\, \overline{K}^{-(\alpha_1+\alpha_2)} + (\beta - 1)\, k(x)\, \overline{K}^{-1}$$

$$\times \left[\frac{\alpha_1 \overline{K}^{-\alpha_1}}{e^{-\left\{-\frac{1-\overline{K}^{\alpha_1}}{\overline{K}^{\alpha_1}}\right\}} - 1} - \frac{\alpha_2 \overline{K}^{-\alpha_2}}{e^{-\left\{-\frac{1-\overline{K}^{\alpha_2}}{\overline{K}^{\alpha_2}}\right\}} - 1}\right] < 0.$$

Thus, $f_1(x)/f_2(x)$ is decreasing in x and hence $X_1 \leq_{lr} X_2$. □

4. OGE2-Fréchet Distribution

In this section, we study the first special model defined in Section 2.2, the OGE2-Fréchet (OGE2Fr), in view of its practical application.

The OGE2Fr model can be defined from (1) by taking $K(x; \psi) = e^{-(a/x)^b}$ and $k(x; \psi) = b\, a^b x^{-(b+1)} e^{-(a/x)^b}$, as cdf and pdf of the baseline Fréchet distribution with $a, b > 0$, respectively. The cdf and pdf of OGE2Fr distribution are, respectively, given by

$$F(x; \alpha, \beta, a, b) = \left[1 - e^{1 - \left\{1 - e^{-\left(\frac{a}{x}\right)^b}\right\}^{-\alpha}}\right]^{\beta}, \quad x > 0 \quad \alpha, \beta, a, b > 0, \tag{17}$$

and

$$f(x; \alpha, \beta, a, b) = a^b \alpha b \beta x^{-b-1} e^{1 - \left(\frac{a}{x}\right)^b - \left(1 - e^{-\left(\frac{a}{x}\right)^b}\right)^{-\alpha}} \left(1 - e^{-\left(\frac{a}{x}\right)^b}\right)^{-\alpha - 1}$$

$$\times \left[1 - e^{1 - \left(1 - e^{-\left(\frac{a}{x}\right)^b}\right)^{-\alpha}}\right]^{\beta - 1}, \tag{18}$$

where α, β and b are shape parameters while a is scale parameter.

The hrf and qf of the OGE2Fr distribution are obtained as

$$h(x) = a^b \alpha b \beta x^{-b-1} e^{1 - \left(\frac{a}{x}\right)^b - \left\{1 - e^{-\left(\frac{a}{x}\right)^b}\right\}^{-\alpha}} \left[1 - e^{-\left(\frac{a}{x}\right)^b}\right]^{-\alpha - 1}$$

$$\times \left[1 - e^{1 - \left\{1 - e^{-\left(\frac{a}{x}\right)^b}\right\}^{-\alpha}}\right]^{1-\beta} \left[1 - \left\{1 - e^{1 - \left(1 - e^{-\left(\frac{a}{x}\right)^b}\right)^{-\alpha}}\right\}^{\beta}\right] \tag{19}$$

$$Q(u) = \left[a\left\{-\log\left(1 - \left[1 - \log\left(1 - u^{1/\beta}\right)\right]^{-1/\alpha}\right)\right\}^{-1/b}\right]. \tag{20}$$

Figure 1 depicts a visualisation of the pdf and hrf functions, exhibiting the range of shapes that all these functions can take at random input parametric values. The OGE2Fr distribution's pdf can be gradually decreasing, unimodal, and right-skewed, with different curves, tail, and asymmetric aspects, as shown in Figure 1. The hrf, on the other hand, offers an extensive range of increasing, decreasing, unimodal, and increasing-decreasing-increasing (IDI) forms. Given a wide variety of hrf shapes being offered, the OGE2Fr distribution can in fact be a useful tool to model unpredictable time-to-event phenomena.

4.1. Linear Representation and Related Properties

The cdf of the OGE2Fr distribution is quite straightforward and is achieved by using the result defined in Equation (6) as

$$F(x) = F(x : \alpha, \beta, a, b) = \sum_{\ell=0}^{\infty} \xi_\ell \left[e^{-(a/x)^b}\right]^\ell \quad \ell \geq 1, \tag{21}$$

where ℓ is the power parameter and noting that $\sum_{\ell=0}^{\infty} \xi_\ell$ is unity. For simplicity, we can rewrite the above result as

$$F(x) = F(x : \alpha, \beta, a, b) = \sum_{\ell=0}^{\infty} \xi_\ell e^{-\ell(a/x)^b}.$$

By differentiating the last term, we can express the density of OGE2Fr model as follows

$$f(x : \alpha, \beta, a, b) = \sum_{i,j=1}^{\infty} \xi_\ell \Pi(x; \ell, a, b), \qquad (22)$$

where $\Pi(x; \ell, a, b) = \ell b a^b x^{-b-1} e^{-\ell(\frac{a}{x})^b}$ represents the Fréchet density function with power parameter ℓ. Equation (22) enforces the fact that OGE2Fr density is a linear combination of Fréchet densities. Thus, we can derive various mathematical properties using Fréchet distribution.

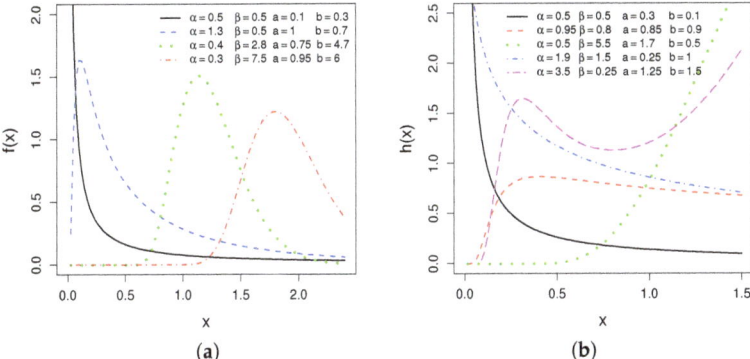

Figure 1. (a) Plots of density and (b) hazard rate of the OGE2Fr model for some random parameter values.

Moments are the heart and soul of any statistical analysis. Moments can be used to evaluate the most essential characteristics such as mean, variance, skewness, and kurtosis of a distribution. We now directly present the mathematical expressions for the moments of OGE2Fr model as follows. Let Y_ℓ be a random variable with density $\Pi(x; \ell, a, b)$. Then, core properties of X can follow from those of Y_ℓ. First, the pth ordinary moment of X can be written as

$$\mu'_p = \sum_{i,j=1}^{\infty} \xi_\ell \ell a^p \frac{\ell^{1-p/b}}{\Gamma(1-p/b)}. \qquad (23)$$

Second, the cumulants (κ_p) of X can be determined recursively from (23) as $\kappa_s = \mu'_s - \sum_{k=1}^{s-1} \binom{s-1}{k-1} \kappa_k \mu'_{s-k}$, respectively, where $\kappa_1 = \mu'_1$. The skewness $\gamma_1 = \kappa_3/\kappa_2^{3/2}$ and kurtosis $\gamma_2 = \kappa_4/\kappa_2^2$ of X can be calculated from the third and fourth standardized cumulants. Plots of mean, variance, skewness and kurtosis of the OGE2Fr distribution are displayed in Figure 2. These plots signifies the significant role of the parameters α and β in modeling the behaviors of X.

Third, the pth incomplete moment of X, denoted by $m_p(y) = E(X^p \mid X \leq y) = \int_0^y x^p f_{OGE2Fr}(x) dx$, is easily found changing variables from the lower incomplete gamma function $\gamma(v, u\,x) = \int_0^\infty x^{v-1} e^{-ux} dx$ when calculating the corresponding moment of Y_ℓ. Then, we obtain

$$m_p(y) = \sum_{i,j=1}^{\infty} \xi_\ell a^p \ell^{1+p/b} \Gamma\left(1 - p/b, \ell\,(a/x)^b\right). \qquad (24)$$

Fourth, the first incomplete moment $m_1(z)$ is used to construct the Bonferroni and Lorenz curves as discussed in Section 3.2. Figure 3 provides the income inequality curves (Bonferroni & Lorenz) of the proposed distribution which can easily be derived from (24), respectively, where $q = Q(\pi)$ is the qf of X derived from Equation (20).

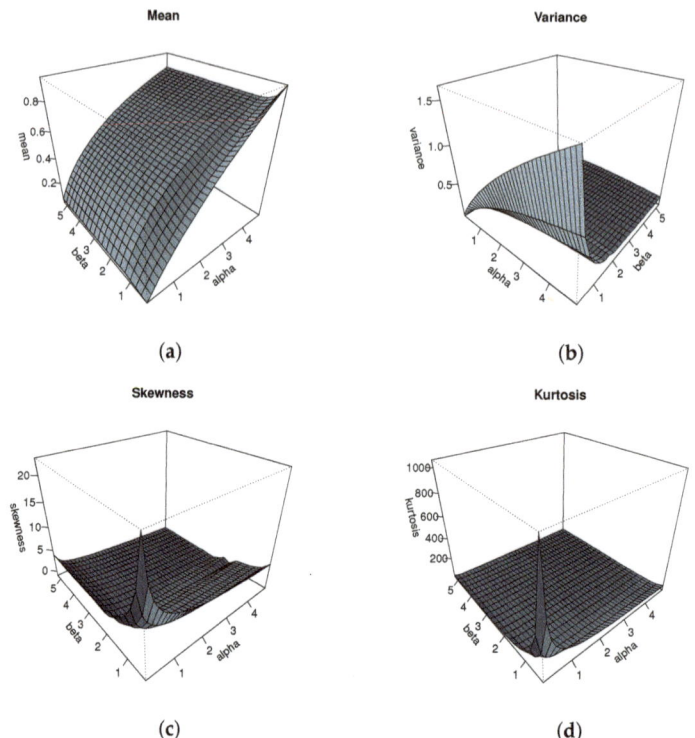

Figure 2. Plots of (**a**) mean, (**b**) variance, (**c**) skewness and (**d**) kurtosis of the OGE2Fr distribution.

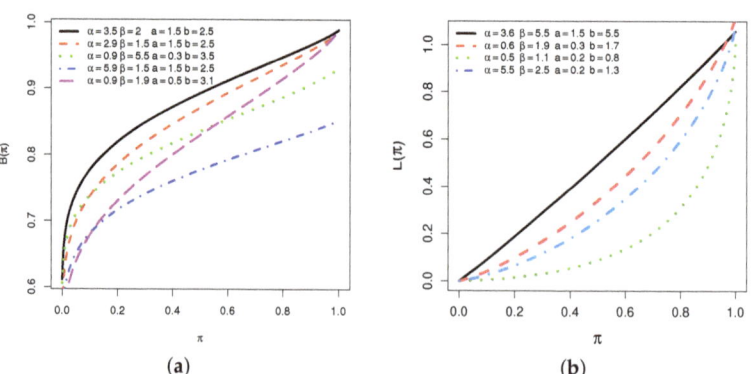

Figure 3. Plots of (**a**) Bonferroni curve and (**b**) Lorenz curve of OGE2Fr model.

4.2. Parameter Estimation

Let $x_1, \ldots, x_n$ be a sample of size n from the OGE2Fr distribution given in Equation (18). The log-likelihood function $\ell = \ell(\Theta)$ for the vector of parameters $\Theta = (\alpha, \beta, a, b)$ is

$$\ell = nb\log(a) + n\log(\alpha\beta b) - (b+1)\sum_{i=1}^{n}\log(x_i) - \sum_{i=1}^{n}\left(\frac{a}{x_i}\right)^b + \sum_{i=1}^{n}\left[1 - \left\{1 - e^{-(a/x_i)^b}\right\}^{-\alpha}\right]$$

$$-(\alpha+1)\sum_{i=1}^{n}\log\left[1 - e^{-\left(\frac{a}{x_i}\right)^b}\right] + (\beta-1)\sum_{i=1}^{n}\log\left[1 - e^{1-\left(1-e^{-\left(\frac{a}{x_i}\right)^b}\right)^{-\alpha}}\right]. \qquad (25)$$

The components of score vectors $U(\Theta)$ are

$$U_\alpha = \frac{n}{\alpha} - \sum_{i=1}^{n}\log\left[1 - e^{-\left(\frac{a}{x_i}\right)^b}\right] + \sum_{i=1}^{n}\left[1 - e^{-\left(\frac{a}{x_i}\right)^b}\right]^{-\alpha}\log\left[1 - e^{-\left(\frac{a}{x_i}\right)^b}\right]$$

$$+ (\beta-1)\sum_{i=1}^{n}\frac{\left\{1 - e^{-\left(\frac{a}{x_i}\right)^b}\right\}^{-\alpha}\log\left\{1 - e^{-\left(\frac{a}{x_i}\right)^b}\right\}}{1 - e^{-1+\left\{1-e^{-\left(\frac{a}{x_i}\right)^b}\right\}^{-\alpha}}},$$

$$U_\beta = \frac{n}{\beta} + \sum_{i=1}^{n}\log\left[1 - e^{1-\left\{1-e^{-\left(\frac{a}{x_i}\right)^b}\right\}^{-\alpha}}\right],$$

$$U_a = \frac{nb}{a} - \frac{a^b b}{a}\sum_{i=1}^{n}x_i^{-b} - \frac{a^b b(\alpha+1)}{a}\sum_{i=1}^{n}\frac{x_i^{-b}}{e^{\left(\frac{a}{x_i}\right)^b} - 1} - \frac{a^b b\alpha}{a}\sum_{i=1}^{n}\frac{x_i^{-b}\left\{1 - e^{-\left(\frac{a}{x_i}\right)^b}\right\}^{-\alpha}}{1 - e^{-\left(\frac{a}{x_i}\right)^b}}$$

$$+ \frac{\alpha(\beta-1)a^b b}{a}\sum_{i=1}^{n}\frac{x_i^{-b}\left\{1 - e^{-\left(\frac{a}{x_i}\right)^b}\right\}^{-\alpha}}{\left[1 - e^{\left(\frac{a}{x_i}\right)^b}\right]\left[1 - e^{-1+\left\{1-e^{-\left(\frac{a}{x_i}\right)^b}\right\}^{-\alpha}}\right]},$$

$$U_b = \frac{n}{b} + n\log(a) - \sum_{i=1}^{n}\log(x_i) - a^b\sum_{i=1}^{n}x_i^{-b}\log\left(\frac{a}{x_i}\right)$$

$$-(\alpha+1)a^b\sum_{i=1}^{n}\frac{x_i^{-b}\log\left(\frac{a}{x_i}\right)}{e^{\left(\frac{a}{x_i}\right)^b} - 1} + \alpha a^b\sum_{i=1}^{n}\frac{x_i^{-b}\log\left(\frac{a}{x_i}\right)\left\{1 - e^{-\left(\frac{a}{x_i}\right)^b}\right\}^{-\alpha}}{e^{\left(\frac{a}{x_i}\right)^b} - 1}$$

$$+ \alpha a^b(\beta-1)\sum_{i=1}^{n}\frac{x_i^{-b}\log\left(\frac{a}{x_i}\right)\left\{1 - e^{-\left(\frac{a}{x_i}\right)^b}\right\}^{-\alpha}}{\left[e^{\left(\frac{a}{x_i}\right)^b} - 1\right]\left[1 - e^{-1+\left\{1-e^{-\left(\frac{a}{x_i}\right)^b}\right\}^{-\alpha}}\right]}.$$

4.3. Order Statistics

For a random sample of $X_1, \ldots, X_n$ taken from the OGE2Fr distribution with $X_{i:n}$ as the ith order statistic. For $i = 1, 2, 3, \ldots, n$, the pdf corresponding to $X_{i:n}$ can be expressed as

$$f_{i:n}(x) = \frac{1}{\beta(i, n-i+1)} f(x) F(x)^{i-1} \{1 - F(x)\}^{n-i}.$$

$$= \frac{1}{\beta(i, n-i+1)} \sum_{j=0}^{n-i} (-1)^j \binom{n-i}{j} f(x) F(x)^{j+i-1},$$

where $f(x)$ and $F(x)$ are the pdf and cdf of OGE2Fr distribution, respectively. Inserting Equations (17) and (18), and using the result defined in Section 3, we have

$$f_{i:n}(x; m\, a, b) = \sum_{j=0}^{n-i} \eta_j \, m\, b\, a^b\, x^{-b-1} e^{-m(a/x)^b}, \qquad (26)$$

where

$$\eta_j = \frac{(-1)^j}{\beta(i, n-i+1)} \binom{n-i}{j} \sum_{m=0}^{\infty} \zeta_m^*$$

and

$$\zeta_m^* = (-1)^m \sum_{i,k=0}^{\infty} \sum_{l=0}^{i} \frac{(-1)^{i+k+l}(k+1)^i \Gamma\{\beta(i+j)\}}{i! k! \Gamma\{\beta(i+j) - k\}} \binom{i}{l} \binom{-\alpha(i+l+1) - 1}{m}.$$

$f_{i:n}(x; m\, a, b)$ is the probability density function of the OGE2Fr distribution with parameters $m\, a$ and b.

4.4. Stochastic Ordering

In several areas of probability and statistics, stochastic ordering and disparities are being adhered to at an accelerating rate. For example, in analyzing the contrast of investment returns to random cash flows; two manufacturers may use distinct technologies to make gadgets with the same function, resulting in non-identical life distributions or comparing the strength of dependent structures. Here, we use the term stochastic ordering to refer to any ordering relation on a space of probability measures in a wide sense. Let X and Y be two rvs from OGE2Fr distributions, with assumptions previously mentioned in Section 3. Given that $a_1 < a_2$, and for $X_1 \leq_{lr} X_2$, $f_1(x)/f_2(x)$ shall be decreasing in x if and only if the following result holds Let X and Y be two rvs from OGE2Fr distributions, with assumptions previously mentioned in Section 3. Given that $a_1 < a_2$, and for $X_1 \leq_{lr} X_2$, $f_1(x)/f_2(x)$ shall be decreasing in x if the following result holds

$$\frac{d}{dx} \log\left[\frac{f_1(x)}{f_2(x)}\right] = (\alpha_2 - \alpha_1) b\, a^b x^{-(b+1)} e^{-(a/x)^b} 1 - e^{-(a/x)^b - (\alpha_1 + \alpha_2)}$$

$$+ (\beta - 1)\left[b\, a^b x^{-(b+1)} e^{-(a/x)^b}\right]\left(1 - e^{-(a/x)^b}\right)^{-1}$$

$$\times \left[\frac{\alpha_1\left(1 - e^{-(a/x)^b}\right)^{-\alpha_1}}{e^{-\left(1 - e^{-(a/x)^b}\right)^{-\alpha_1} - 1} - 1}\right]$$

$$+ (1 - \beta)\left[b\, a^b x^{-(b+1)} e^{-(a/x)^b}\right]\{1 - e^{-(a/x)^b}\}^{-1}$$

$$\times \left[\frac{\alpha_1\left(1 - e^{-(a/x)^b}\right)^{-\alpha_2}}{e^{-\left(1 - e^{-(a/x)^b}\right)^{-\alpha_2} - 1} - 1}\right] < 0.$$

4.5. Simulation Study

By using the result defined in Equation (25), we evaluate the sensitivity of the method of estimations using the MLEs of OGE2Fr distribution parameters by Monte Carlo simulation technique. The simulation study is conducted for sample sizes $n = 50, 100, 200, 300, 500, 600$ and parameter combinations, denoted by $w_{(.)}$, are:

- w_1: $\alpha = 0.3$, $\beta = 1.7$, $a = 0.8$ and $b = 0.5$;
- w_2: $\alpha = 0.5$, $\beta = 1.5$, $a = 0.8$ and $b = 0.7$;
- w_3: $\alpha = 1.5$, $\beta = 2.4$, $a = 1.5$ and $b = 0.5$.

We use Equation (20) to generate the random observations. For each $w_{(.)}$, the empirical bias and MSE values are the average of the values from $N = 1000$ simulated samples for given sample size n. The formula to evaluate the mean squared error (MSEs) and the average bias (Bias) of each parameter, is given below

$$MSE(\hat{\Theta}) = \sum_{i=1}^{N} \frac{(\hat{\Theta}_i - \Theta)^2}{N} \quad \text{and} \quad Bias(\hat{\Theta}) = \sum_{i=1}^{N} \frac{\hat{\Theta}_i}{N} - \Theta.$$

We report the results of the AE, Bias and MSE for the parameters α, β, a and b in Table 2. The MSE of the estimators increases when the assumed model deviates from the genuine model, as anticipated. When the sample size grows larger and the symmetry degrades, the MSE shrinks. Generally speaking, the MSE decreases when the kurtosis grows. Similarly, when the asymmetry rises, the bias grows, and vice versa. As the kurtosis grows, the bias becomes smaller. In conclusion, it is apparent that the MSEs and Biases decrease when the sample size n increases. Thus, we can say that the MLEs perform satisfactorily well in estimating the parameters of the OGE2Fr distribution.

Table 2. AEs, MSEs and Biases for w_1, w_2 & w_3.

	θ	w_1			w_2			w_3		
		AE	MSE	Bias	AE	MSE	Bias	AE	MSE	Bias
$n = 50$	α	1.14	2.267	0.982	1.97	0.997	1.787	2.14	2.892	0.447
	β	2.77	1.367	0.531	2.14	1.459	0.508	3.04	1.667	0.771
	a	1.70	1.119	0.539	1.45	1.517	0.621	2.12	1.486	0.541
	b	1.23	0.997	0.408	1.67	0.899	0.447	1.19	1.035	0.546
$n = 100$	α	0.65	1.892	0.877	1.88	0.901	1.205	2.02	2.793	0.420
	β	2.61	1.213	0.509	1.99	1.312	0.472	2.91	1.522	0.656
	a	1.31	1.092	0.511	1.11	1.349	0.555	1.93	1.397	0.502
	b	0.82	0.901	0.388	1.40	0.835	0.420	1.08	0.923	0.522
$n = 300$	α	0.52	1.407	0.853	1.56	0.866	0.773	1.72	2.771	0.407
	β	2.33	1.809	0.477	1.83	1.292	0.443	2.67	1.487	0.629
	a	1.19	0.934	0.483	0.92	1.293	0.507	1.86	1.203	0.488
	b	0.78	0.866	0.363	1.32	0.801	0.417	0.87	0.847	0.497
$n = 400$	α	0.39	0.775	0.639	0.89	0.519	0.651	1.55	1.636	0.374
	β	1.89	0.686	0.393	1.59	0.897	0.370	2.53	0.883	0.409
	a	0.93	0.473	0.411	0.85	0.945	0.477	1.59	0.860	0.359
	b	0.55	0.519	0.287	0.81	0.569	0.374	0.57	0.580	0.338
$n = 500$	α	0.32	0.701	0.497	0.54	0.298	0.455	1.48	1.475	0.325
	β	1.67	0.529	0.376	0.51	0.774	0.323	2.46	0.661	0.373
	a	0.81	0.355	0.337	0.83	0.670	0.435	1.52	0.663	0.323
	b	0.49	0.393	0.264	0.75	0.411	0.325	0.49	0.444	0.317
$n = 600$	α	0.31	0.472	0.316	0.51	0.252	0.424	1.45	1.437	0.311
	β	1.65	0.333	0.288	0.49	0.554	0.311	2.45	0.516	0.361
	a	0.80	0.271	0.298	0.80	0.655	0.409	1.50	0.577	0.305
	b	0.50	0.313	0.224	0.71	0.405	0.317	0.50	0.440	0.313

5. Application of OGE2Fr to Premium Data

Most skewed distributions are suitable to measure risk measures associated with actuarial data. The risks involve credit, portfolio, capital, premiums losses, and stocks prices among others. We focus our attention on the stakes based on premiums. Premiums are the payments for insurance that the customer pay to the company to which they are insured. In this section, we apply the OGE2Fr lifetime model for the statistical analysis of two real life data sets both of which include premium losses. Our aim is to compare the fits of the OGE2Fr model with other well-known generalizations of the Fréchet (Fr) models given in Table 3.

The first premium data set, designated as PD1, is derived from complaints upheld against vehicle insurance firms as a proportion of their overall business over a two-year period. The study was conducted by DFR (Darla Fry Ross) insurance and investment company (2009–2016), registered in New York state. The most common complaints are over delays in the settlement of no-fault claims and non-renewal of insurance. Top of the list are insurers with the fewest upheld complaints per million USD of premiums. The companies with the greatest complaint ratios are at the bottom of the list. The data understudy is from the year 2016. The second premium data, denoted by PD2, signifies the net premiums written (in billions of USD) to insurers which, under Article 41 of the New York Insurance Law, are required to meet minimum financial security requirements. Table 4: Descriptives statistics of PD1 and PD2.

Table 3. The comparative fitted models.

Distribution	Author(s)	Θ
BFr	Nadarajah and Gupta [38]; Barreto and Souza [39]	(α, β, a, b)
KwFr	Cordiero et al. [40]	(α, β, a, b)
EGFr	Cordiero et al. [41]	(α, β, a, b)
MOFr	Krishna et al. [42]	(θ, a, b)
EFr	Nadarajah and Kotz [43]	(θ, a, b)
GaFr	Da Silva et al. [44]	(γ, a, b)
TLFr	Abbas et al. [45]	(θ, a, b)
OLiFr	Silva et al. [29]	(λ, a, b)
Fr	Fréchet [46]	(a, b)

Table 4. The descriptive statistics related to PD1 & PD2.

Data	Sample Size	μ	σ	Lowest	Highest	Skewness	Kurtosis
PD1	89	14.08	638.38	1.048	204.17	5.31	34.97
PD2	34	3629.40	59,372,161	7.567	36,502.53	3.06	9.18

The OGE2Fr model is validated through the discriminatory criterions (DCs) we considered for each data set. It includes the negative log-likelihood ($-\hat{\ell}$) of the model taken at the corresponding MLEs, the Akaike Information Criterion (AICs), Bayesian Information Criterion (BICs), Anderson-Darling (AD), Cramér–von Mises (CvM), and Kolmogrov-Smirnov (KS) as well as the p-value (P-KS) of the related KS test. We use the method of maximum likelihood estimation to estimate the unknown parameters as presented in Section 4.2. For each criterion (except p-value (KS)) with highest value), the smallest values is gained by the OGE2Fr model, indicating the best fit among its competitive models.

Some descriptive statistics related to these data are given in Table 4. The skewness and kurtosis are indicative of exponentially tailed data (reversed-J shape). The TTT plots for the both data sets are given in Figure 4. In particular, the TTT plots show largely decreasing hrf, permitting to fit OGE2Fr model on these data sets. The estimated hrf in Figure 5 matches Figure 4. In Table 5, we present the estimates (MLEs) along with their respective standard errors(SEs) while the DCs are listed in Table 6 for PD1 & PD2, respectively. For a more visual view, the estimated pdf, cdf, sf and Q-Q plots of the OGE2Fr model for two data sets are displayed in Figures 6 and 7. Furthermore, the PP-plots of OGE2Fr and its three other competitive 4-parameter models for PD1 and PD2 are displayed in Figures 8 and 9. The log-likelihood function profiles for PD1 and PD2, respectively, are provided in Figures 10 and 11 to highlight the universality of the MLEs of Θ vector. The graphical visualizations are indicative of nice fits for the OGE2Fr model.

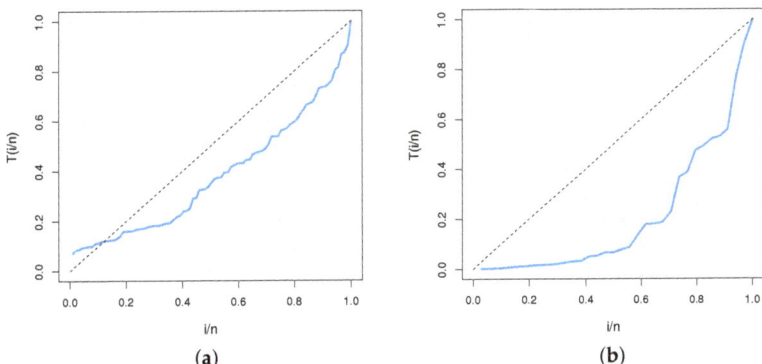

Figure 4. TTT plots of (**a**) PD1 and (**b**) PD2.

Table 5. Estimates and standard errors for PD1 & PD2.

Distribution	Θ	MLE(PD1)	SE(PD1)	MLE(PD2)	SE(PD2)
OGE2Fr	α	0.065	0.004	2.202	0.649
	β	1.177	0.145	0.298	0.143
	a	2.336	0.099	24.064	19.485
	b	5.685	0.109	0.327	0.124
BFr	α	5.623	4.692	30.671	13.743
	β	1.699	1.324	34.622	16.797
	a	0.855	0.646	11.391	9.267
	b	0.759	0.453	0.175	0.126
KwFr	α	6.581	4.779	6.282	3.189
	β	1.409	1.161	15.235	4.679
	a	0.606	0.496	5.735	3.726
	b	0.858	0.390	0.157	0.124
EGFr	α	12.927	9.199	6.758	5.059
	β	62.076	36.099	53.635	39.338
	a	21.399	17.982	22.629	16.084
	b	0.158	0.119	0.106	0.091
MOFr	θ	105.267	67.873	105.566	88.076
	a	0.060	0.028	0.302	0.224
	b	14.866	0.177	0.723	0.107
EFr	θ	1.409	1.161	1.097	0.554
	a	5.442	4.611	167.306	163.093
	b	0.858	0.391	0.452	0.128
GaFr	γ	5.642	3.889	14.715	5.016
	a	0.186	0.460	0.008	0.002
	b	2.060	0.769	1.603	0.395
TLFr	θ	0.075	0.009	0.122	0.098
	a	53.724	46.329	78.317	54.389
	b	0.953	0.114	0.425	0.089
OLiFr	λ	23.260	14.666	35.788	8.969
	a	6.036	0.653	8.583	1.458
	b	0.274	0.049	0.124	0.050
Fr	a	4.178	0.564	10.630	3.207
	b	1.042	0.087	0.469	0.061

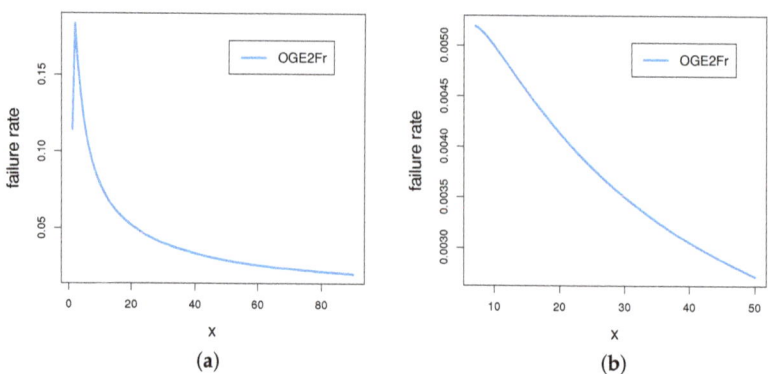

Figure 5. Estimated hazard rate plots of (**a**) PD1 and (**b**) PD2 of OGE2Fr.

Table 6. The statistics ℓ, AIC, CAIC, BIC, HQIC, AD, CvM, KS and p-value (KS) for the PD1 & PD2.

Distribution	ℓ	AIC	CAIC	BIC	HQIC	AD	CvM	KS	p-Value (KS)
Premium data 1									
OGE2Fr	302.22	612.44	612.92	622.39	616.45	0.38	0.077	0.074	0.69
BFr	306.63	621.25	621.72	631.23	625.27	0.86	0.158	0.093	0.39
KwFr	306.70	621.40	621.85	631.35	625.42	0.88	0.164	0.092	0.41
EGFr	306.76	621.51	621.99	631.47	625.52	0.84	0.152	0.098	0.34
MOFr	311.09	628.17	628.46	635.64	631.18	1.12	0.178	0.110	0.22
EFr	306.70	619.40	619.69	626.86	622.41	0.88	0.164	0.092	0.41
GaFr	305.72	617.44	617.72	624.90	620.44	0.77	0.146	0.090	0.45
TLFr	305.65	617.29	617.58	624.76	620.30	0.71	0.133	0.090	0.43
OLiFr	308.403	622.81	623.09	630.24	625.80	0.981	0.140	0.116	0.17
Fr	306.79	617.58	617.72	622.56	619.59	0.95	0.180	0.094	0.39
Premium data 2									
OGE2Fr	286.09	580.18	581.56	586.29	582.26	0.18	0.027	0.083	0.96
BFr	287.43	582.87	584.25	588.97	584.95	0.29	0.042	0.101	0.84
KwFr	287.45	582.89	584.27	588.99	584.97	0.30	0.044	0.100	0.86
EGFr	288.21	584.41	585.79	590.52	586.50	0.39	0.053	0.102	0.84
MOFr	288.66	583.32	584.11	587.89	584.86	0.40	0.060	0.103	0.83
EFr	288.70	583.40	584.20	587.98	584.96	0.47	0.063	0.119	0.68
GaFr	287.62	581.24	582.04	585.82	582.81	0.33	0.045	0.101	0.85
TLFr	287.70	581.39	582.19	585.97	582.96	0.35	0.047	0.102	0.84
OLiFr	287.52	581.54	581.84	586.62	582.60	0.310	0.077	0.094	0.894
Fr	288.79	581.58	581.97	584.63	582.62	0.49	0.065	0.104	0.82

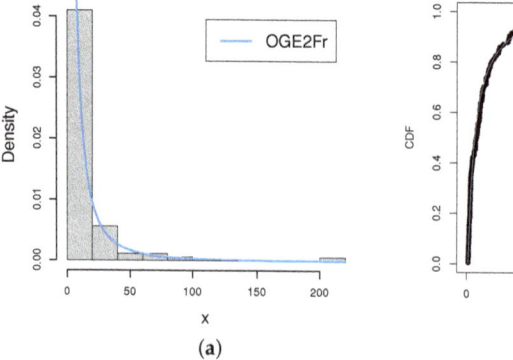

Figure 6. *Cont.*

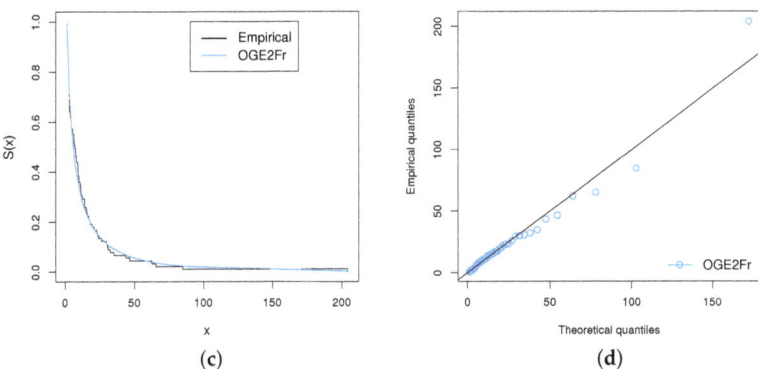

Figure 6. Estimated (**a**) density, (**b**) cdf, (**c**) sf, and (**d**) QQ-plot for PD1.

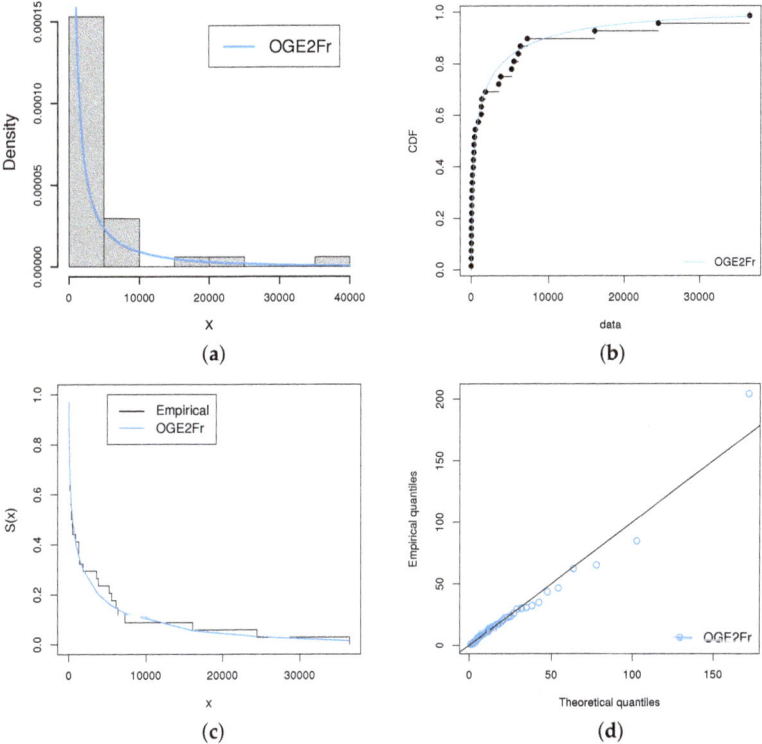

Figure 7. Estimated (**a**) density (**b**) cdf (**c**) sf, and (**d**) QQ-plot for PD2.

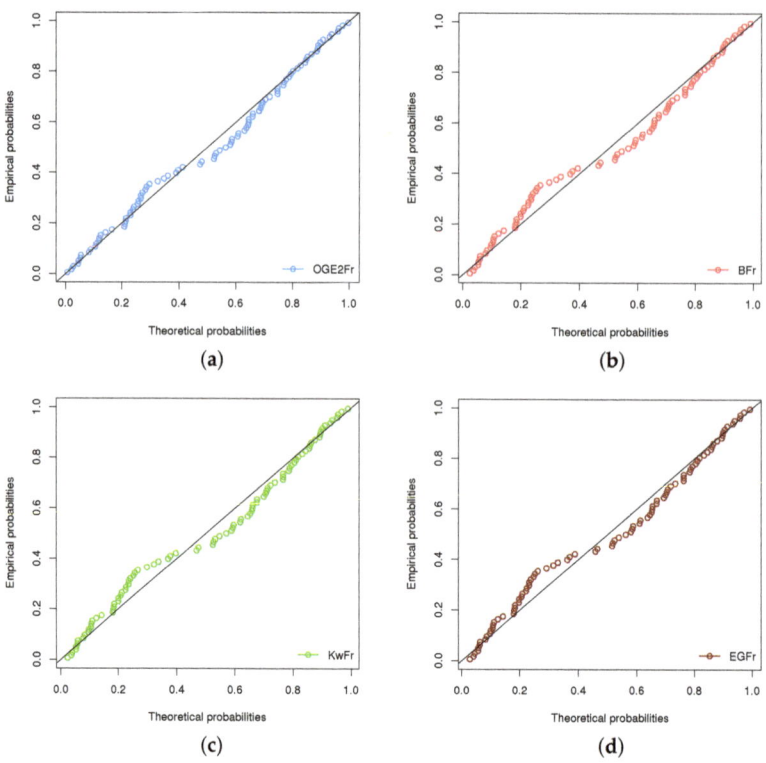

Figure 8. PP-plots of (**a**) OGE2Fr alongside competitive (**b**) BFr, (**c**) KwFr and (**d**) EGFr (4-parameter models) for PD1.

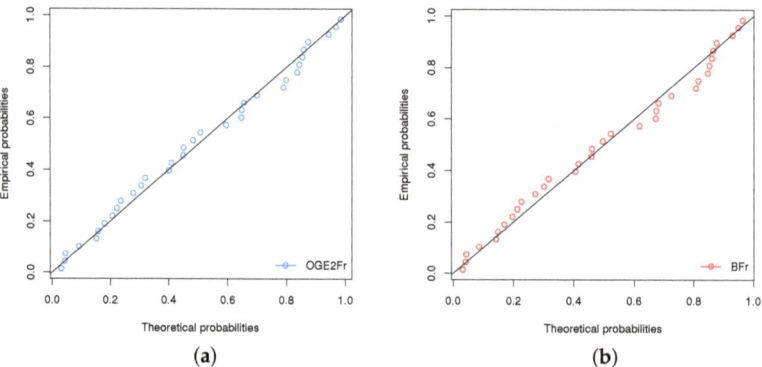

Figure 9. *Cont.*

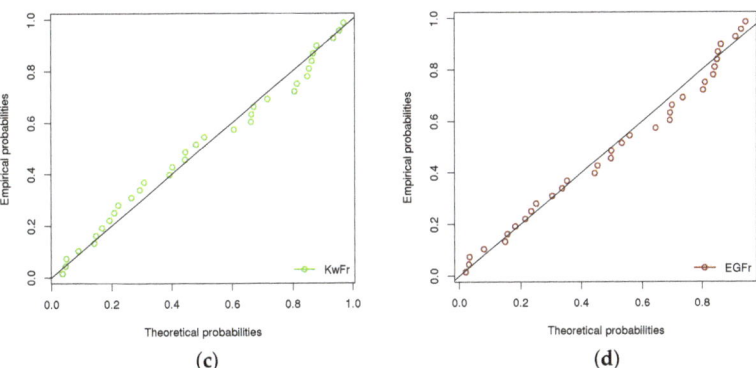

Figure 9. PP-plots of (**a**) OGE2Fr alongside competitive (**b**) BFr, (**c**) KwFr and (**d**) EGFr (4-parameter models) for PD2.

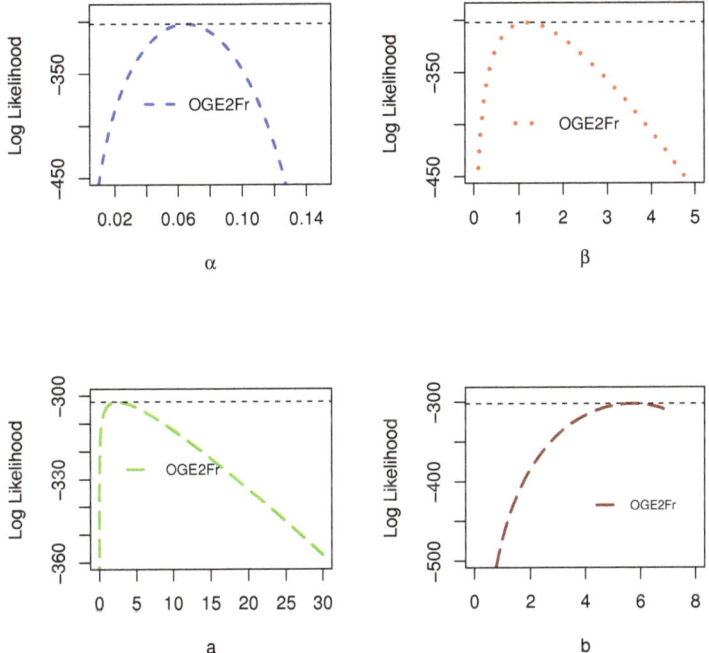

Figure 10. Profiles of the log-likelihood function for the parameters α, β, a and b, respectively, of the OGE2Fr for the PD1.

5.1. Actuarial Measures

One of the most important duties of actuarial sciences organizations is to assess market risk in a portfolio of instruments, which originates from changes in underlying factors such as equities prices, interest rates, or currency rates.One of the most important duties of actuarial sciences organizations is to assess market risk in a portfolio of instruments, which originates from changes in underlying factors such as equities prices, interest rates, or currency rates. We compute several important risk measures for the suggested distribution in this section, such as Value at Risk (VaR) and Expected Shortfall (ES), which are important in portfolio optimization under uncertainty.

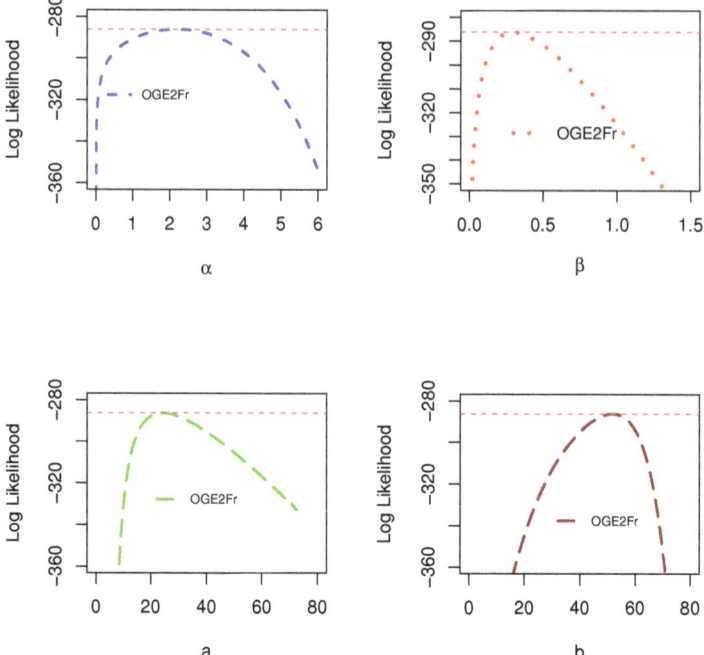

Figure 11. Profiles of the log-likelihood function for the parameters α, β, a and b, respectively, of the OGE2Fr for the PD2.

5.1.1. Value at Risk

The quantile premium principal of the distribution of aggregate losses, commonly known as Value at risk (VaR), is the most widely used measure to evaluate exposure to risk in finance. VaR of a rv is the pth quantile of its cdf. If $X \sim$ OGE2Fr denotes a random variable with cdf (17), then its VaR is

$$VaR_p = \left[a \left\{ -\log \left(1 - \left[1 - \log \left(1 - p^{1/\beta} \right) \right]^{-1/\alpha} \right) \right\} \right]^{-1/b}. \tag{27}$$

5.1.2. Expected Shortfall

Artzner et al. [47,48] recommended the use of conditional VaR instead of VaR, famously called Expected Shortfall (ES). The ES is a metric that quantifies the average loss in situations where the VaR level is exceeded. It is defined by the following expression

$$ES_p = \frac{1}{p} \int_0^p VaR_x \, dx, \quad \text{where} \quad 0 < p < 1.$$

The ES of OGE2Fr is given by

$$ES_p = \frac{1}{p} \int_0^p \left[a \left\{ -\log \left(1 - \left[1 - \log \left(1 - p^{1/\beta} \right) \right]^{-1/\alpha} \right) \right\} \right]^{-1/b} dx. \tag{28}$$

Figure 12 illustrates VaR and ES for some random parameter combinations of OGE2Fr.

5.1.3. Numerical Calculation of VaR and ES

The results of OGE2Fr presented in Section 4 allowed us to further explore its application to these risk measures. From Table 5, we take the values of MLEs of PD1 and PD2, respectively, to measure the volatility associated with these measures. Higher values of these risk measures signify heavier tails while lower values indicate a much lighter tail behavior of the model. It is worth mentioning that the OGE2Fr model produced substantially more significant results than its counterparts, indicating that the model has a heavier tail. In Table 7, we show the numerical results of VaRs and ESs of PD1 and PD2, respectively, of the proposed model. For the convenience of the reader, Figure 13 show the results graphically.

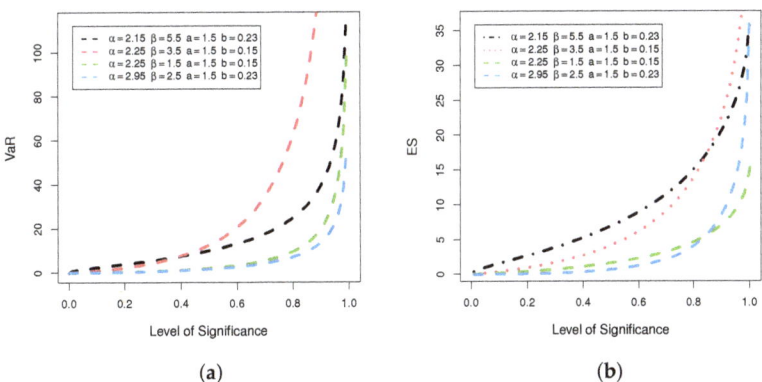

Figure 12. Plots of (**a**) VaR (**b**) ES for some parameter values.

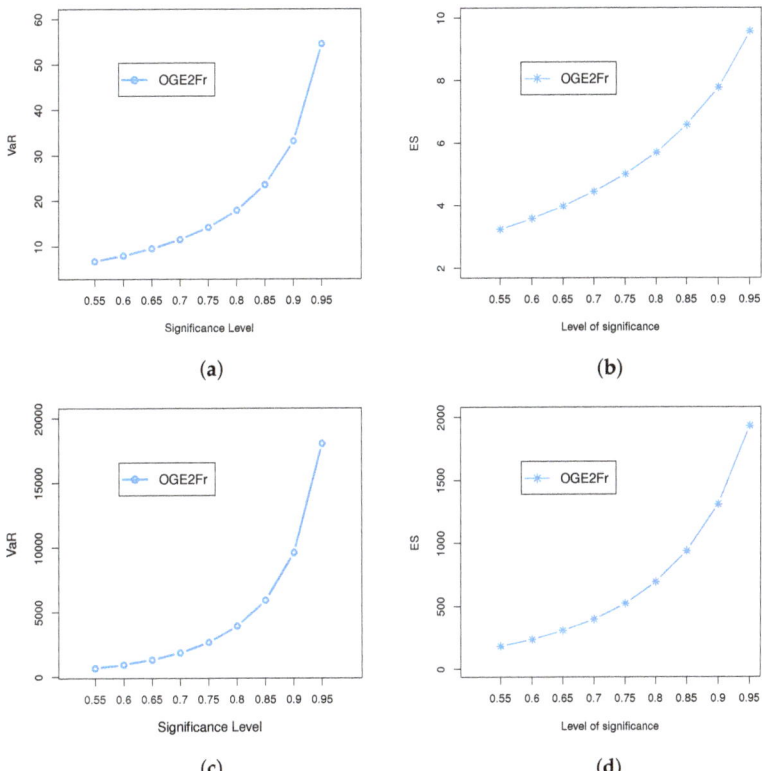

Figure 13. Estimated VaR (**a,c**) with ES (**b,d**) for PD1 & PD2.

Table 7. Numerical measures of VaRs and ESs of PD1 & PD2.

Level of Significance	VaRs(PD1)	ESs(PD1)	VaRs(PD2)	ESs(PD2)
0.55	6.782	3.245	698.117	184.508
0.60	8.023	3.589	965.385	237.819
0.65	9.581	3.988	1343.206	307.461
0.70	11.588	4.456	1887.655	399.670
0.75	14.263	5.016	2693.364	523.906
0.80	18.005	5.704	3932.723	695.305
0.85	23.638	6.581	5957.838	1309.704
0.90	33.238	7.768	9636.239	1933.041
0.95	54.610	9.578	18,069.512	3659.730

6. Discussion

The *OGE2-G* class of distribution is proposed and studied with some mathematical properties such as ordinary and incomplete moments, mean deviations and generating functions. The maximum likelihood approach is used to estimate the model parameters. Then, we focussed our attention to one of the special member of the family defined with the Fréchet distribution, called the OGE2Fr distribution. We established the optimized maximum likelihood methodology in particular, with the goal of effectively estimating model parameters and validated their convergence by a simulation study, ensuring that the projections have asymptotic properties. To demonstrate the potentiality of the proposed model, two applications to real data sets are provided. The creation of various regression models, Bayesian parameter estimates, and studies of new data sets will all be part of a future effort. We feel that the OGE2-G family can be useful for professionals in statistical analyses beyond the scope of this research because of its several other features.

Author Contributions: Conceptualization: S.K. and M.H.T.; Methodology: W.A.; Software: O.S.B.; Validation: M.H.T., W.A. and A.A.A.; Formal analysis: S.K.; Investigation: S.K.; Resources: M.H.T.; Data curation: O.S.B. and W.A.; Writing—original draft preparation:, S.K.; Writing—review and editing: S.K.; Visualization: S.K.; Supervision: A.A.A.; Project administration: O.S.B. All authors have read and agreed to the published version of the manuscript.

Funding: This manuscript is supported by Digiteknologian TKI-ymparisto project A74338(ERDF, 357 Regional Council of Pohjois-Savo.

Data Availability Statement: https://data.world/datasets/insurance/ (accesed on 28 June 2021).

Acknowledgments: The authors would like to thank the reviewers for their thoughtful remarks and recommendations, which considerably enhanced the paper's presentation.

Conflicts of Interest: The authors state that they have no conflicting interests to declare in this work.

Abbreviations

The following abbreviations are used in this manuscript:

GE	generalized exponential
LA-I	Lehmann alternatives I
LA-II	Lehmann alternatives II
OGE-G	Odd generalized exponential
OGE1-G	generalized odd generalized exponentia distributionl
OGE2-G	generalized Odd generalized exponential distribution
sf	survival function
hrf	hazard rate function
pdf	probability density function
cdf	cumulative distribution function
rv	random variable
OGE2Fr	generalized Odd generalized exponential distribution
Fr	Fréchet

References

1. Marshall, A.W.; Olkin, I. A new method for adding parameters to a family of distributions with application to the exponential and Weibull families. *Biometrika* **1997**, *10*, 641–652. [CrossRef]
2. Gleaton, J.U.; Lynch, J.D. Properties of generalized log-logistic families of lifetime distributions. *J. Probab. Stat. Sci.* **2006**, *4*, 51–64.
3. Cooray, K. Generalization of the Weibull distribution: The odd Weibull family. *Stat. Model. Int. J.* **2006**, *6*, 265–277. [CrossRef]
4. Bourguignon, M.; Silva, R.B.; Cordeiro, G.M. The Weibull–G family of probability distributions. *J. Data Sci.* **2014**, *12*, 53–68. [CrossRef]
5. Alzatreh, A.; Famoye, F.; Lee, C. A new method for generating families of continuous distributions. *Metron* **2013**, *71*, 63–79. [CrossRef]
6. Ahsan ul Haq, M.; Elgarhy, M. The Odd Fréchet-G family of Probability distributions. *J. Stat. Appl. Probab.* **2017**, *7*, 185–201. [CrossRef]
7. Alizadeh, M.; Cordeiro, G.M.; Nascimento, A.D.C. Odd-Burr generalized family of distributions with some applications. *J. Stat. Comput. Simul.* **2016**, *87*, 367–389. [CrossRef]
8. Afify, A.Z.; Altun, E.; Alizadeh, M.; Ozel, G.; Hamedani, G.G. The Odd Exponentiated Half-Logistic-G Family: Properties, Characterizations and Applications. *Chil. J. Stat.* **2017**, *8*, 65–91.
9. Bakouch, H.; Chesneau, C.; Khan, M.N. The Extended Odd Family of Probability Distributions with Practice to a Submodel. *Filomat* **2018**, *33*, 3855–3867. [CrossRef]
10. Cordeiro, G.M.; Yousof, H.M.; Ramires, T.G.; Ortega, E.M.M. The Burr XII System of densities: Properties, regression model and applications. *J. Stat. Comput. Simul.* **2017**, *87*, 1–25. [CrossRef]
11. Chesneau, C.; Toufik, E.A. Modified Odd Weibull Family of Distributions: Properties and Applications. *J. Indian Soc. Probab. Stat.* **2019**, *21*, 259–286. [CrossRef]
12. El-Morshedy, M.; Eliwa, M.S. The odd flexible Weibull-H family of distributions: Properties and estimation with applications to complete and upper record data. *Filomat* **2019**, *33*, 2635–2652. [CrossRef]
13. Haghbin, H.; Ozel, G.; Alizadeh, M.; Hamedani, G.G. A new generalized odd log-logistic family of distributions. *Commun. Stat. Theory Methods* **2016**, *46*, 9897–9920. [CrossRef]
14. Jamal, F.; Nasir, M.; Tahir, M.H.; Montazeri, N. The odd Burr-III family of distributions. *J. Stat. Appl. Probab.* **2017**, *6*, 105–122. [CrossRef]
15. Torabi, H.; Montazari, N.H. The gamma-uniform distribution and its application. *Kybernetika* **2012**, *48*, 16–30.
16. Elmorshedy, M.; Eliwa, M.S.; Afify, A.Z. The Odd Chen Generator of Distributions: Properties and Estimation Methods with Applications in Medicine and Engineering. *J. Natl. Sci. Found. Sri Lanka* **2020**, *48*, 113–130.
17. Almamy, J.A.; Ibrahim, M.; Eliwa, M.S.; Al-mualim, S.; Yousof, H.M. The Two-Parameter Odd Lindley Weibull Lifetime Model with Properties and Applications. *Int. J. Stat. Probab.* **2018**, *7*, 57. [CrossRef]
18. Nasiru, S. Extended Odd Fréchet-G Family of Distributions. *J. Probab. Stat.* **2018**, *2018*, 2931326. [CrossRef]
19. Afify, A.Z.; Cordiero, G.M.; Mead, M.E.; Alizadeh, M.; Al-Mofleh, H.; Nofal, Z.M. The Generalized Odd Lindley-G Family: Properties and Applications. *Ann. Braz. Acad. Sci.* **2019**, *91*, e20180040. [CrossRef]
20. Korkamaz, M.C. A new family of the continuous distributions: The extended Weibull-G family. *Commun. Fac. Sci. Univ. Ank. Ser. Math. Stat.* **2018**, *68*, 248–70. [CrossRef]
21. Alex, er C.; Cordeiro, G.M.; Ortega, E.M.M.; Sarabia, J.M. Generalized beta-generated distributions. *Comput. Stat. Data Anal.* **2012**, *56*, 1880–1897. [CrossRef]
22. Korkamaz, M.C.; Genc, A.I. A new generalized gwo-sided class of distributions with an emphasis on two-sided generalized normal distribution. *Commun. Stat.-Simul. Comput.* **2015**, *46*, 1441–1460. [CrossRef]
23. Korkamaz, M.C.; Cordiero, G.M.; Yousof, H.M.; Pescim, R.R.; Afify, A.Z.; Nadarajah, S. The Weibull Marshall-Olkin family: Regression model and application to censored data. *Commun. Stat.-Theory Methods* **2018**, *48*, 4171–4194. [CrossRef]
24. Korkamaz, M.C.; Yousof, H.M.; Hamedani, G.G. The Exponential Lindley Odd Log-Logistic-G Family: Properties, Characterizations and Applications. *J. Stat. Theory Appl.* **2018**, *17*, 554–571. [CrossRef]
25. Korkamaz, M.C.; Altun, E.; Yousof, H.M.; Afify, A.Z.; Nadarajah, S. The Burr-X Pareto Distribution: Properties, Applications and VaR Estimation. *J. Risk Financ. Manag.* **2017**, *11*, 1. [CrossRef]
26. Korkamaz, M.C.; Alizadeh, M.; Yousof, H.M.; Butt, N.S. The Generalized Odd Weibull Generated Family of Distributions: Statistical Properties and Applications. *Pak. J. Stat. Oper. Res.* **2018**, *542*, 541–556. [CrossRef]
27. Korkamaz, M.C.; Yousof, H.M.; Alizadeh, M.; Hamedani, G.G. The Topp-Leone Generalized Odd Log-Logistic Family of Distributions: Properties, Characterizations and Applications. *Commun. Fac. Sci. Univ. Ank. Ser. A1 Math. Stat.* **2018**, *68*, 1506–1527. [CrossRef]
28. Alizadeh, M.; Korkamaz, M.C.; Almanay, J.A.; Afify, A.Z. Another odd log-logistic logarithmic class of continuous distributions. *J. Stat. Stat. Actuar. Sci.* **2018**, *2*, 55–72.
29. Silva, F.G.; Ramos, M.W.; Percontini, A.; Venâncio, R.; De Brito, E.; Cordeiro, G.M. The Odd Lindley-G Family of Distributions. *Austrian J. Stat.* **2017**, *35*, 281–308. [CrossRef]
30. Korkamaz, M.C.; Yousof, H.M.; Ali, M.M. Some Theoretical and Computational Aspects of the Odd Lindley Fréchet Distribution. *J. Stat. Stat. Actuar. Sci.* **2017**, *2*, 129–140.

31. Korkamaz, M.C.; Altun, E.; Yousof, H.M.; Hamedani, G.G. The Hjorth's IDB generator of distributions: Properties, characterizations, regression modelling and applications. *J. Stat. Theory Appl.* **2020**, *19*, 59–74. [CrossRef]
32. Tahir, M.H.; Cordeiro, G.M.; Alizadeh, M.; Mansoor, M.; Zubair, M.; Hamedani, G.G. The odd generalized exponential family of distributions with applications. *J. Stat. Distrib. Appl.* **2015**, *2*, 1. [CrossRef]
33. Morad, A.; Ghosh, I.; Yusuf, H.M.; Rasekhi, M.; Hamedani, G.G. The generalized odd generalized exponential family of distributions. *J. Data Sci.* **2017**, *15*, 443–465. [CrossRef]
34. Tahir, M.H.; Nadarajah, S. Parameter induction in continuous univariate distributions: Well-established G families. *AABC* **2015**, *87*, 539–568. [CrossRef]
35. Aarset, M.V. How to identify bathtub hazard rate. *IEEE* **1987**, *36*, 106–108. [CrossRef]
36. Rényi, A. On measures of entropy and information. In Proceedings of the 4th Berkeley Symposium on Mathematical Statistics and Probability, Berkeley, CA, USA, 20–30 July 1960; Volume 1, pp. 547–561.
37. Shaked, M.; Shantikumar, J.G. *Stochastic Orders and Their Applications*; Springer: New York, NY, USA, 1994.
38. Nadarajah, S.; Gupta, A.K. The Beta Fréchet distribution. *Far East J. Theor. Stat.* **2004**, *14*, 15–24.
39. Souza, W.B.; Cordeiro, G.M.; Simas, A.B. Some Results for Beta Fréchet Distribution. *Commun. Stat.-Theory Methods* **2011**, *40*, 798–811. [CrossRef]
40. Cordeiro, G.M.; De-Castro, M. A new family of generalized distributions. *J. Stat. Comput. Simul.* **2011**, *81*, 883–898. [CrossRef]
41. Cordeiro, G.M.; Ortega, E.M.M.; Cunha, D.C.C. The exponentiated generalized class of distributions. *J. Data Sci.* **2013**, *11*, 1–27. [CrossRef]
42. Krishna, E.; Jose, K.K.; Ristic, M.M. Application of Marshall-olkin Fréchet distribution. *Commun. Stat.-Simul. Comput.* **2013**, *42*, 76–89. [CrossRef]
43. Nadarajah, S.; Kotz, S. The exponentiated Fréchet distribution. *Interstat Electron. J.* **2003**, *92*, 97–111.
44. Da Silva, R.V.; De Andrade, T.A.N.; Maciel, D.B.M.; Campos, R.P.S.; Cordeiro, G.M. A New Lifetime Model: The Gamma Extended Frechet Distribution. *J. Stat. Theory Appl.* **2013**, *12*, 39–54. [CrossRef]
45. Abbas, S.; Taqi, S.A.; Mustafa, F.; Murtaza, M.; Shahbaz, M.Q. Topp-Leone Inverse Weibull Distribution: Theory and Application. *Eur. J. Pure Appl. Math.* **2017**, *10*, 1005–1022.
46. Fréchet, M. Sur la loi de probabilite de lecart maximum. *APM* **1927**, *6*, 110–116.
47. Artzner, P.; Delbaen, F.; Eber, J.M.; Heath, D. Thinking Coherently. *Risk* **1997**, *10*, 68–71.
48. Artzner, P. Application of coherent risk measures to capital requirements in insurance. *NAAJ* **1999**, *3*, 11–25. [CrossRef]

Article

Optimal Plan of Multi-Stress–Strength Reliability Bayesian and Non-Bayesian Methods for the Alpha Power Exponential Model Using Progressive First Failure

Ehab M. Almetwally [1,2], Refah Alotaibi [3], Aned Al Mutairi [3], Chanseok Park [4,*] and Hoda Rezk [5]

1. Department of Statistical, Faculty of Business Administration, Delta University for Science and Technology, Gamasa 11152, Egypt; ehabxp_2009@hotmail.com
2. Department of Mathematical Statistical, Faculty of Graduate Studies for Statistical Research, Cairo University, Cairo 12613, Egypt
3. Department of Mathematical Sciences, College of Science, Princess Nourah Bint Abdulrahman University, P.O. Box 84428, Riyadh 11671, Saudi Arabia; rmalotaibi@pnu.edu.sa (R.A.); aoalmutairi@pnu.edu.sa (A.A.M.)
4. Applied Statistics Laboratory, Department of Industrial Engineering, Pusan National University, Busan 46241, Korea
5. Department of Statistics, Al-Azhar University, Cairo 11751, Egypt; hodaragab2009@yahoo.com
* Correspondence: cpark2@gmail.com

Abstract: It is extremely frequent for systems to fail in their demanding operating environments in many real-world contexts. When systems reach their lowest, highest, or both extreme operating conditions, they usually fail to perform their intended functions, which is something that researchers pay little attention to. The goal of this paper is to develop inference for multi-reliability using unit alpha power exponential distributions for stress–strength variables based on the progressive first failure. As a result, the problem of estimating the stress–strength function R, where X, Y, and Z come from three separate alpha power exponential distributions, is addressed in this paper. The conventional methods, such as maximum likelihood for point estimation, Bayesian and asymptotic confidence, boot-p, and boot-t methods for interval estimation, are also examined. Various confidence intervals have been obtained. Monte Carlo simulations and real-world application examples are used to evaluate and compare the performance of the various proposed estimators.

Keywords: multi-stress–strength; progressive first failure censoring; balanced loss functions; Lindley's approximation; Markov Chain Monte Carlo; symmetric and asymmetric loss functions; bootstrap confidence intervals

1. Introduction

Systems failing to perform in their harsh working settings is a common occurrence in real-life scenarios. When crossing their lower, upper, or both extreme operating conditions, systems frequently fail to perform their intended roles. Stress–strength reliability, often known as $R = p(X < Y)$, has been extensively investigated in the literature. When the applied stress exceeds the system's strength, a system working under such stress–strength conditions fail to function. Refs. [1–11] are only a few of the significant efforts in this direction. Moreover, the study of stress–strength models has been expanded to multi-component systems, which are systems with several components. Despite the fact that Ref. [12] developed the multi-component stress–strength model decades ago, it has garnered a lot of attention in recent years and has been explored by numerous scholars for both complete and filtered data [13–17]. Stress–strength reliability, $R = P(X < Y)$, has been extensively investigated as a stress–strength model, and the research has also been extended to multi-component systems. However, an equally important practical scenario in which equipment fails in extreme lower and upper working environments receives significantly less attention. When electrical equipment is placed below or above a specified power supply, for example, it will fail. A person's systolic and diastolic pressure limits should not be exceeded at the same time. There are a plethora of such applications, many of them are straightforward and natural, reflecting sound correlations between diverse real-world events. It is a valuable relationship in a variety of subfields of genetics and psychology, where strength Y should not only be more than stress X, but also less than stress Z. For numerous statistical models, several scholars have examined the estimation of the stress–strength parameter. Refs. [18–20] investigated the estimation of $R = P(X < Y < Z)$ based on independent samples. Ref. [21] obtained the estimation in the stress–strength model with the assumption that a component's strength lies in an interval and the probability $R = P(X_1 < Y < X_2)$, where X_1 and X_2 are random stress variables and Y is a random strength variable. When $(Y_1, Y_2, \ldots, Y_k)$ are normal random variables, X is another independent normal random variable, and the estimation of $R = P[\max(Y_1, Y_2, \ldots, Y_k) < X]$ is considered. Ref. [22] calculated the reliability of a component that was subjected to two separate stresses that were unrelated to the component's strength. Ref. [23] used a multi-component series stress–strength model to predict system reliability. Using current U-statistics, Ref. [24] proposed a straightforward computation procedure for $P(X < Y < Z)$ and its variance. $P(X < Y < Z)$ was used by Ref. [24] to study the cascade system. Nonparametric statistical inference for $P(X < Y < Z)$ was studied by Ref. [25]. Ref. [26] achieved inference of $R = P(X < Y < Z)$ for the n-Standby System: a Monte-Carlo simulation approach. Ref. [27] discussed $R = P(X < Y < Z)$ for the progressive first failure of the Kumaraswamy model.

Many articles appeared in the censored sample, including a multi-component stress–strength model with adaptive hybrid progressive censored data. Ref. [28] discussed Bayesian and maximum likelihood estimation methods of reliability. Weibull distribution is a type of probability distribution. Using progressively first-failure censored data, Ref. [29] determined the reliability of a multi-component stress–strength system based on the Burr XII distribution. Under adaptive hybrid progressive censoring, Ref. [30] proposed multi-component stress–strength estimation of a non-identical component strengths system. Ref. [31] used progressive Type-II censoring data to estimate the reliability of multi-component stress–strength with a generalized linear failure rate distribution. Ref. [32] studied the estimation of multi-component reliability based on progressively Type-II censored data from unit Weibull distribution.

When dealing with reliability features in statistical analysis, even when it is known that some efficiency loss may occur, different censoring strategies, or early deletions of active units, are frequently utilized to save time and money. The Type-II censoring scheme, progressive Type-II censoring system, and progressive first failure censoring method, for example, are all well-known censoring schemes. Ref. [33] presented the progressive first failure censoring scheme, which combines progressive Type-II censoring and first failure censoring strategies to create a new life-test plan.

The progressive first failure censoring system can be summarized as follows. Assume that a life test is administered to n independent groups, each having k items. The R_1 units and the group in which the first failure is identified are randomly withdrawn from the experiment once the first failure $Y_{1;m,n,k}$ has occurred. The R_2 units and the group in which the second failure is observed are randomly withdrawn from the remaining live $(n - R_1 - 2)$ groups at the moment of the second failure $Y_{2;m,n,k}$. When the m-th observation $Y_{m;m,n,k}$ fails at the end, the remaining living units R_m are removed from the test. The resultant ordered observations $Y_{1;m,n,k}, \ldots, Y_{m;m,n,k}$ are then referred to as progressive first-failure censored with a progressive censored scheme described by $R = (R_1, R_2, \ldots, R_m)$, where m are failures and the sum of all removals equals n, that is, $n = m + \sum_{i=1}^{m} R_i$. The progressive first-failure censoring scheme is reduced to a first-failure censoring scheme when $R_1 = R_2 = \ldots = R_m = 0$. Similarly, first-failure Type-II censoring is a special instance of this censoring technique when $R_1 = R_2 = \ldots = R_{m-1} = 0$ and $R_m = n - m$. The progressive first-failure censoring scheme is simplified to the progressive Type-II censoring scheme with the premise that each group contains precisely one unit, $k = 1$. Progressive first-failure censoring is a generalization of progressive censoring.

Letting $Y_{1;m,n,k}, \ldots, Y_{m;m,n,k}$ denote a progressive first-failure Type-II censored population sample with probability density function (PDF) $f_X(.)$ and cumulative distribution function (CDF) $F_X(.)$ and the progressive censoring scheme of R, on the basis of considering progressive first-failure, the likelihood function is based on Ref. [34]. The following is a censored sample:

$$f_{1,2,\ldots,m}(Y_{1;m,n,k},\ldots,Y_{m;m,n,k}) = AK^m \prod_{i=1}^{m} f(Y_{i;m,n,k})[1 - F(Y_{i;m,n,k})]^{k(R_i+1)-1}, 0 < Y_{1;m,n,k},\ldots,Y_{m;m,n,k} < \infty, \quad (1)$$

where $A = n(n - R_1 - 1)(n - R_1 - R_2 - 2) \ldots \left(n - \sum_{i=1}^{m-1} R_i - m + 1\right)$.

Ref. [35] constructed the APE distribution from the exponential baseline distribution and explored its essential aspects as well as parameter estimation. Ref. [36] developed the alpha power Weibull distribution and demonstrated that it outperforms certain other variants of the Weibull distribution using two real data sets. Ref. [37] used the generalized exponential baseline distribution and the APE approach to introduce the alpha power generalized exponential (APGE) distribution. Closed-form formulas for the APGE distribution's moment properties were established by Ref. [38]. Because of APE flexibility, recently, many studies gave been conducted, such as in Refs. [39,40]. The PDF and hazard functions of the APE distribution are similar to the Weibull, gamma, and GE distributions. As a result, it can be used to replace the popular Weibull, gamma, and GE distributions. Because the APE distribution's CDF may be precisely defined, it can also be used to evaluate censored data. The PDF, CDF, and hazard rate function of the APE with parameters α and β are described by

$$f(y; \alpha, \beta) = \frac{\beta \log(\alpha) e^{-\beta y} \alpha^{1-e^{-\beta y}}}{\alpha - 1}, \ y \geq 0, \alpha, \beta > 0, \quad (2)$$

$$F(y; \alpha, \beta) = \frac{\alpha^{1-e^{-\beta y}}}{\alpha - 1}, \ y \geq 0, \alpha, \beta > 0, \quad (3)$$

and

$$h(y; \alpha, \beta) = \frac{\beta \log(\alpha) e^{-\beta y} \alpha^{1-e^{-\beta y}}}{1 - \alpha^{1-e^{-\beta y}}}, \ y \geq 0, \alpha, \beta > 0, \quad (4)$$

To the best of our knowledge, statistical inference and optimality on multi-component stress–strength models have been derived for some well-known models using progressively censored sample conditions; this subject has not received much attention under censored data. As a result, we plan to introduce multi-component reliability inference where stress–strength variables follow unit APE based on progressive first-failure. This work addresses the problem of predicting the stress–strength function R, where X, Y, and Z are three independent APE. The moments, skewness, and kurtosis measures of APE are computed. The assessment of likelihood based on increasing first-failure point estimation filtered, asymptotic confidence interval, boot-p, and boot-t approaches are also covered. Using Markov chain Monte Carlo (MCMC), Bayesian estimate methods based on progressive first-failure censoring are produced. A Bayesian estimate has made use of both symmetric and asymmetric loss functions. Based on progressive first-failure censored samples, the balanced and unbalanced loss functions were utilized to assess the reliability of the multi-stress–strength APE distribution. The different optimal schemes of the progressively censored samples are obtained. Monte Carlo simulations and real-world application examples are utilized to assess and compare the performance of the various proposed estimators.

The remainder of the paper is structured as follows: Moments of APE are calculated in Section 2. Section 3 considers the traditional point estimates, maximum likelihood estimation of R, and the parameter model under progressive first failure. Fisher information matrix of the parameter model is obtained in Section 4, while confidence intervals, namely asymptotic intervals, boot-p, and boot-t, are computed in Section 5. In Section 6, the

Bayesian approach is considered. Optimization criterion is used to choose the appropriate progressive censoring approach in Section 7. Simulation research is carried out to demonstrate the relative effectiveness of multi-stress–strength reliability under progressive first failure based on different censoring methods in Section 8. Section 9 provides real-world data application examples. Finally, Section 10 has the concluding remarks of this paper.

2. Moments

Let $X \sim APE(\alpha, \beta)$ and $Y \sim APE(\alpha, 1)$. Then, we have $X = Y/\beta$. Thus, we have $E(X) = \frac{1}{\beta}E(Y)$ and $E(X^2) = \frac{1}{\beta^2}E(Y^2)$.

Lemma 1. *We have*

$$E(Y) = \frac{\alpha}{\alpha - 1}\{\log\log(\alpha) + \Gamma(0, \log(\alpha)) + \gamma\},$$

where Γ is the incomplete gamma function defined by $\Gamma(s, x) = \int_x^\infty t^{s-1} e^{-t} dt$, and γ is the Euler-Mascheroni constant given by $\gamma \approx 0.5772156649$.

Proof. First, we derive $E(Y)$. The PDF of Y is given by

$$f(y) = \frac{\alpha \log(\alpha)}{\alpha - 1} e^{-y} \alpha^{-e^{-y}} = \frac{\alpha \log(\alpha)}{\alpha - 1} e^{-y} e^{-\log(\alpha) e^{-y}}.$$

Using the change of variable ($t = e^{-y} \log \alpha$), we have

$$E(Y) = \int_0^\infty y f(y)\, dy = \frac{\alpha}{\alpha - 1} \int_0^{\log \alpha} (\log\log(\alpha) - \log(t)) e^{-t} dt, \tag{5}$$

$$= \log\log(\alpha) - \frac{\alpha}{\alpha - 1} \int_0^{\log(\alpha)} \log(t) e^{-t} dt.$$

Then, it suffices to obtain $\int_0^{\log(\alpha)} e^{-t} \log(t)\, dt$. It should be noted that $\gamma = -\int_0^\infty e^{-t} \log(t)\, dt$. For more details, refer to Identity (6) of Ref. [41]. Thus, we have

$$\int_0^{\log(\alpha)} e^{-t} \log(t)\, dt = \int_0^\infty e^{-t} \log(t)\, dt - \int_{\log \alpha}^\infty e^{-t} \log(t)\, dt = -\gamma - \int_{\log \alpha}^\infty e^{-t} \log(t)\, dt \tag{6}$$

Using the integration by parts, we have

$$\int_{\log(\alpha)}^\infty e^{-t} \log(t)\, dt = [-\log(t) e^{-t}]_{\log(\alpha)}^\infty + \int_{\log(\alpha)}^\infty \frac{1}{t} e^{-t} dt = \frac{\log\log(\alpha)}{\alpha} + \Gamma(0, \log(\alpha)). \tag{7}$$

Substituting (8) into (7), we have

$$\int_0^{\log(\alpha)} e^{-t} \log(t)\, dt = -\gamma - \frac{\log\log(\alpha)}{\alpha} - \Gamma(0, \log(\alpha)). \tag{8}$$

Substituting (9) into (6), we have

$$E(Y) = \int_0^\infty y f(y) dy = \log\log(\alpha) + \frac{\alpha}{\alpha - 1}\left\{\gamma + \frac{\log\log(\alpha)}{\alpha} + \Gamma(0, \log(\alpha))\right\} = \frac{\alpha}{\alpha - 1}\{\log\log(\alpha) + \Gamma(0, \log(\alpha)) + \gamma\},$$

which completes the proof. □

Thus, we have

$$E(X) = \frac{1}{\beta} \cdot \frac{\alpha}{\alpha - 1}\{\log\log(\alpha) + \Gamma(0, \log(\alpha)) + \gamma\}.$$

Lemma 2. We have

$$E(Y^2) = \frac{2\alpha \log(\alpha)}{\alpha - 1} \cdot {}_3F_3(1,1,1;2,2,2;-\log\alpha).$$

here, ${}_pF_q(\cdot)$ is the generalized hypergeometric function [42,43] defined as

$$_pF_q(a_1,\ldots,a_p;b_1,\ldots,b_q;z) = \sum_{n=0}^{\infty} \frac{(a_1)_n \cdots (a_p)_n}{(b_1)_n \cdots (b_q)_n} \frac{z^n}{n!},$$

where $(a)_n$ is the Pochhammer symbol for the rising factorial defined as $(a)_0 = 1$ and $(a)_n = a(a+1)\cdots(a+n-1)$ for $n = 1,2,\ldots$.

Proof. Using the change of variable ($t = e^{-y}\log\alpha$), we have

$E(Y^2) = \int_0^\infty y^2 f(y) dy = \frac{\alpha}{\alpha-1} \int_0^{\log \alpha} (\log\log\alpha - \log t)^2 e^{-t} dt = \frac{\alpha}{\alpha-1}[(\log\log\alpha)^2 \int_0^{\log \alpha} e^{-t} dt - 2\log\log\alpha \int_0^{\log \alpha} \log t \, e^{-t} dt + \int_0^{\log \alpha} (\log t)^2 e^{-t} dt]$

Since $\int_0^{\log(\alpha)} e^{-t} dt = 1 - 1/\alpha$ and $\int_0^{\log(\alpha)} \log t \, e^{-t} dt = -\gamma - \log\log\alpha/\alpha - \Gamma(0,\log\alpha)$ from (8), we have

$$E(Y^2) = \frac{\alpha}{\alpha-1}[(\log\log(\alpha))^2\left(1-\frac{1}{\alpha}\right) = -2\log\log(\alpha)\left\{-\gamma - \frac{1}{\alpha}\log\log(\alpha) - \Gamma(0,\log(\alpha))\right\}$$
$$+ \int_0^{\log \alpha} (\log(t))^2 e^{-t} dt = \frac{\alpha}{\alpha-1}[(\log\log(\alpha))^2\left(1+\frac{1}{\alpha}\right) + 2\log\log(\alpha)\{\gamma + \Gamma(0,\log(\alpha))\} + \int_0^{\log(\alpha)} (\log(t))^2 e^{-t} dt. \quad (9)$$

Now, it suffices to evaluate $\int_0^{\log(\alpha)} (\log(t))^2 e^{-t} dt$, which is in the last term in (5). After tedious calculus and algebra along with the help of Mathematica [44], we have

$$\int (\log(t))^2 e^{-t} dt = 2t \cdot {}_3F_3(1,1,1;2,2,2;-t) - \log(t)\{(1+e^{-t})\log(t) + 2\Gamma(0,t) + 2\gamma\}$$

along with $\int_0^1 (\log(t))^2 e^{-t} dt = 2{}_3F_3(1,1,1;2,2,2;-1)$. Thus, we have

$\int_0^{\log(\alpha)} (\log(t))^2 e^{-t} dt = \int_0^1 (\log(t))^2 e^{-t} dt + \int_1^{\log \alpha} (\log(t))^2 e^{-t} dt$
$= 2\log(\alpha) \cdot {}_3F_3(1,1,1;2,2,2;-\log(\alpha)) - \log\log(\alpha)\left\{\left(1+\frac{1}{\alpha}\right)\log\log(\alpha) + 2\Gamma(0,\log(\alpha)) + 2\gamma\right\}$
$= 2\log(\alpha) \cdot {}_3F_3(1,1,1;2,2,2;-\log(\alpha)) - (\log\log(\alpha))^2\left(1+\frac{1}{\alpha}\right) - 2\log\log(\alpha)\{\Gamma(0,\log(\alpha)) + \gamma\}$

Substituting the above into (10), we have

$$E(Y^2) = \frac{2\alpha \log(\alpha)}{\alpha-1} \cdot {}_3F_3(1,1,1;2,2,2;-\log(\alpha))$$

which completes the proof. □

Then, using Lemmas 1 and 2, we have

$$E(X) = \frac{1}{\beta} \cdot \frac{\alpha}{\alpha-1}\{\log\log(\alpha) + \Gamma(0,\log(\alpha)) + \gamma\}$$
$$E(X^2) = \frac{2\alpha \log(\alpha)}{\beta^2(\alpha-1)} \cdot {}_3F_3(1,1,1;2,2,2;-\log(\alpha)). \quad (10)$$

$$\mathrm{Var}(X) = \frac{1}{\beta^2}\left[\frac{2\alpha\log(\alpha)}{(\alpha-1)} \cdot {}_3F_3(1,1,1;2,2,2;-\log(\alpha)) - \frac{\alpha^2}{(\alpha-1)^2}\{\log\log(\alpha) + \Gamma(0,\log(\alpha)) + \gamma\}^2\right]$$

Using $E(X)$ and $E(X^2)$ in the above, we can obtain the method-of-moments estimate as follows. We can set

$$\frac{E(X^2)}{\{E(X)\}^2} = \frac{2(\alpha-1)\log(\alpha) \cdot {}_3F_3(1,1,1;2,2,2;-\log(\alpha))}{\alpha\{\log\log(\alpha) + \Gamma(0,\log(\alpha)) + \gamma\}^2} = \frac{\frac{1}{n}\sum_{i=1}^{n} X_i^2}{\left(\frac{1}{n}\sum_{i=1}^{n} X_i\right)^2}.$$

Thus, by solving the above for α, we can estimate α. We denote this estimate as $\hat{\alpha}$. Then, the estimate of β can be explicitly obtained by setting $E(X) = \frac{1}{n}\sum_{i=1}^{n} X_i$ with (11), which is given by $\hat{\beta} = \frac{1}{\frac{1}{n}\sum_{i=1}^{n} X_i} \cdot \frac{\hat{\alpha}}{\hat{\alpha}-1}\{\log\log(\hat{\alpha}) + \Gamma(0,\log(\hat{\alpha})) + \gamma\}$.

Figure 1 shows the skewness (SK) and kurtosis (KT) by using moment measures of quartile with different values of parameters. Table 1 discusses the first quartile, median, and third quartile and well as SK and KT of the APE distribution with different values.

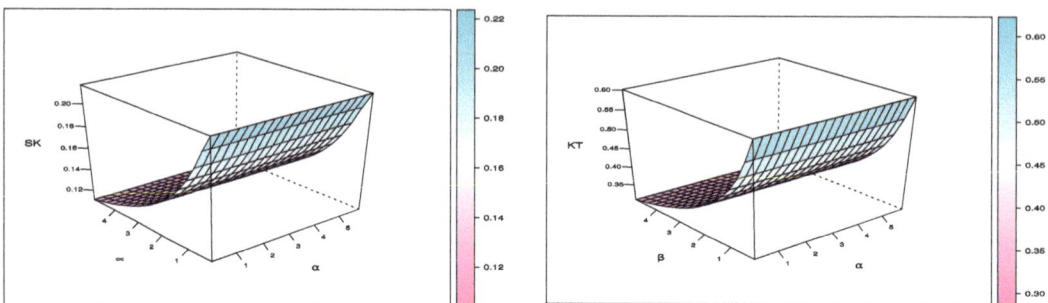

Figure 1. Three-dimensional plot of skewness and kurtosis with different values of parameters.

Table 1. Different measures of the moment by different values of parameters.

α	β	Q_1	Median	Q_3	SK	KT
	0.15	0.8973	2.2992	5.1031	0.33333	0.93528
	1.3	0.1035	0.2653	0.5888	0.33330	0.93527
0.15	2.45	0.0549	0.1408	0.3124	0.33333	0.93536
	3.6	0.0374	0.0958	0.2126	0.33342	0.93537
	4.75	0.0283	0.0726	0.1611	0.33342	0.93564
	0.15	2.2878	5.3284	10.2600	0.23720	0.63055
	1.3	0.2640	0.6148	1.1838	0.23721	0.63060
1.5	2.45	0.1401	0.3262	0.6282	0.23723	0.63052
	3.6	0.0953	0.2220	0.4275	0.23719	0.63057
	4.75	0.0722	0.1683	0.3240	0.23715	0.63062
	0.15	3.0063	6.5448	11.8495	0.19972	0.53889
	1.3	0.3469	0.7552	1.3673	0.19971	0.53887
2.85	2.45	0.1841	0.4007	0.7255	0.19978	0.53887
	3.6	0.1253	0.2727	0.4937	0.19972	0.53893
	4.75	0.0949	0.2067	0.3742	0.19967	0.53882
	0.15	3.5129	7.3072	12.7711	0.18033	0.49144
	1.3	0.4053	0.8431	1.4736	0.18035	0.49140
4.2	2.45	0.2151	0.4474	0.7819	0.18030	0.49140
	3.6	0.1464	0.3045	0.5321	0.18043	0.49148
	4.75	0.1109	0.2308	0.4033	0.18031	0.49143

3. Estimation in the Classical Style

In this part, the classical point and interval estimation methods are discussed, namely maximum likelihood estimation for finding point estimates of R and asymptotic, boot-p, and boot-t intervals for R for obtaining interval estimates.

Maximum Likelihood R Estimation

Let $X \sim APE(\beta_1, \alpha)$, $Y \sim APE(\beta_2, \alpha)$ and $Z \sim APE(\beta_3, \alpha)$ be independent functions. Assuming α is known in this the case, we have

$$R = p(X < Y < Z) = \int_{-\infty}^{\infty} F_X(y) dF_Y(y) - \int_{-\infty}^{\infty} F_X(y) F_Z(y) dF_Y(y), \quad (11)$$

$$= \frac{\beta_1 \left[2\beta_1^2 + 2\beta_2^2 + 0.5\beta_3^2 + 1.5\beta_1\beta_3 + 3\beta_1\beta_2\right]}{(\beta_1 + \beta_2)(\beta_1 + 2\beta_2)(\beta_1 + \beta_3)(2\beta_1 + \beta_3)}$$

Figure 2 shows the different plot of multi-stress–strength reliability for different values of parameters, which explains that the multi-stress–strength reliability has different ranges.

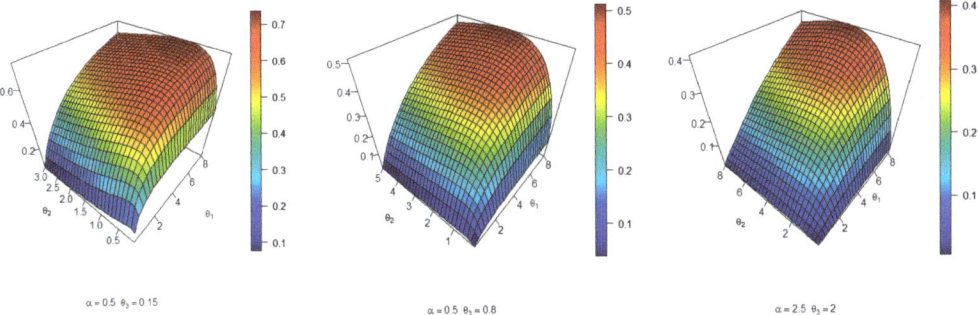

Figure 2. Three-dimensional plot of multi-stress–strength reliability with different values of parameters.

To obtain the MLE of R, we must first obtain the MLEs of β_1, β_2 and β_3. Let $(X_{1;m_1,n_1,k_1}, \ldots, X_{n_1;m_1,n_1,k_1})$, $(Y_{1;m_2,n_2,k_2}, \ldots, Y_{n_2;m_2,n_2,k_2})$, and $(Z_{1;m_3,n_3,k_3}, \ldots, Z_{n_3;m_3,n_3,k_3})$ be three progressively first-failure censored samples from $APE(\beta_i, \alpha)$ distribution with censoring schemes $\underline{R}_x = (R_{x_1}, \ldots, R_{x_{m_1}}), \underline{R}_y = (R_{y_1}, \ldots, R_{y_{m_2}}), \underline{R}_z = (R_{z_1}, \ldots, R_{z_{m_3}})$. Using the formulas from (2) and (3), the likelihood function of β_1, β_2 and β_3 is given by

$$L(\beta_1, \beta_2, \beta_3)$$
$$\propto \prod_{j=1}^{3} (\beta_j k_j)^{m_j} \left(\frac{\log \alpha}{\alpha - 1}\right)^{(m_1+m_2+m_3)} \prod_{i=1}^{m_1} e^{-\beta_1 x_i(k_1 R_{x_i}+1)} \alpha^{1-e^{-\beta_1 x_i(R_{x_i}+1)}} \prod_{i=1}^{m_2} e^{-\beta_2 y_i(k_2 R_{y_i}+1)} \alpha^{1-e^{-\beta_2 y_i(k_2 R_{y_i}+1)}} \quad (12)$$
$$\prod_{i=1}^{m_3} e^{-\beta_3 z_i(k_3 R_{z_i}+1)} \alpha^{1-e^{-\beta_3 z_i(k_3 R_{z_i}+1)}},$$

We use x_i instead of $X_{i_1;m_1,n_1,k_1}$ to simplify notation. Similarity between y_i and z_i. The log-likelihood function, ℓ can now be written as follows:

$$\ell(\beta_1, \beta_2, \beta_3) \propto \sum_{j=1}^{3} m_j \left(\ln k_j + \ln \beta_j\right) + (m_1 + m_2 + m_3)[\ln(\log \alpha) - \ln(\alpha - 1)]$$
$$- \sum_{i=1}^{m_1} \beta_1 x_i(k_1 R_{x_i}+1) + \sum_{i=1}^{m_1} \left(1 - e^{-\beta_1 x_i(R_{x_i}+1)}\right) \ln(\alpha) - \sum_{i=1}^{m_2} \beta_2 y_i(k_2 R_{y_i}+1) \quad (13)$$
$$+ \sum_{i=1}^{m_2} 1 - e^{-\beta_2 y_i(k_2 R_{y_i}+1)} \ln(\alpha) - \sum_{i=1}^{m_3} \beta_3 z_i(k_3 R_{z_i}+1) + \sum_{i=1}^{m_3} 1 - e^{-\beta_3 z_i(k_3 R_{z_i}+1)} \ln(\alpha)$$

Taking the derivative of (14) with respect to β_1, β_2 and β_3, we obtain

$$\frac{\partial \ell}{\partial \beta_1} = \frac{m_1}{\beta_1} - \sum_{i=1}^{m_1} x_i(k_1 R_{x_i}+1) + \ln(\alpha) \sum_{i=1}^{m_1} x_i(R_{x_i}+1) e^{-\beta_1 x_i(R_{x_i}+1)}, \quad (14)$$

$$\frac{\partial \ell}{\partial \beta_2} = \frac{m_2}{\beta_2} - \sum_{i=1}^{m_2} y_i(k_2 R_{y_i} + 1) + \ln(\alpha) \sum_{i=1}^{m_2} y_i(k_2 R_{y_i} + 1) e^{-\beta_2 y_i (k_2 R_{y_i} + 1)} \qquad (15)$$

$$\frac{\partial \ell}{\partial \beta_3} = \frac{m_3}{\beta_3} - \sum_{i=1}^{m_3} z_i(k_3 R_{z_i} + 1) + \ln(\alpha) \sum_{i=1}^{m_3} z_i(k_3 R_{z_i} + 1) e^{-\beta_3 z_i (k_3 R_{z_i} + 1)} \qquad (16)$$

It is noted that the MLEs of β_1, β_2 and β_3 can not be found in closed form. Thus, by solving the system of nonlinear Equations (15)–(17), numerical solutions to the nonlinear system in (15)–(17) can be found using an iterative approach, such as Newton–Raphson. Then, the MLEs $\hat{\beta}_1$, $\hat{\beta}_2$ and $\hat{\beta}_3$ can be obtained. To obtain the MLE of R, by replacing β_1, β_2 and β_3 in (5) with $\hat{\beta}_1$, $\hat{\beta}_2$ and $\hat{\beta}_3$ as follows:

$$\hat{R} = \frac{\hat{\beta}_1 \left[2\hat{\beta}_1^2 + 2\hat{\beta}_2^2 + 0.5\hat{\beta}_3^2 + 1.5\hat{\beta}_1 \hat{\beta}_3 + 3\hat{\beta}_1 \hat{\beta}_2 \right]}{(\hat{\beta}_1 + \hat{\beta}_2)(\hat{\beta}_1 + 2\hat{\beta}_2)(\hat{\beta}_1 + \hat{\beta}_3)(2\hat{\beta}_1 + \hat{\beta}_3)} \qquad (17)$$

4. Fisher Information

The Fisher information matrix of the $\varphi = (\beta_1, \beta_2, \beta_3)$ is expressed as

$$I_{3\times 3} = -E \begin{bmatrix} A_{11} & A_{12} & A_{13} \\ A_{21} & A_{22} & A_{23} \\ A_{31} & A_{32} & A_{33} \end{bmatrix}, \qquad (18)$$

where $A_{11} = E\left(\frac{\partial^2 \ell}{\partial \beta_1^2}\right)$, $A_{12} = A_{21} = E\left(\frac{\partial^2 \ell}{\partial \beta_2 \partial \beta_1}\right)$, $A_{13} = A_{31} = E\left(\frac{\partial^2 \ell}{\partial \beta_1 \partial \beta_3}\right)$, $A_{22} = E\left(\frac{\partial^2 \ell}{\partial \beta_2^2}\right)$, $A_{23} = A_{32} = E\left(\frac{\partial^2 \ell}{\partial \beta_2 \partial \beta_3}\right)$, $A_{33} = E\left(\frac{\partial^2 \ell}{\partial \beta_3^2}\right)$,

$$\frac{\partial^2 \ell}{\partial \beta_1^2} = \frac{-m_1}{\beta_1^2} + \ln(\alpha) \sum_{i=1}^{m_1} [x_i(R_{x_i} + 1)]^2 e^{-\beta_1 x_i (R_{x_i} + 1)},$$

$$\frac{\partial^2 \ell}{\partial \beta_2 \partial \beta_1} = \frac{\partial^2 \ell}{\partial \beta_1 \partial \beta_3} = \frac{\partial^2 \ell}{\partial \beta_2 \partial \beta_3} = 0$$

$$\frac{\partial^2 \ell}{\partial \beta_2^2} = \frac{-m_2}{\beta_2} + \ln(\alpha) \sum_{i=1}^{m_2} [y_i(k_2 R_{y_i} + 1)]^2 e^{-\beta_2 y_i (k_2 R_{y_i} + 1)},$$

$$\frac{\partial^2 \ell}{\partial \beta_3^2} = \frac{-m_3}{\beta_3} + \ln(\alpha) \sum_{i=1}^{m_3} [z_i(k_3 R_{z_i} + 1)]^2 e^{-\beta_3 z_i (k_3 R_{z_i} + 1)}.$$

5. Confidence Intervals

In this section, the parameters' confidence intervals (CIs) are computed. Because our point estimate is the most likely value for the parameter, we should build the confidence intervals on it. CIs are a set of values (intervals) that serve as good approximations of an unknown population parameter. In this investigation, two types of CIs were computed.

5.1. Approximate Confidence Intervals

Because the APE distribution's PDF is not symmetric, asymptotic CIs based on normality do not perform well. The underlying distribution is assumed to be APE. As a result, we believe that the parametric bootstrap percentile interval is preferable to the nonparametric one. Furthermore, it is well known that the nonparametric bootstrap percentile interval does not perform well in general. See Section 5.3.1 of Ref. [45] for more information. The parametric bootstrap interval with normal approximation or Studentization can be used. However, because this CI is symmetric, it may not be suitable for our asymmetric instance. According to large sample theory, the MLE results are consistent and regularly distributed, subject to certain regularity restrictions. According to large sample theory, the MLE results are consistent and regularly distributed, subject to certain regularity restrictions. Because parameter MLE values are not in closed form, correct CIs cannot be obtained; instead, asymptotic CIs based on the asymptotic normal distribution of MLE values are computed.

Assume that $\varphi = (\beta_1, \beta_2, \beta_3, R)$. $[(\hat{\beta}_1 - \beta_1), (\hat{\beta}_2 - \beta_2), (\hat{\beta}_3 - \beta_3), (\hat{R} - R)]$ is known to yield the asymptotic distribution of MLE values of $N(0, \sigma)$, where $\sigma = \sigma_{ij}$, $i, j = 1, 2, 3$, is the variance–covariance matrix of the unknown parameters. As previously established, the inverse of the Fisher information matrix is an estimator of the asymptomatic variance–covariance matrix.

The approximate $100(1 - \omega)\%$ two-sided CIs for φ are provided by

$$(\hat{\varphi}_{iL}, \hat{\varphi}_{iU}) : \hat{\varphi}_i \mp z_{1-\frac{\omega}{2}} \sqrt{\hat{\sigma}_{ij}}, i = 1, 2, 3, 4. \tag{19}$$

where $z_{1-\frac{\omega}{2}}$ is the $100(1 - \frac{\omega}{2})$-th upper percentile of the standard normal distribution.

5.2. Bootstrap Confidence Intervals

In this paragraph, we propose to employ two additional confidence intervals based on parametric bootstrap methods: percentile bootstrap technique (Boot-p) and bootstrap-t method (Boot-t). Obtaining the step-by-step illustrations of the two ways is shown briefly below; for more information, see Ref. [46].

5.2.1. Methods of Boot-p

- Use the sample $\{X_{1;m_1,n_1,k_1}, \ldots, X_{m_1;m_1,n_1,k_1}\}$, $\{Y_{1;m_2,n_2,k_2}, \ldots, Y_{m_2;m_2,n_2,k_2}\}$, and $\{Z_{1;m_3,n_3,k_3}, \ldots, Z_{m_3;m_3,n_3,k_3}\}$ to compute $\hat{\beta}_1, \hat{\beta}_2$ and $\hat{\beta}_3$.
- Based on $\underline{R}_x$ censoring technique, a bootstrap progressive first-failure Type-II censored sample indicated by $X^*_{1;m_1,n_1,k_1}, \ldots, X^*_{m_1;m_1,n_1,k_1}$ is constructed from the APE(α, β_1). From the APE(α, β_2), a bootstrap progressive first-failure Type-II censored sample designated by $Y^*_{1;m_2,n_2,k_2}, \ldots, Y^*_{m_2;m_2,n_2,k_2}$ is constructed using $\underline{R}_y$ censoring scheme. Based on $\underline{R}_z$ censoring scheme, a bootstrap progressive first-failure Type-II censored sample, indicated by $Z^*_{1;m_3,n_3,k_3}, \ldots, Z^*_{m_3;m_3,n_3,k_3}$, is constructed from the APE(α, β_3). Based on $\{X^*_{1;m_1,n_1,k_1}, \ldots, X^*_{m_1;m_1,n_1,k_1}\}, \{Y^*_{1;m_2,n_2,k_2}, \ldots, Y^*_{m_2;m_2,n_2,k_2}\}$, and $\{Z^*_{1;m_3,n_3,k_3}, \ldots, Z^*_{m_3;m_3,n_3,k_3}\}$, construct the bootstrap sample estimate of R using (5), say $\hat{R}^*$.
- Step 2 should be repeated N_p times.
- Assume $G(x) = P(\hat{R}^* \leq x)$, where $\hat{R}^*$ is the cumulative distribution function. For a given x, define $\hat{R}_{Boot-p}(x) = G^{-1}(x)$. The approximation of $100(1 - \omega)\%$ percent confidence interval of R is given by

$$\left(\hat{R}_{Boot-p}\left(\frac{\omega}{2}\right), \hat{R}_{Boot-p}\left(1 - \frac{\omega}{2}\right)\right).$$

5.2.2. Methods of Boot-t

- Use the sample $\{X_{1;m_1,n_1,k_1}, \ldots, X_{m_1;m_1,n_1,k_1}\}$, $\{Y_{1;m_2,n_2,k_2}, \ldots, Y_{m_2;m_2,n_2,k_2}\}$, and $\{Z_{1;m_3,n_3,k_3}, \ldots, Z_{m_3;m_3,n_3,k_3}\}$ to compute $\hat{\beta}_1, \hat{\beta}_2$ and $\hat{\beta}_3$.
- Use $\hat{\beta}_1$ to generate a bootstrap sample $X^*_{1;m_1,n_1,k_1}, \ldots, X^*_{m_1;m_1,n_1,k_1}, \hat{\beta}_2$ to generate a bootstrap sample $Y^*_{1;m_2,n_2,k_2}, \ldots, Y^*_{m_2;m_2,n_2,k_2}$, and similarly, $\hat{\beta}_3$ to generate a bootstrap sample $Z^*_{1;m_3,n_3,k_3}, \ldots, Z^*_{m_3;m_3,n_3,k_3}$. Based on $\{X^*_{1;m_1,n_1,k_1}, \ldots, X^*_{m_1;m_1,n_1,k_1}\}$, $\{Y^*_{1;m_2,n_2,k_2}, \ldots, Y^*_{m_2;m_2,n_2,k_2}\}$ and $\{Z^*_{1;m_3,n_3,k_3}, \ldots, Z^*_{m_3;m_3,n_3,k_3}\}$, compute the bootstrap sample estimate of R using (5), say $\hat{R}^*$ and the following statistic:

$$T^* = \frac{\sqrt{m}\left(\hat{R}^* - \hat{R}\right)}{\sqrt{V(\hat{R}^*)}}$$

- Step 2 should be repeated N_p times.
- After obtaining N_p a number of T^* values, the boundaries $100(1-\omega)\%$ of R percent confidence interval are determined as follows: Assume T^* has a cumulative distribution function given by $H(x) = P(T^* \leq x)$. Define $\hat{R}_{Boot-t} = \hat{R} + \sqrt{V(\hat{R})} mH^{-1}(x)$ for a given x.
- $100(1-\omega)\%$ percent boot-t confidence interval of R is calculated as $(\hat{R}_{Boot-t}(\frac{\omega}{2}), \hat{R}_{Boot-t}(1-\frac{\omega}{2}))$
- To achieve better estimates of parameters or any function of parameters, it is often advantageous to incorporate prior knowledge about the parameters, which could be prior data, expert opinion, or some other medium of knowledge. A Bayesian technique is used to include such prior knowledge into the estimation process. As a result, we now go through the Bayesian approach of estimation in depth, which incorporates previous knowledge in the form of prior distributions.

6. Bayesian Approach

Bayesian inference has gained appeal in a variety of sectors in recent years, including engineering, clinical medicine, biology, and so on. Its capacity to analyze data using prior knowledge makes it valuable in dependability studies, where data availability is a major issue. The model parameters $\beta_1, \beta_2, \beta_3$ and R Bayesian estimates, as well as the corresponding credible intervals, are derived in this section.

6.1. Prior Information and Loss Function

Because the gamma distribution can take on different shapes based on the parameter values, using various gamma priors is simple and can result in more expressive posterior density estimates. As a result, we investigated gamma density priors, which are more adaptable than other challenging prior distributions and APE distribution under progressive first-failure censoring model parameters. As a result, under progressive first-failure censoring model parameters gamma $(a_j, b_j); j = 1, \ldots, 4$, independent gamma PDFs are assumed for the APE distribution. The joint prior is as follows

$$\pi(\beta_1, \beta_2, \beta_3, R) \propto \beta_1^{a_1-1} e^{-b_1\beta_1} \beta_2^{a_2-1} e^{-b_2\beta_2} \beta_3^{a_3-1} e^{-b_3\beta_3} R^{a_4-1} e^{-b_4 R}, \qquad (20)$$

where $a_j, b_j; j = 1, \ldots, 4$ indicate prior knowledge of the unknown parameters $\beta_1, \beta_2, \beta_3$ and R and are anticipated to be non-negative.

According to the literature, choosing the symmetric loss function (SLF), (squared loss function) (SEL) is a critical issue in Bayesian analysis. The SEL function is the most often utilized SLF in this study for estimating the considered unknown values.

$$\mathcal{L}(R, \widetilde{R}) = (\widetilde{R} - R)^2, \mathcal{L}(\beta_1, \widetilde{\beta_1}) = (\widetilde{\beta_1} - \beta_1)^2, \mathcal{L}(\beta_2, \widetilde{\beta_2}) = (\widetilde{\beta_2} - \beta_2)^2, \mathcal{L}(\beta_3, \widetilde{\beta_3}) = (\widetilde{\beta_3} - \beta_3)^2,$$

where $\widetilde{R}, \widetilde{\beta_1}, \widetilde{\beta_2}$ and $\widetilde{\beta_3}$ are approximations of R, β_1, β_2 and β_3. The posterior mean of R, θ_1, θ_2 and θ_3 is utilized to compute the objective estimate of $\widetilde{R}, \widetilde{\theta_1}, \widetilde{\theta_2}$, and $\widetilde{\theta_3}$. In contrast, any other loss function can be easily incorporated.

6.2. Posterior Analysis by SLF

Observing the APE distribution under progressive first-failure censoring sample data from the likelihood function and the prior knowledge given both yield the joint posterior density function.

$$L(R, \beta_1, \beta_2, \beta_3|\underline{t}) \propto \pi(R, \beta_1, \beta_2, \beta_3) \prod_{i=1}^{3} \prod_{j=1}^{n_i} g(t_{ij}) (1 - G(t_{ij}))^{c_i}, \qquad (21)$$

The Bayesian estimator of R, θ_1, θ_2 and θ_3 such as $\widetilde{R}, \widetilde{\theta_1}, \widetilde{\theta_2}$, and $\widetilde{\theta_3}$, under the SEL function, is the posterior expectation of R, θ_1, θ_2 and θ_3. The marginal posterior distributions for each of the parameters (R, θ_1, θ_2 and θ_3) must be gathered in order to generate these estimates. However, due to the implied mathematical calculations, precise formulations for the marginal PDFs for each unknown parameter are plainly not realistic. As a result, we would like to generate Bayesian estimates and credible intervals utilizing simulation approaches such as MCMC.

The Metropolis–Hastings (MH) algorithm, which is used to generate random samples using the posterior density distribution and an independent proposal distribution to approximate Bayesian estimates and to create the associated Highest Posterior Density (HPD) credible intervals, is one of the most useful MCMC algorithms. In addition, this method provides a chain version of the Bayesian estimate that is simple to use in practice.

7. Optimization Criterion

In recent years, there has been a lot of interest in finding the optimal censoring scheme in the statistical literature; for example, see Refs. [47–53]. Possible censoring schemes refer to any $R_1, \ldots, R_m$ combinations such that $n = m + \sum_{i=1}^{m} R_i$ and finding the optimum sampling approach means locating the progressive censoring scheme that offers the most information about the unknown parameters among all conceivable progressive censoring schemes for fixed n and m. The first difficulty is, of course, how to generate unknown parameter information measures based on specific progressive censoring data, and the second is how to compare two distinct information measures based on two different progressive censoring techniques. The next subsections go through some of the optimality criteria that were employed in this situation. In practice, we want to select the filtering scheme that delivers the most information about the unknown parameters; see Ref. [54] for further information. In our example, Table 2 presents a number of regularly used measures to help us choose the appropriate progressive censoring approach.

Table 2. Some practical censoring plan optimum criteria.

Criterion	Method
O_1	Maximize trace $[\mathbf{I}_{3\times 3}(.)]$
O_2	Minimize trace $[\mathbf{I}_{3\times 3}(.)]^{-1}$
O_3	Minimize det $[\mathbf{I}_{3\times 3}(.)]^{-1}$
O_4	Minimize $\mathbf{Var}[\log(\hat{t}_p)]$, $0 < p < 1$

In terms of O_1, our goal is to maximize the observed Fisher $\mathbf{I}_{3\times 3}(.)$ information values. Furthermore, our goal for criterion O_2 and O_3 is to minimize the determinant and trace of $[\mathbf{I}_{3\times 3}(.)]^{-1}$. Comparing multiple criteria is simple when dealing with single-parameter distributions; however, when dealing with unknown multi-parameter distributions, comparing the two Fisher information matrices becomes more difficult because the criterion O_2 and O_3 are not scale-invariant; see Ref. [55]. However, the optimal censoring scheme of multi-parameter distributions can be chosen using scale-invariant criteria O_4. The criterion O_4, which is dependent on the value of p, clearly tends to minimize the variance of logarithmic MLE of the p-th quantile, $\log(\hat{t}_p)$. As a result, the logarithmic for $\hat{t}_p$ of the APE distribution is supplied by

$$\log(\hat{t}_p) = \log\left\{\frac{-1}{\beta}\log\left[1 - \frac{\log(p(\alpha-1))}{\log \alpha}\right]\right\}, \ 0 < p < 1,$$

The delta approach is applied to (3) to produce the approximated variance for $\log(\hat{t}_p)$ of the APE distribution as

$$\mathrm{Var}(\log(\hat{t}_p)) = [\nabla \log(\hat{t}_p)]^T I_{3\times 3}^{-1}(\hat{\beta}_1, \hat{\beta}_2, \hat{\beta}_3)[\nabla \log(\hat{t}_p)],$$

where

$$[\nabla \log(\hat{f}_p)]^T = \left[\frac{\partial}{\partial \beta_1}\log(\hat{f}_p), \frac{\partial}{\partial \beta_2}\log(\hat{f}_p), \frac{\partial}{\partial \beta_3}\log(\hat{f}_p)\right]_{(\beta_1=\hat{\beta}_1,\beta_2=\hat{\beta}_2,\beta_3=\hat{\beta}_3)}.$$

The optimal progressive censoring, however, corresponds to a maximum value of the criterion O_1 and a minimum value of the criteria O_i i, = 1, 2, 3, 4.

8. Simulation Study

A simulation study is carried out to illustrate the relative efficiency of multi-stress–strength reliability under the progressive first failure based on different censored schemes and to evaluate it as a function of changing factors of a parameter. For a better understanding of this model, we use the following procedure to produce samples from the progressive first failure based on different censored schemes for APE distribution described in Section 3.

A large number N = 1000 of progressively first-failure censored samples for a true value of parameters α, β_1, β_2, and β_3 different combinations of n (number of groups), m (progressively first-failure-censoring data), and k (number of items within each group) are generated from the APE by using the algorithm described in Balakrishnan and Sandhu (1995). In each case, the MLE and Bayesian of the multi-stress–strength reliability are computed. The asymptotic CIs and two parametric bootstrap CIs are used for MLE computation purposes. The HPD CIs are used for Bayesian computation purposes. The MSE and Bias values are used to compare different estimators. The average lengths are also used to compare the performances of the two-sided 95% asymptotic CI/HPD credible intervals, where the length of asymptotic CI is (LACI), length of bootstrap-p CI is (LBPCI), length of bootstrap-t CI is (LBTCI), and length of credible CI is (LCCI). Comparison between censoring schemes is made with respect to their optimum criteria measures; see Table 1, where we consider the various sampling schemes listed as follows:

Scheme I: $R_m = n - m$ and $R_i = 0; i = 1, \ldots, m-1$,
Scheme II: $R_1 = n - m$ and $R_i = 0; i = 2, \ldots, m$.

The simulation study was conducted with various values of (k, n, m), such as n = 20, 50, and k = 2 and 4 for each group size. When the number of failed participants reaches or exceeds a specified value m, the test is over, where m =12 and 18 when n = 20, and m = 35 and 45 when n = 50. The joint posterior distribution of the unknown four parameters is proportional to the likelihood function based on the non-informative priors of hyper-parameters ai, bi for I = 1, ... , 4. As a result, we employed an informative prior of, and using elective hyper-parameters, the values of hyper-parameters are chosen to satisfy the prior mean, resulting in the expected value of the corresponding parameter; see Refs. [56,57]. The Bayesian estimation based on 12,000 MCMC samples and discarding the first 2000 values as "burn-in" are generated using the M-H sampler technique introduced in Section 3.

The progressive first failure of censored samples was generated from APE distribution for four sets of parametric values:

In Table 2: $\alpha = 0.8$, $\beta_1 = 1.8$, $\beta_2 = 0.8$, $\beta_3 = 0.2$ and $\alpha = 2$, $\beta_1 = 1.8$, $\beta_2 = 0.8$, $\beta_3 = 0.2$.
In Table 3: $\alpha = 0.8$, $\beta_1 = 3$, $\beta_2 = 2$, $\beta_3 = 1.5$ and $\alpha = 2$, $\beta_1 = 3$, $\beta_2 = 2$, $\beta_3 = 1.5$.

In computational analysis, extensive computations were carried out using the R statistical programming language software, with the "coda" package proposed by Ref. [58], and the "maxLik" package proposed by Henningsen and Toomet (2011), which uses the Newton–Raphson method of maximizing the computations. The average results of MLE and Bayesian for multi-stress–strength reliability are presented in Tables 2 and 3.

Table 3. MLE and Bayesian point and interval estimations for multi-stress–strength reliability with optimality measures when $\beta_1 = 1.8, \beta_2 = 0.8, \beta_3 = 0.2$.

$\beta_1=1.8, \beta_2=0.8, \beta_3=0.2$				MLE		Bayesian		MLE		HPD		Optimality		
α	n	k	Scheme	m	Bias	MSE	Bias	MSE	LACI	LBPCI	LBTCI	LCCI	O_1	O_2	O_3
0.8	20	2	I	12	0.0244	0.0051	0.0491	0.0038	0.2621	0.0085	0.0083	0.1397	21.3816	0.00079670	1315.0742
				18	0.0137	0.0031	0.0487	0.0029	0.2099	0.0065	0.0064	0.0909	4.1313	0.00000699	1860.8153
			II	12	0.0142	0.0051	0.0257	0.0019	0.2750	0.0083	0.0086	0.1332	6.5200	0.00010403	1137.2594
				18	0.0152	0.0027	0.0402	0.0021	0.1966	0.0063	0.0062	0.0807	3.2014	0.00000570	1541.9155
		4	I	12	0.0231	0.0043	0.0215	0.0041	0.2271	0.0072	0.0071	0.1299	32.0128	0.00002417	4326.9511
				18	0.0110	0.0023	0.0103	0.0021	0.1695	0.0054	0.0053	0.0757	7.1082	0.00000042	5887.7508
			II	12	0.0218	0.0038	0.0179	0.0037	0.2274	0.0071	0.0072	0.1124	13.6802	0.00001076	4260.3735
				18	0.0278	0.0024	0.0020	0.0020	0.1602	0.0052	0.0052	0.0689	5.7489	0.00000036	4892.7823
	50	2	I	35	−0.0026	0.0019	0.0025	0.0015	0.1694	0.0076	0.0076	0.1309	5.4335	0.00000781	2173.0070
				45	−0.0018	0.0013	0.0016	0.0013	0.1399	0.0062	0.0062	0.0876	0.9871	0.00000027	2673.3238
			II	35	0.0038	0.0027	−0.0034	0.0008	0.2033	0.0093	0.0095	0.1027	1.4849	0.00000062	1446.0044
				45	0.0026	0.0020	0.0233	0.0010	0.1764	0.0079	0.0080	0.0801	1.0515	0.00000015	1889.7725
		4	I	35	0.0016	0.0029	−0.0039	0.0005	0.2119	0.0099	0.0099	0.0795	2.7322	0.00000005	4818.0247
				45	0.0054	0.0018	0.0341	0.0016	0.1642	0.0070	0.0071	0.0688	1.8893	0.000000008	6547.6266
			II	35	0.0148	0.0016	0.0408	0.0015	0.1434	0.0062	0.0062	0.0693	1.9652	0.00000001	12,058.2247
				45	0.0171	0.0010	0.0740	0.0010	0.1042	0.0047	0.0047	0.0534	1.4447	0.000000002	14,466.0555
2	20	2	I	12	0.0252	0.0053	0.0389	0.0029	0.2687	0.0122	0.0118	0.1378	44.8698	0.00028752	1298.6571
				18	0.0138	0.0025	0.0383	0.0019	0.1901	0.0083	0.0083	0.0824	10.6874	0.000007058	1724.2822
			II	12	0.0118	0.0047	0.0151	0.0012	0.2650	0.0118	0.0119	0.1133	18.6539	0.00006624	1221.1348
				18	0.0138	0.0028	0.0319	0.0014	0.1998	0.0090	0.0090	0.0797	10.2767	0.000007664	1692.4905
		4	I	12	0.0362	0.0044	0.0958	0.0041	0.2189	0.0098	0.0097	0.1120	71.0129	0.00003361	3458.2427
				18	0.0305	0.0023	0.0739	0.0022	0.1469	0.0064	0.0065	0.0646	17.4184	0.000000603	4725.7657
			II	12	0.0284	0.0053	0.0352	0.0018	0.2632	0.0123	0.0124	0.0918	30.5605	0.000007690	3241.6188
				18	0.0311	0.0027	0.0570	0.0025	0.1628	0.0072	0.0073	0.0606	14.7362	0.00000051	4491.3445
	50	2	I	35	0.0149	0.0018	0.0475	0.0018	0.1565	0.0069	0.0071	0.0939	6.3239	0.000000503	3853.6782
				45	0.0119	0.0012	0.0396	0.0011	0.1287	0.0058	0.0056	0.0564	2.9557	0.00000007	4607.4580
			II	35	0.0120	0.0016	0.0029	0.0004	0.1479	0.0066	0.0067	0.0780	3.5200	0.000000218	3587.6918
				45	0.0135	0.0011	0.0278	0.0010	0.1215	0.0053	0.0054	0.0543	2.6907	0.00000007	4509.7376
		4	I	35	0.0305	0.0020	0.0796	0.0017	0.1285	0.0059	0.0058	0.0817	13.5622	0.000000060	9487.8097
				45	0.0247	0.0013	0.0652	0.0012	0.1001	0.0046	0.0047	0.0521	5.5558	0.00000001	12,885.4276
			II	35	0.0264	0.0019	0.0119	0.0003	0.1350	0.0060	0.0060	0.0459	5.9567	0.000000015	10,036.4394
				45	0.0253	0.0014	0.0402	0.0013	0.1085	0.0048	0.0048	0.0480	4.1892	0.00000000	12,893.1857

Tables 3 and 4 show that APE based on the multi-stress–strength model MLE and Bayesian of multi-stress–strength reliability is excellent in terms of MSE, Bias, and CI length (LCI). The MSE, Bias, and LCI drop as n and m rise, as expected. Furthermore, the MSE, Bias, and LCI drop as group size k grows. In terms of MSE, Bias, and LCI, Bayesian estimation utilizing gamma informative prior is also superior to MLE because it includes prior knowledge. In terms of the length of CI values, HPD credible intervals outperform asymptotic CI for interval estimation. As a result, we recommend using the M-H approach to estimate multi-stress–strength reliability using Bayesian point and interval estimates. Furthermore, when comparing Scheme I and Scheme II, it is obvious that the MLE optimum criteria measures for Scheme II are higher than for Scheme I.

Table 4. MLE and Bayesian point and interval estimations for multi-stress–strength reliability with optimality measures when $\beta_1 = 3, \beta_2 = 2, \beta_3 = 1.5$.

$\beta_1=3, \beta_2=2, \beta_3=1.5$					MLE		Bayesian		MLE		HPD		Optimality		
α	n	k	Scheme	m	Bias	MSE	Bias	MSE	LACI	LBPCI	LBTCI	LCCI	O_1	O_2	O_3
0.8	20	2	I	12	0.0141	0.0035	0.0204	0.0015	0.2243	0.0098	0.0095	0.1263	32.7192	0.851629	59.1656
				18	0.0062	0.0020	0.0075	0.0004	0.1737	0.0079	0.0078	0.0721	5.3389	0.007162	95.2781
			II	12	0.0054	0.0041	0.0079	0.0010	0.2489	0.0109	0.0109	0.1141	8.4620	0.140559	93.5644
				18	0.0041	0.0020	0.0066	0.0004	0.1755	0.0076	0.0077	0.0753	3.8724	0.005310	68.8098
		4	I	12	0.0086	0.0017	0.0514	0.0014	0.1601	0.0069	0.0071	0.1405	41.6896	0.040229	181.3487
				18	0.0101	0.0011	0.0207	0.0008	0.1233	0.0056	0.0057	0.0726	8.0888	0.000366	197.4359
			II	12	0.0060	0.0029	0.0252	0.0017	0.2111	0.0093	0.0093	0.1170	10.7009	0.005277	123.4315
				18	0.0108	0.0014	0.0160	0.0006	0.1426	0.0062	0.0061	0.0715	5.8162	0.000307	140.7154
	50	2	I	35	0.0053	0.0011	0.0412	0.0010	0.1291	0.0056	0.0055	0.1019	5.5126	0.000537	262.9994
				45	0.0019	0.0006	0.0163	0.0006	0.0982	0.0043	0.0042	0.0641	1.7133	0.000035	247.1240
			II	35	0.0038	0.0010	0.0161	0.0008	0.1262	0.0056	0.0057	0.0920	1.4508	0.000110	130.4385
				45	0.0002	0.0007	0.0114	0.0004	0.1059	0.0048	0.0047	0.0648	1.0404	0.000031	148.3842
		4	I	35	0.0028	0.0005	0.0923	0.0004	0.0857	0.0038	0.0039	0.1058	7.7591	0.000029	704.7141
				45	0.0025	0.0003	0.0411	0.0002	0.0723	0.0033	0.0033	0.0717	2.8182	0.000002	710.6756
			II	35	0.0046	0.0009	0.0333	0.0006	0.1163	0.0052	0.0053	0.0854	2.1859	0.000007	399.3411
				45	0.0055	0.0005	0.0279	0.0004	0.0836	0.0037	0.0039	0.0686	1.6343	0.000002	465.4802
2	20	2	I	12	0.0111	0.0030	0.0250	0.0019	0.2118	0.0095	0.0094	0.1366	48.2769	0.309823	47.0611
				18	0.0096	0.0021	0.0070	0.0004	0.1750	0.0078	0.0080	0.0737	12.2381	0.008539	65.7453
			II	12	0.0031	0.0036	0.0084	0.0011	0.2352	0.0106	0.0105	0.1259	19.2689	0.059121	39.0353
				18	0.0088	0.0020	0.0062	0.0004	0.1710	0.0073	0.0074	0.0710	10.0978	0.006465	53.7042
		4	I	12	0.0121	0.0018	0.0592	0.0015	0.1611	0.0071	0.0071	0.1328	73.0888	0.029018	112.0391
				18	0.0117	0.0011	0.0215	0.0009	0.1243	0.0056	0.0056	0.0815	17.7696	0.000577	137.7838
			II	12	0.0064	0.0027	0.0247	0.0015	0.2010	0.0090	0.0091	0.1186	16.6365	0.001927	101.0923
				18	0.0106	0.0013	0.0151	0.0006	0.1342	0.0060	0.0062	0.0770	11.7618	0.000317	136.2249
	50	2	I	35	0.0033	0.0009	0.0416	0.0008	0.1198	0.0055	0.0055	0.0975	6.9337	0.000501	111.1543
				45	0.0022	0.0007	0.0165	0.0006	0.1023	0.0045	0.0045	0.0632	3.0112	0.000064	143.9309
			II	35	0.0034	0.0011	0.0105	0.0006	0.1271	0.0059	0.0058	0.0869	3.6038	0.000188	110.5934
				45	0.0040	0.0008	0.0100	0.0004	0.1094	0.0049	0.0049	0.0686	2.6286	0.000058	140.2241
		4	I	35	0.0113	0.0006	0.0822	0.0005	0.0895	0.0039	0.0037	0.0869	13.8108	0.000054	281.3838
				45	0.0089	0.0005	0.0375	0.0004	0.0780	0.0036	0.0036	0.0656	5.6687	0.000006	388.0669
			II	35	0.0100	0.0010	0.0195	0.0007	0.1191	0.0054	0.0056	0.0689	5.7857	0.000014	313.3802
				45	0.0093	0.0004	0.0238	0.0004	0.0839	0.0037	0.0036	0.0595	4.3141	0.000004	395.1895

9. Application of Real Data

The analysis of real data is presented in this part for demonstration reasons. We look at data from three distinct voltages of 36, 34, and 32 KV that show times to breakdown of an insulating fluid between electrodes. This information is taken from page 105 of [59].

Data set 1: Times to breakdown of an insulated fluid at 32 KV (Z): 0.27, 0.40, 0.69, 0.79, 0.75, 2.75, 3.91, 9.88, 13.95, 15.93, 27.80, 53.24, 82.85, 89.29, 100.58, 215.10.

Data set 2: Times to breakdown of an insulated fluid at 34 KV (Y): 0.19, 0.78, 0.96, 1.31, 2.78, 3.16, 4.15, 4.67, 4.85, 6.50, 7.35, 8.01, 8.27, 12.06, 31.75, 32.52, 33.91, 36.71, 72.89.

Data set 3: Times to breakdown of an insulated fluid at 36 KV (X): 0.35, 0.59, 0.96, 0.99, 1.69, 1.97, 2.07, 2.58, 2.71, 2.90, 3.67, 3.99, 5.35, 13.77, 25.50.

Ref. [60] discusses the estimation of R = P[Y < X < Z] of the Weibull distribution. Table 5 discusses parameter estimation with stander error (SE) for this model and R = P[Y < X < Z] by the MLE method.

Table 5. MLE with SE and R = P[Y < X < Z] for the Weibull model.

	Estimates	SE	Lower	Upper
β	0.6813	0.0911	0.5026	0.8599
θ_1	0.6861	0.2586	0.1793	1.1928
θ_2	0.4150	0.1424	0.1358	0.6942
θ_3	0.2266	0.0892	0.0518	0.4015
R		0.3342		

First, we check the fitting of APE distribution to this data; see Table 6. Distance of Kolmogorov–Smirnov (DKS) with p values (PVKS) for three distinct voltages data. The values of KSD statistics are found to be 0.2598, 0.1612, and 0.1427 with corresponding PVKS 0.2214, 0.6492, and 0.8786. The p values indicate that the APE distribution with the above-mentioned parameters is a suitable model for modeling these three data sets. The plots of the estimated PDF, CDF, and PP plot of the three data sets in Figures 3–5 also confirm the same.

Table 6. MLE with SE, KSD, and different measures for three distinct voltages data.

		Estimates	SE	KSD	PVKS	VAIC	VBIC	VCVM	VAD
x1	α	0.0854	0.1495	0.2598	0.2214	142.1859	143.6020	0.0431	0.3264
	β	0.0147	0.0082						
x2	α	0.1094	0.2142	0.1612	0.6492	140.8927	142.7816	0.0584	0.3580
	β	0.0409	0.0253						
x3	α	0.0421	0.1392	0.1427	0.8786	77.8128	79.2289	0.0669	0.4317
	β	0.0943	0.0885						

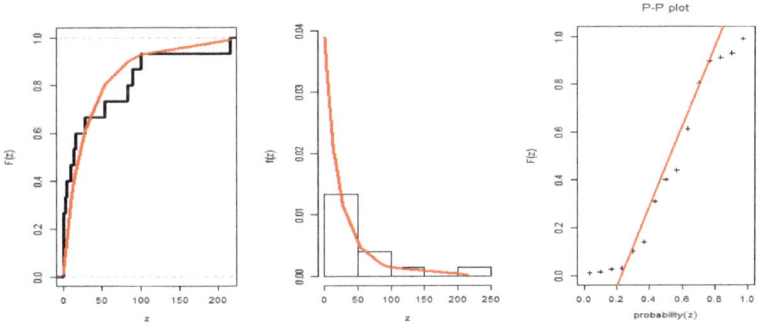

Figure 3. Plots of the estimated PDF, CDF, and PP of APE distribution in data set I.

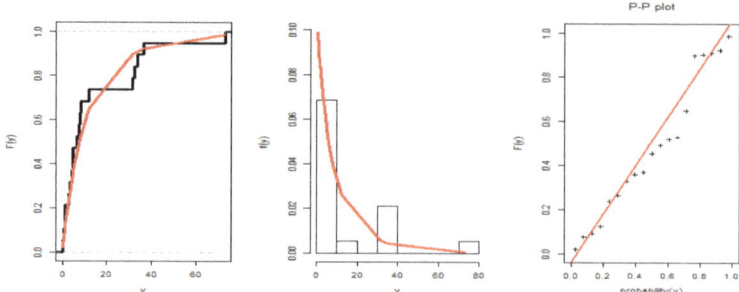

Figure 4. Plots of the estimated PDF, CDF and PP plot of APE distribution in data set II.

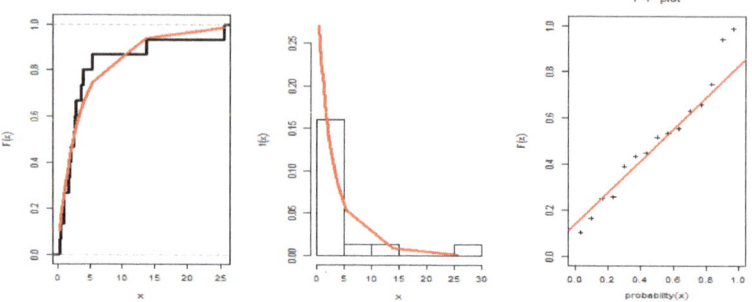

Figure 5. Plots of the estimated PDF, CDF, and PP plot of APE distribution in data set III.

Based on the complete data, the MLE and Bayesian estimate for the APE model of R = P[Y < X < Z] are found to be 0.4523 and 0.4570, respectively, as shown in Table 7. Here, it is to be noted in the Bayesian estimation of parameters that we use informative priors, as gamma prior is available regarding the model parameters. From the results of Table 7, we show that the Bayesian estimation is the best estimation of this model where the multi-stress–strength reliability R = P[Y < X < Z] is larger than MLE. In addition, the SE of Bayesian is smaller than MLE. Figure 6 shows the contour plot of the log-likelihood function of this model with different values of parameters to check the unique and global values of these parameters. Figure 7 discusses the MCMC trace, convergence, and plot of the posterior distribution of this model.

Table 7. MLE and Bayesian estimation for the parameters and R = P[Y < X < Z] for the APE model.

	MLE				Bayesian			
	Estimates	SE	Lower	Upper	Estimates	SE	Lower	Upper
α	0.0811	0.0168	0.0481	0.2791	0.0837	0.0125	0.0426	0.1297
β_1	0.1126	0.0515	0.0116	0.2135	0.1252	0.0444	0.0485	0.2212
β_2	0.0375	0.0173	0.0036	0.0714	0.0405	0.0102	0.0167	0.0663
β_3	0.0145	0.0066	0.0014	0.0275	0.0156	0.0035	0.0053	0.0275
R		0.4523				0.4570		

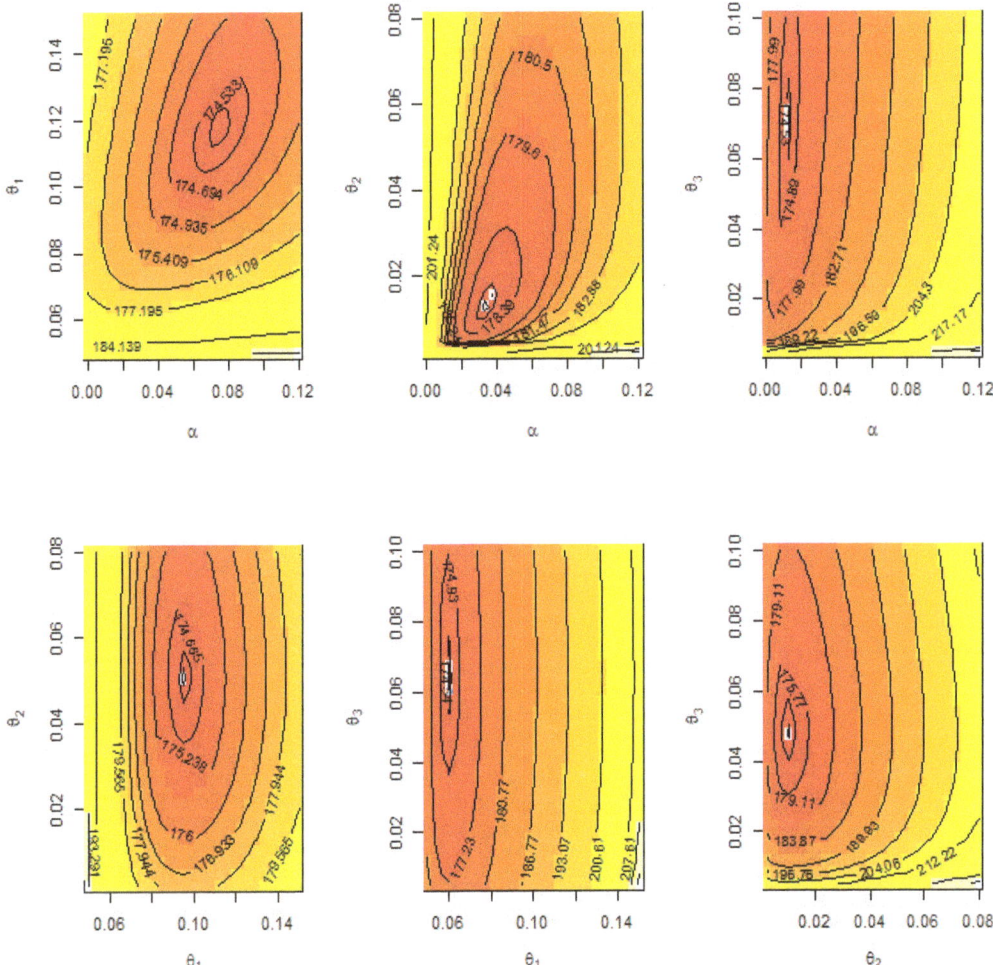

Figure 6. Contour plot of log-likelihood function with different values of parameters; complete sample.

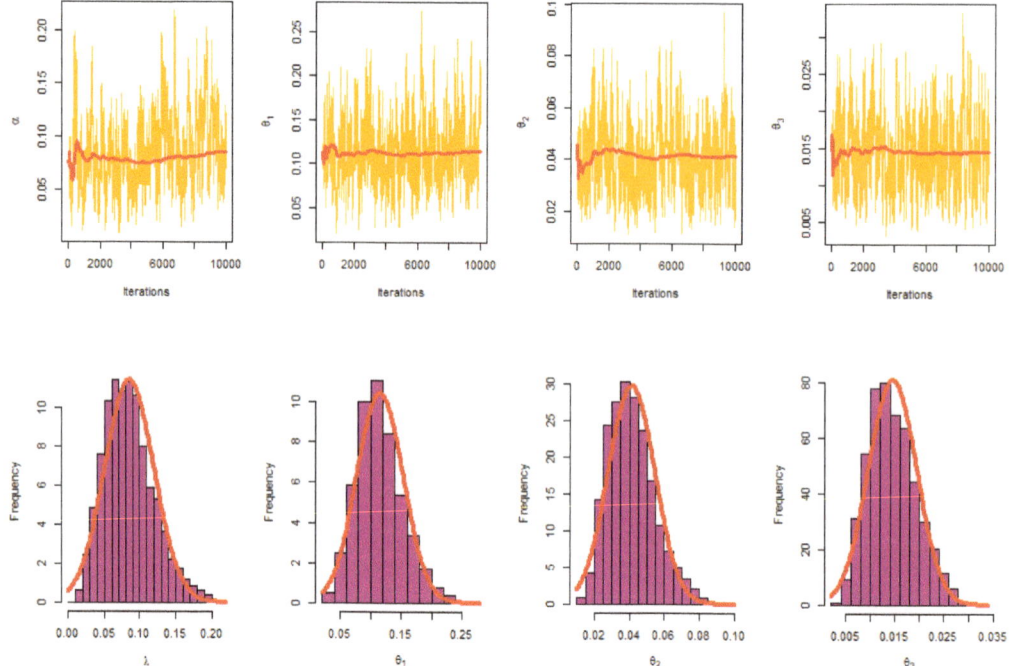

Figure 7. MCMC trace, convergence and plot of posterior distribution; complete sample.

10. Conclusions

In this paper, inference for multi-reliability using unit alpha power exponential distributions for stress–strength variables based on the progressive first failure is considered. The conventional methods such as maximum likelihood and Bayesian methods for point estimation of the parameter model and R are obtained. The Fisher information and confidence intervals such as asymptotic, boot-p, and boot-t methods are also examined. Various optimal criteria have been found. Monte Carlo simulations and real-world application examples are used to evaluate and compare the performance of the various proposed estimators.

Author Contributions: Investigation, R.A., E.M.A., A.A.M., C.P., and H.R.; methodology, R.A., C.P., and H.R.; software, R.A. and E.M.A.; validation, R.A., A.A.M., E.M.A., C.P., and H.R.; writing, R.A., E.M.A., and H.R.; funding acquisition, R.A. All authors have read and agreed to the published version of the manuscript.

Funding: This research was funded by Princess Nourah bint Abdulrahman University Researchers Supporting Project number (PNURSP2022R50), Princess Nourah bint Abdulrahman University, Riyadh, Saudi Arabia.

Institutional Review Board Statement: Not applicable.

Informed Consent Statement: Not applicable.

Data Availability Statement: The data used to support the findings of this study are included within the article.

Acknowledgments: The authors extend their appreciation to Princess Nourah bint Abdulrahman University Researchers Supporting Project number (PNURSP2022R50), Princess Nourah bint Abdulrahman University, Riyadh, Saudi Arabia.

Conflicts of Interest: The authors declare no conflict of interest.

References

1. Weerahandi, S.; Johnson, R.A. Testing reliability in a stress-strength model when X and Y are normally distributed. *Technometrics* **1992**, *34*, 83–91. [CrossRef]
2. Surles, J.G.; Padgett, W.J. Inference for reliability and stress-strength for a scaled Burr Type X distribution. *Lifetime Data Anal.* **2001**, *7*, 187–200. [CrossRef] [PubMed]
3. Al-Mutairi, D.K.; Ghitany, M.E.; Kundu, D. Inferences on stress-strength reliability from Lindley distributions. *Commun. Stat.—Theory Methods* **2013**, *42*, 1443–1463. [CrossRef]
4. Rao, G.S.; Aslam, M.; Kundu, D. Burr-XII distribution parametric estimation and estimation of reliability of multicomponent stress-strength. *Commun. Stat.—Theory Methods* **2015**, *44*, 4953–4961. [CrossRef]
5. Singh, S.K.; Singh, U.; Yaday, A.; Viswkarma, P.K. On the estimation of stress strength reliability parameter of inverted exponential distribution. *Int. J. Sci. World* **2015**, *3*, 98–112. [CrossRef]
6. Abo-Kasem, O.E.; Almetwally, E.M.; Abu El Azm, W.S. Inferential Survival Analysis for Inverted NH Distribution Under Adaptive Progressive Hybrid Censoring with Application of Transformer Insulation. *Ann. Data Sci.* **2022**, 1–48. [CrossRef]
7. Alshenawy, R.; Sabry, M.A.; Almetwally, E.M.; Almongy, H.M. Product Spacing of Stress-Strength under Progressive Hybrid Censored for Exponentiated-Gumbel Distribution. *Comput. Mater. Contin.* **2021**, *66*, 2973–2995. [CrossRef]
8. Alamri, O.A.; Abd El-Raouf, M.M.; Ismail, E.A.; Almaspoor, Z.; Alsaedi, B.S.; Khosa, S.K.; Yusuf, M. Estimate stress-strength reliability model using Rayleigh and half-normal distribution. *Comput. Intell. Neurosci.* **2021**, 7653581. [CrossRef]
9. Sabry, M.A.; Almetwally, E.M.; Alamri, O.A.; Yusuf, M.; Almongy, H.M.; Eldeeb, A.S. Inference of fuzzy reliability model for inverse Rayleigh distribution. *AIMS Math.* **2021**, *6*, 9770–9785. [CrossRef]
10. Abu El Azm, W.S.; Almetwally, E.M.; Alghamdi, A.S.; Aljohani, H.M.; Muse, A.H.; Abo-Kasem, O.E. Stress-Strength Reliability for Exponentiated Inverted Weibull Distribution with Application on Breaking of Jute Fiber and Carbon Fibers. *Comput. Intell. Neurosci.* **2021**, 4227346. [CrossRef]
11. Okabe, T.; Otsuka, Y. Proposal of a Validation Method of Failure Mode Analyses based on the Stress-Strength Model with a Support Vector Machine. *Reliab. Eng. Syst. Saf.* **2021**, *205*, 107247. [CrossRef]
12. Bhattacharyya, G.K.; Johnson, R.A. Estimation of reliability in a multicomponent stress-strength model. *J. Am. Stat. Assoc.* **1974**, *69*, 966–970. [CrossRef]
13. Kotb, M.S.; Raqab, M.Z. Estimation of reliability for multi-component stress–strength model based on modified Weibull distribution. *Stat. Pap.* **2021**, *62*, 2763–2797. [CrossRef]
14. Maurya, R.K.; Tripathi, Y.M. Reliability estimation in a multicomponent stress-strength model for Burr XII distribution under progressive censoring. *Braz. J. Probab. Stat.* **2020**, *34*, 345–369. [CrossRef]
15. Mahto, A.K.; Tripathi, Y.M.; Kızılaslan, F. Estimation of Reliability in a Multicomponent Stress-Strength Model for a General Class of Inverted Exponentiated Distributions Under Progressive Censoring. *J. Stat. Theory Pract.* **2020**, *14*, 58. [CrossRef]
16. Alotaibi, R.M.; Tripathi, Y.M.; Dey, S.; Rezk, H.R. Bayesian and non-Bayesian reliability estimation of multicomponent stress–strength model for unit Weibull distribution. *J. Taibah Univ. Sci.* **2020**, *14*, 1164–1181. [CrossRef]
17. Maurya, R.K.; Tripathi, Y.M.; Kayal, T. Reliability Estimation in a Multicomponent Stress-Strength Model Based on Inverse Weibull Distribution. *Sankhya B* **2022**, *84*, 364–401. [CrossRef]
18. Chandra, S.; Owen, D.B. On estimating the reliability of a component subject to several different stresses (strengths). *Nav. Res. Logist. Quart.* **1975**, *22*, 31–39.
19. Dutta, K.; Sriwastav, G.L. An n-standby system with P(X < Y < Z). *IAPQR Trans.* **1986**, *12*, 95–97.
20. Ivshin, V.V. On the estimation of the probabilities of a double linear inequality in the case of uniform and two-parameter exponential distributions. *J. Math. Sci.* **1998**, *88*, 819–827. [CrossRef]
21. Singh, N. On the estimation of $\Pr(X_1 < Y < X_2)$. *Commun. Statist. Theory Meth.* **1980**, *9*, 1551–1561.
22. Hlawka, P. *Estimation of the Parameter p = P(X < Y < Z)*; No.11, Ser. Stud. i Materiaty No. 10 Problemy Rachunku Prawdopodobienstwa; Prace Nauk. Inst. Mat. Politechn.: Wroclaw, Poland, 1975; pp. 55–65.
23. Hanagal, D.D. Estimation of system reliability in multicomponent series stress-strength model. *J. Indian Statist. Assoc.* **2003**, *41*, 1–7.
24. Waegeman, W.; De Baets, B.; Boullart, L. On the scalability of ordered multi-class ROC analysis. *Comput. Statist. Data Anal.* **2008**, *52*, 33–71. [CrossRef]
25. Chumchum, D.; Munindra, B.; Jonali, G. Cascade System with $\Pr(X < Y < Z)$. *J. Inform. Math. Sci.* **2013**, *5*, 37–47.
26. Patoway, A.N.; Sriwastav, G.L.; Hazarika, J. Inference of R = P(X < Y < Z) for n-Standby System: A Monte-Carlo Simulation Approach. *J. Math.* **2016**, *12*, 18–22.
27. Yousef, M.M.; Almetwally, E.M. Multi stress-strength reliability based on progressive first failure for Kumaraswamy model: Bayesian and non-Bayesian estimation. *Symmetry* **2021**, *13*, 2120. [CrossRef]
28. Kohansal, A.; Shoaee, S. Bayesian and classical estimation of reliability in a multicomponent stress-strength model under adaptive hybrid progressive censored data. *Stat. Pap.* **2021**, *62*, 309–359. [CrossRef]
29. Saini, S.; Tomer, S.; Garg, R. On the reliability estimation of multicomponent stress–strength model for Burr XII distribution using progressively first-failure censored samples. *J. Stat. Comput. Simul.* **2022**, *92*, 667–704. [CrossRef]
30. Kohansal, A.; Fernández, A.J.; Pérez-González, C.J. Multi-component stress–strength parameter estimation of a non-identical component strengths system under the adaptive hybrid progressive censoring samples. *Statistics* **2021**, *55*, 925–962. [CrossRef]

31. Hassan, M.K. On Estimating Standby Redundancy System in a MSS Model with GLFRD Based on Progressive Type II Censoring Data. *Reliab. Theory Appl.* **2021**, *16*, 206–219.
32. Alotaibi, R.; Tripathi, Y.; Dey, S.; Rezk, H. Estimation of multicomponent reliability based on progressively Type II censored data from unit Weibull distribution. *WSEAS Trans. Math.* **2021**, *20*, 288–299. [CrossRef]
33. Wu, S.J.; Kus, C. On estimation based on progressive first-failure-censored sampling. *Comput. Stat. Data Anal.* **2009**, *53*, 3659–3670. [CrossRef]
34. Balakrishnan, N.; Aggarwala, R. *Progressive Censoring: Theory, Methods, and Applications*; Springer Science & Business Media Birkhauser Boston: Cambridge, MA, USA, 2000.
35. Mahdavi, A.; Kundu, D. A new method for generating distributions with an application to exponential distribution. *Commun. Stat. Theory Methods* **2017**, *46*, 6543–6557. [CrossRef]
36. Nassar, M.; Alzaatreh, A.; Mead, M.; Abo-Kasem, O. Alpha power Weibull distribution: Properties and applications. *Commun. Stat.—Theory Methods* **2017**, *46*, 10236–10252. [CrossRef]
37. Dey, A.; Alzaatreh, A.; Zhang, C.; Kumar, D. A new extension of generalized exponential distribution with application to ozone data. *Ozone Sci. Eng.* **2017**, *39*, 273–285. [CrossRef]
38. Nadarajah, S.; Okorie, I.E. On the moments of the alpha power transformed generalized exponential distribution. *Ozone Sci. Eng.* **2018**, *40*, 330–335. [CrossRef]
39. Alotaibi, R.; Elshahhat, A.; Rezk, H.; Nassar, M. Inferences for Alpha Power Exponential Distribution Using Adaptive Progressively Type-II Hybrid Censored Data with Applications. *Symmetry* **2022**, *14*, 651. [CrossRef]
40. Alotaibi, R.; Al Mutairi, A.; Almetwally, E.M.; Park, C.; Rezk, H. Optimal Design for a Bivariate Step-Stress Accelerated Life Test with Alpha Power Exponential Distribution Based on Type-I Progressive Censored Samples. *Symmetry* **2022**, *14*, 830. [CrossRef]
41. Dence, T.P.; Dence, J.B. A survey of Euler's constant. *Math. Mag.* **2009**, *82*, 255–265. [CrossRef]
42. Abramowitz, M.; Stegun, I.A. *Handbook of Mathematical Functions: With Formulas, Graphs, and Mathematical Tables*; 55 of National Bureau of Standards Applied Mathematics Series; U.S. Government Printing Office: Washington, DC, USA, 1964.
43. Seaborn, J.B. *Hypergeometric Functions and Their Applications*; Springer: New York, NY, USA, 1991.
44. Wolfram Research, Inc. *Mathematica—Wolfram/Alpha*; Davison and Hinkley: Champaign, IL, USA, 1997.
45. Davison, A.C.; Hinkley, D.V. *Bootstrap Methods and Their Application*; Cambridge University Press: Cambridge, UK, 1997.
46. Tibshirani, R.; Efron, B. *An Introduction to the Bootstrap*; Chapman & Hall, Inc.: New York, NY, USA, 1993.
47. Ng, H.K.T.; Chan, C.S.; Balakrishnan, N. Optimal progressive censoring plans for the Weibull distribution. *Technometrics* **2004**, *46*, 470–481. [CrossRef]
48. Balasooriya, U.; Balakrishnan, N. Reliability sampling plans for log-normal distribution, based on progressively-censored samples. *IEEE Trans. Reliab.* **2000**, *49*, 199–203. [CrossRef]
49. Balasooriya, U.; Saw, S.L.C.; Gadag, V. Progressively censored reliability sampling plans for the Weibull distribution. *Technometrics* **2000**, *42*, 160–167. [CrossRef]
50. Burkschat, M.; Cramer, E.; Kamps, U. Optimality criteria and optimal schemes in progressive censoring. *Commun. Stat.—Theory Methods* **2007**, *36*, 1419–1431. [CrossRef]
51. Burkschat, M.; Cramer, E.; Kamps, U. On optimal schemes in progressive censoring. *Stat. Probab. Lett.* **2006**, *76*, 1032–1036. [CrossRef]
52. Burkschat, M. On optimality of extremal schemes in progressive type II censoring. *J. Stat. Plan. Inference* **2008**, *138*, 1647–1659. [CrossRef]
53. Pradhan, B.; Kundu, D. On progressively censored generalized exponential distribution. *Test* **2009**, *18*, 497–515. [CrossRef]
54. Elshahhat, A.; Rastogi, M.K. Estimation of parameters of life for an inverted Nadarajah–Haghighi distribution from Type-II progressively censored samples. *J. Indian Soc. Probab. Stat.* **2021**, *22*, 113–154. [CrossRef]
55. Gupta, R.D.; Kundu, D. On the comparison of Fisher information of the Weibull and GE distributions. *J. Stat. Plan. Inference* **2006**, *136*, 3130–3144. [CrossRef]
56. Almongy, H.M.; Alshenawy, F.Y.; Almetwally, E.M.; Abdo, D.A. Applying transformer insulation using Weibull extended distribution based on progressive censoring scheme. *Axioms* **2021**, *10*, 100. [CrossRef]
57. El-Sherpieny, E.S.A.; Almetwally, E.M.; Muhammed, H.Z. Bayesian and non-bayesian estimation for the parameter of bivariate generalized Rayleigh distribution based on clayton copula under progressive type-II censoring with random removal. *Sankhya A* **2021**, 1–38. [CrossRef]
58. Plummer, M.; Best, N.; Cowles, K.; Vines, K. CODA: Convergence diagnosis and output analysis for MCMC. *R News* **2006**, *6*, 7–11.
59. Nelson, W.B. *Applied Life Data Analysis*; John Wiley & Sons.: Hoboken, NJ, USA, 2003.
60. Choudhary, N.; Tyagi, A.; Singh, B. Estimation of R = P[Y < X < Z] under Progressive Type-II Censored Data from Weibull Distribution. *Lobachevskii J. Math.* **2021**, *42*, 318–335.

Article

Simple Closed-Form Formulas for Conditional Moments of Inhomogeneous Nonlinear Drift Constant Elasticity of Variance Process

Kittisak Chumpong [1,2], Raywat Tanadkithirun [3,*] and Chanon Tantiwattanapaibul [3]

[1] Division of Computational Science, Faculty of Science, Prince of Songkla University, Songkhla 90110, Thailand; kittisak.ch@psu.ac.th
[2] Statistics and Applications Research Unit, Faculty of Science, Prince of Songkla University, Songkhla 90110, Thailand
[3] Department of Mathematics and Computer Science, Faculty of Science, Chulalongkorn University, Bangkok 10330, Thailand; chanon.tanti@gmail.com
* Correspondence: raywat.t@chula.ac.th

Abstract: The stochastic differential equation (SDE) has been used to model various phenomena and investigate their properties. Conditional moments of stochastic processes can be used to price financial derivatives whose payoffs depend on conditional moments of underlying assets. In general, the transition probability density function (PDF) of a stochastic process is often unavailable in closed form. Thus, the conditional moments, which can be directly computed by applying the transition PDFs, may be unavailable in closed form. In this work, we studied an inhomogeneous nonlinear drift constant elasticity of variance (IND-CEV) process, which is a class of diffusions that have time-dependent parameter functions; therefore, their sample paths are asymmetric. The closed-form formulas for conditional moments of the IND-CEV process were derived without having a condition on eigenfunctions or the transition PDF. The analytical results were examined through Monte Carlo simulations.

Keywords: conditional moment; constant elasticity of variance process; Feynman–Kac formula

MSC: 34A30; 60G65; 62M20; 65C05

1. Introduction

The stochastic differential equation (SDE) has been used to model various phenomena and investigate their properties, such as the moments, variance and conditional moments, which are beneficial for estimating parameters that play significant roles in several practical applications. For example, financial derivative prices, such as moment swaps, can be obtained by calculating the conditional moments of their payoffs under the risk neutral measure; see for more concrete studies Araneda et al. [1], Cao et al. [2], He and Zhu [3] and Nonsoong et al. [4]. Actually, such moments can be directly computed by employing SDE's transition probability density function (PDF). However, the transition PDF is often unavailable in closed form; so is the formula for those conditional moments of the SDE. Investigating properties of those SDEs is still imperative and challenging.

There are several empirical studies confirming that a mean-reverting drift process, such as the Vašíček, Ornstein–Uhlenbeck (OU) [5] and Cox–Ingersoll–Ross (CIR) [6] processes, should not necessarily be linear. Indeed, the behaviors and dynamics of interest rate and its derivatives prefer nonlinearity in the mean-reverting drift rather than linear drift processes; see for more details in [7–10]. In order to extend the OU process, a nonlinear diffusion process was introduced by Cox [11], namely, the constant elasticity of variance (CEV) process. The CEV process is useful and has many applications in various fields. However, the drift term of Cox's CEV process is still linear. For many reasons described in the existing literature [7,8], an extended case of Cox's CEV process was first studied by Marsh and Rosenfeld [12]. The process is sometimes called the Marsh–Rosenfeld (MR) process, and its transition PDF that can be straightforwardly calculated by using Itô's lemma and the transition PDF of the CIR process are very complicated; the closed-form formula for conditional moments of the MR process is also complicated or unavailable in general; see for more details in [13]. It gets even more complicated for an inhomogeneous-time MR process that extends the MR process by replacing the constant parameters in the process with time-dependent functions. From now on, we subsequently call the inhomogeneous-time MR process in general an inhomogeneous nonlinear drift constant elasticity of variance (IND-CEV) process.

Conditional moments have been extensively used in modern financial markets. For example, they can be used to price moment swaps. Unfortunately, the conditional moments, which can be directly computed by applying the transition PDFs, are often unavailable in closed form because the transition PDFs are hardly known. The Feynman–Kac technique is used to overcome this problem for calculating the conditional moments of many stochastic processes. There has still been little research on the analytical formula for conditional moments regarding the IND-CEV process. In this work, a novel approach is developed based on the Feynman–Kac theorem, where the partial differential equation (PDE) is solved analytically, and some combinatorial techniques are used to simplify the system of recursive ordinary differential equations (ODEs) associated with the conditional moment.

The rest of the paper is organized as follows. Section 2 provides an overview of the IND-CEV process and sufficient conditions of the time-dependent parameter functions in the process. The key methodology and main results are given in Section 3. Section 4 proposes some essential properties such as conditional moments, conditional variance and central moments, conditional mixed moments, conditional covariance and correlation. Section 5 provides the formula of the unconditional moments of the IND-CEV process with constant parameters. Experimental validations for our results applied with Monte Carlo (MC) simulations are addressed in Section 6. Conclusions, limitations and future researches are discussed in Section 7.

2. IND-CEV Process

This section presents the IND-CEV process and sufficient assumptions for the process in order to have a unique positive solution. The dynamics of the short-term interest rate over time are assumed to follow the SDE:

$$dr_t = \kappa(t)\left(\theta(t)r_t^{2\beta-1} - r_t\right)dt + \sigma(t)r_t^{\beta}dW_t, \tag{1}$$

with the initial condition $r_0 > 0$, where $\kappa(t), \theta(t)$ and $\sigma(t)$ are smooth and bounded time-dependent parameter functions and W_t is a standard Brownian motion, which has asymmetric sample paths, under a probability space $(\Omega, \mathcal{F}, \mathcal{P})$ with filtration $\{\mathcal{F}_t\}_{t\geq 0}$. In this study, we only focus on the case that $\beta < 1$ in the SDE (1). Let $\ell := 2 - 2\beta$. Henceforth, the dynamics of the process r_t are considered via the following SDE:

$$dr_t = \kappa(t)\left(\theta(t)r_t^{-(\ell-1)} - r_t\right)dt + \sigma(t)r_t^{-\left(\frac{\ell-2}{2}\right)}dW_t \tag{2}$$

where $\ell > 0$. The process r_t in (2) is called an IND-CEV process. In addition, the SDE (2) is called the extended Cox–Ingersoll–Ross (ECIR) process when $\ell = 1$; see for more details in [14–17]. From (2), if the parameters $\kappa(t), \theta(t)$ and $\sigma(t)$ are constants written by κ, θ and σ, respectively, then the SDE (2) can be rewritten as:

$$dr_t = \kappa\left(\theta r_t^{-(\ell-1)} - r_t\right)dt + \sigma r_t^{-\left(\frac{\ell-2}{2}\right)}dW_t \tag{3}$$

where $\ell > 0$. We will consider SDEs (2) and (3) on a time domain $[0, T]$.

We first discuss the solution of SDE (2).

Assumption 1. *The parameter functions $\theta(t), \kappa(t)$ and $\sigma(t)$ in SDE (2) are strictly positive and continuously differentiable on $[0, T]$. Moreover, $\kappa(t)/\sigma^2(t)$ is locally bounded on $[0, T]$.*

Assumption 2. $2\kappa(t)\theta(t) > \sigma^2(t)$ *for all $t \in [0, T]$.*

Theorem 1. *For SDE (2), if Assumptions 1 and 2 hold with $r_0 > 0$, then there exists a pathwise unique strong solution process $r_t > 0$ for all $t \in [0, T]$.*

Proof. Transforming $v_t = r_t^\ell$ with the Itô lemma yields:

$$dv_t = (\ell)r_t^{\ell-1}\left(\kappa(t)\left(\theta(t)r_t^{-(\ell-1)} - r_t\right)dt + \sigma(t)r_t^{-\frac{\ell-2}{2}}dW_t\right) + \frac{1}{2}(\ell)(\ell-1)r_t^{\ell-2}\left(\sigma(t)r_t^{-\frac{\ell-2}{2}}dW_t\right)^2$$

$$= \left(\ell\kappa(t)\left(\theta(t) - r_t^\ell\right) + \frac{1}{2}(\ell)(\ell-1)\sigma^2(t)\right)dt + \ell\sigma(t)r_t^{\frac{1}{2}\ell}dW_t$$

$$= \ell\kappa(t)\left(\theta(t) - r_t^\ell + \frac{(\ell-1)\sigma^2(t)}{2\kappa(t)}\right)dt + \ell\sigma(t)r_t^{\frac{1}{2}\ell}dW_t$$

$$= \ell\kappa(t)\left(\theta(t) + \frac{(\ell-1)\sigma^2(t)}{2\kappa(t)} - v_t\right)dt + \ell\sigma(t)\sqrt{v_t}dW_t$$

$$= A_\ell(t)(B_\ell(t) - v_t)dt + C_\ell(t)\sqrt{v_t}dW_t,$$

where $A_\ell(t) = \ell\kappa(t)$, $B_\ell(t) = \theta(t) + (\ell-1)\sigma^2(t)/2\kappa(t)$ and $C_\ell(t) = \ell\sigma(t)$. Thus, v_t is an ECIR process. Under Assumptions 1 and 2, the functions A_ℓ, B_ℓ and C_ℓ are strictly positive, smooth and continuous time-dependent parameter functions on $[0, T]$. Additionally, we have that:

$$2A_\ell(t)B_\ell(t) = 2\ell\kappa(t)\left(\theta(t) + \frac{(\ell-1)\sigma^2(t)}{2\kappa(t)}\right)$$

$$= \ell\left(2\kappa(t)\theta(t) + (\ell-1)\sigma^2(t)\right)$$

$$> \ell\left(\sigma^2(t) + (\ell-1)\sigma^2(t)\right) = C_\ell^2(t).$$

By the Feller condition [18], the SDE (2) has a pathwise unique strong solution in which v_t avoids zero almost surely under measure $\mathcal{P}$ for all $0 < t \leq T$ and so does r_t. □

From now on, we will always assume Assumptions 1 and 2 with $r_0 > 0$.

3. Main Results

In this section, we give the closed-form formula of conditional moments of processes (2) and (3). Applying the Feynman–Kac technique and assuming a special form of the conditional moment, we can express the solution of the resulting PDE as an infinite series and solve the system of recursive ODEs to obtain coefficients for the closed-form formula. The results for some special cases are also displayed.

In this work, under the probability measure $\mathcal{P}$ and σ–field $\mathcal{F}_t$, we first propose the integral-form formula for the conditional moment of an IND-CEV process for $\gamma > 0$:

$$u_\ell^{\langle\gamma\rangle}(r,\tau) := \mathbf{E}\left[r_T^\gamma \mid r_t = r\right], \tag{4}$$

for all $r > 0$ and $\tau := T - t \in (0, T]$. Obviously, $u_\ell^{\langle\gamma\rangle}(r,0) = r^\gamma$. The key idea involves a system with a recurrence differential equation that brings about the PDE by involving an asymmetric matrix. The form of PDE's solution associated with the conditional moment (4) is a polynomial expression motivated by [16,17,19–24]. Hence, we can solve its coefficients to obtain a closed-form formula directly.

Theorem 2. Let r_t be an IND-CEV process satisfying (2). Assume that the γth conditional moment can be expressed in the form:

$$u_\ell^{\langle\gamma\rangle}(r,\tau) = \sum_{k=0}^{\infty} A_\ell^{\langle k\rangle}(\tau) r^{\gamma-\ell k} \tag{5}$$

in which the infinite series uniformly converges on $D_\ell^{\langle\gamma\rangle} \subseteq (0,\infty) \times (0,T]$. Then, the coefficients in (5) can be expressed recursively by:

$$\begin{aligned}
A_\ell^{\langle 0\rangle}(\tau) &:= e^{-\int_0^\tau P_\ell^{\langle 0\rangle}(T-\xi)d\xi}, \\
A_\ell^{\langle k\rangle}(\tau) &:= \int_0^\tau e^{-\int_\eta^\tau P_\ell^{\langle k\rangle}(T-\xi)d\xi} Q_\ell^{\langle k-1\rangle}(T-\eta) A_\ell^{\langle k-1\rangle}(\eta) d\eta,
\end{aligned} \tag{6}$$

for all $k \in \mathbb{N}$, where:

$$P_\ell^{\langle j\rangle}(\tau) := (\gamma - \ell j)\kappa(\tau), \tag{7}$$

$$Q_\ell^{\langle j\rangle}(\tau) := (\gamma - \ell j)\left(\frac{1}{2}(\gamma - \ell j - 1)\sigma^2(\tau) + \kappa(\tau)\theta(\tau)\right). \tag{8}$$

Proof. Applying the Feynman–Kac formula to the SDE (2), we have that the function $u := u_\ell^{\langle\gamma\rangle}(r,\tau)$ satisfies the PDE:

$$u_\tau - \frac{1}{2}\sigma^2(T-\tau)r^{-(\ell-2)}u_{rr} - \kappa(T-\tau)\left(\theta(T-\tau)r^{-(\ell-1)} - r\right)u_r = 0 \tag{9}$$

for all $r > 0$ and $0 < \tau \leq T$, with the initial condition:

$$u_\ell^{\langle\gamma\rangle}(r,0) = \mathbb{E}[r_T^\gamma \mid r_T = r] = r^\gamma. \tag{10}$$

From (5), $u_\ell^{\langle\gamma\rangle}(r,0) = \sum_{k=0}^{\infty} A_\ell^{\langle k\rangle}(0) r^{\gamma-\ell k}$. Comparing this with (10) implies that $A_\ell^{\langle 0\rangle}(0) = 1$ and $A_\ell^{\langle k\rangle}(0) = 0$ for all $k \in \mathbb{N}$. Substituting (5) into (9), we have that:

$$\begin{aligned}
0 = &\sum_{k=0}^{\infty} \frac{d}{d\tau} A_\ell^{\langle k\rangle}(\tau) r^{\gamma-\ell k} \\
&- \frac{1}{2}\sigma^2(T-\tau)r^{-(\ell-2)} \sum_{k=0}^{\infty}\left((\gamma-\ell k)(\gamma-\ell k - 1)A_\ell^{\langle k\rangle}(\tau) r^{\gamma-\ell k-2}\right) \\
&- \kappa(T-\tau)\left(\theta(T-\tau)r^{-(\ell-1)} - r\right) \sum_{k=0}^{\infty}\left((\gamma-\ell k)A_\ell^{\langle k\rangle}(\tau) r^{\gamma-\ell k-1}\right)
\end{aligned}$$

or it can be simplified as:

$$\begin{aligned}
0 = &\left(\frac{d}{d\tau}A_\ell^{\langle 0\rangle}(\tau) + \gamma\kappa(T-\tau)A_\ell^{\langle 0\rangle}(\tau)\right)r^\gamma \\
&+ \sum_{k=1}^{\infty}\left(\frac{d}{d\tau}A_\ell^{\langle k\rangle}(\tau) + P_\ell^{\langle k\rangle}(T-\tau)A_\ell^{\langle k\rangle}(\tau) - Q_\ell^{\langle k-1\rangle}(T-\tau)A_\ell^{\langle k-1\rangle}(\tau)\right)r^{\gamma-\ell k}.
\end{aligned}$$

Under the assumption that the solution is in the form (5) over $D_\ell^{\langle\gamma\rangle}$, this equation can be solved through the system of ODEs:

$$\begin{aligned}
0 &= \frac{d}{d\tau}A_\ell^{\langle 0\rangle}(\tau) + \gamma\kappa(T-\tau)A_\ell^{\langle 0\rangle}(\tau), \\
0 &= \frac{d}{d\tau}A_\ell^{\langle k\rangle}(\tau) + P_\ell^{\langle k\rangle}(T-\tau)A_\ell^{\langle k\rangle}(\tau) - Q_\ell^{\langle k-1\rangle}(T-\tau)A_\ell^{\langle k-1\rangle}(\tau),
\end{aligned} \tag{11}$$

with initial conditions $A_\ell^{(0)}(0) = 1$ and $A_\ell^{(k)}(0) = 0$ for $k \in \mathbb{N}$. Hence, the coefficients in the infinite series (5) can be directly acquired by solving the system (11), which turns out to be the recursive relation given in (6). □

Note that when we define variables or notations using the := sign, e.g., Equations (6)–(8), we will use those variables or notations throughout this work.

Observe that (5) becomes a finite sum when one of the two factors for $Q_\ell^{(j)}(\tau)$ in (8) is zero. For fixing $\ell > 0$, we give the consequence of (5) in Theorem 2 when $\gamma/\ell \in \mathbb{Z}^+$. The infinite sum in (5) is cut off at a finite order and can be presented as in the following corollary.

Corollary 1. *Let r_t be an IND-CEV process satisfying (2). For the positive real number γ such that $\gamma/\ell \in \mathbb{Z}^+$, the γth conditional moment is explicitly given by:*

$$u_\ell^{\langle\gamma\rangle}(r,\tau) = \sum_{k=0}^{\gamma/\ell} A_\ell^{(k)}(\tau) r^{\gamma-\ell k}, \tag{12}$$

for all $(r,\tau) \in (0,\infty) \times (0,T]$.

Proof. From (8), when $j = \gamma/\ell$, we acquire that $Q_\ell^{(j)}(\tau) = 0$. From (6), the coefficients $A_\ell^{(k)}(\tau) = 0$ for all integers $k \geq \gamma/\ell + 1$. Hence, the infinite sum (5) is actually just the finite sum (12). Since any integration of a continuous function over a compact set is finite, the finite sum (12) exists for all $(r,\tau) \in (0,\infty) \times (0,T]$; hence, the infinite sum (5) uniformly converges to the finite sum (12) and $D_\ell^{\langle\gamma\rangle} = (0,\infty) \times (0,T]$. □

Another consequence of (5) in Theorem 2 is shown in the following corollary.

Corollary 2. *Assume that r_t follows SDE (2) and there exists $m \in \mathbb{Z}_0^+$ such that:*

$$\gamma = 1 - \frac{2\kappa(\tau)\theta(\tau)}{\sigma^2(\tau)} + \ell m \tag{13}$$

for all $\tau \in (0,T]$. Then,

$$u_\ell^{\langle\gamma\rangle}(r,\tau) = \sum_{k=0}^{m} A_\ell^{(k)}(\tau) r^{\gamma-\ell k}, \tag{14}$$

for all $(r,\tau) \in (0,\infty) \times (0,T]$.

Proof. From (8), when $j = m$, we have that $Q_\ell^{(j)}(\tau) = 0$. From (6), the coefficients $A_\ell^{(k)}(\tau) = 0$ for all integers $k \geq m+1$. With the same reasoning as in the proof of Corollary 1, we acquire the desired result. □

One main concern when we investigate the conditional moments described by the IND-CEV process is that the integral terms (6) in Theorem 2 cannot be directly evaluated. Thus, a very accurate numerical integration scheme is applied via the Chebyshev integration method; see [25–28] for more details.

Next, we consider the case when $\kappa(\tau), \theta(\tau)$ and $\sigma(\tau)$ are constant functions.

Theorem 3. *If r_t follows the SDE (3) and the γth conditional moment can be expressed in the form (5), then the γth conditional moment is given by:*

$$u_\ell^{\langle\gamma\rangle}(r,\tau) = \sum_{k=0}^{\infty} \frac{e^{-\gamma\kappa\tau}}{k!} \left(\frac{e^{\kappa\tau\ell}-1}{\kappa\ell}\right)^k \left(\prod_{j=0}^{k-1} \tilde{Q}_\ell^{(j)}\right) r^{\gamma-\ell k}, \tag{15}$$

for all $(r, \tau) \in D_\ell^{\langle \gamma \rangle}$, where:

$$\tilde{Q}_\ell^{\langle j \rangle} := (\gamma - \ell j)\left(\frac{1}{2}(\gamma - \ell j - 1)\sigma^2 + \kappa\theta\right). \quad (16)$$

Note that the product from 0 to -1, $\prod_{j=0}^{-1} \tilde{Q}_\ell^{\langle j \rangle}$, is defined to be 1.

Proof. We will prove by induction that:

$$A_\ell^{\langle k \rangle}(\tau) = \frac{e^{-\gamma\kappa\tau}}{k!}\left(\frac{e^{\kappa\tau\ell} - 1}{\kappa\ell}\right)^k \left(\prod_{j=0}^{k-1} \tilde{Q}_\ell^{\langle j \rangle}\right)$$

for all $k \in \mathbb{N} \cup \{0\}$. From (6) with the constant parameters κ, θ and σ, we have that $A_\ell^{\langle 0 \rangle}(\tau) = e^{-\gamma\kappa\tau}$ and

$$A_\ell^{\langle k \rangle}(\tau) = \tilde{Q}_\ell^{\langle k-1 \rangle} \int_0^\tau e^{-(\tau - \eta)(\gamma - \ell k)\kappa} A_\ell^{\langle k-1 \rangle}(\eta) d\eta, \quad (17)$$

for all $k \in \mathbb{N}$. By substituting $k = 1$ in (17), we obtain:

$$A_\ell^{\langle 1 \rangle}(\tau) = e^{-\gamma\kappa\tau}\left(\frac{e^{\kappa\tau\ell} - 1}{\kappa\ell}\right)\tilde{Q}_\ell^{\langle 0 \rangle}.$$

Let $k \in \mathbb{N}$. Assume that:

$$A_\ell^{\langle k-1 \rangle}(\tau) = \frac{e^{-\gamma\kappa\tau}}{(k-1)!}\left(\frac{e^{\kappa\tau\ell} - 1}{\kappa\ell}\right)^{k-1}\left(\prod_{j=0}^{k-2} \tilde{Q}_\ell^{\langle j \rangle}\right).$$

From (17), we have that:

$$A_\ell^{\langle k \rangle}(\tau) = e^{-(\gamma - \ell k)\kappa\tau}\tilde{Q}_\ell^{\langle k-1 \rangle} \int_0^\tau e^{(\gamma - \ell k)\kappa\eta} A_\ell^{\langle k-1 \rangle}(\eta) d\eta$$

$$= \frac{e^{-(\gamma - \ell k)\kappa\tau}}{(k-1)!(\kappa\ell)^{k-1}}\left(\prod_{j=0}^{k-1} \tilde{Q}_\ell^{\langle j \rangle}\right) \int_0^\tau e^{-k\ell\kappa\eta}\left(e^{\kappa\eta\ell} - 1\right)^{k-1} d\eta$$

$$= \frac{e^{-\gamma\kappa\tau}}{k!}\left(\frac{e^{\kappa\tau\ell} - 1}{\kappa\ell}\right)^k \left(\prod_{j=0}^{k-1} \tilde{Q}_\ell^{\langle j \rangle}\right). \quad \square$$

From Corollaries 1 and 2, when $\kappa(\tau), \theta(\tau)$ and $\sigma(\tau)$ are constant functions, we have the following corollaries.

Corollary 3. Assume that r_t follows SDE (3). For a positive real number γ such that $\gamma/\ell \in \mathbb{Z}^+$, the γth conditional moment is explicitly given by:

$$u_\ell^{\langle \gamma \rangle}(r, \tau) = \sum_{k=0}^{\gamma/\ell} \frac{e^{-\gamma\kappa\tau}}{k!}\left(\frac{e^{\kappa\tau\ell} - 1}{\kappa\ell}\right)^k \left(\prod_{j=0}^{k-1} \tilde{Q}_\ell^{\langle j \rangle}\right) r^{\gamma - \ell k}, \quad (18)$$

for all $(r, \tau) \in (0, \infty) \times (0, T]$. Note that the product of $\tilde{Q}_\ell^{\langle j \rangle}$ in (18) for $k = 0$ is defined to be 1.

Corollary 4. Assume that r_t follows the SDE (3). If there exists $m \in \mathbb{Z}_0^+$ such that

$$\gamma = 1 - \frac{2\kappa\theta}{\sigma^2} + \ell m, \quad (19)$$

then

$$u_\ell^{\langle\gamma\rangle}(r,\tau) = \sum_{k=0}^{m} \frac{e^{-\gamma\kappa\tau}}{k!}\left(\frac{e^{\kappa\tau\ell}-1}{\kappa\ell}\right)^k \left(\prod_{j=0}^{k-1}\widetilde{Q}_\ell^{\langle j\rangle}\right) r^{\gamma-\ell k}, \qquad (20)$$

for all $(r,\tau) \in (0,\infty) \times (0,T]$.

For SDE (3), characterization for the convergence of the series (15) can be provided.

Theorem 4. *Assume that r_t follows SDE (3) and $\widetilde{Q}_\ell^{\langle j\rangle} \neq 0$ for all $j \in \mathbb{Z}_0^+$. Then, the series (15) diverges for all $(r,\tau) \in (0,\infty) \times (0,T]$.*

Proof. Since $\widetilde{Q}_\ell^{\langle j\rangle} \neq 0$ for all $j \in \mathbb{Z}_0^+$, we have that $\gamma - \ell k \neq 0$ and $(\gamma - \ell k - 1)\sigma^2/2 + \kappa\theta \neq 0$ for all $k \in \mathbb{Z}_0^+$.

$$\lim_{k\to\infty}\left|\frac{A_\ell^{\langle k+1\rangle}(\tau) r^{\gamma-\ell(k+1)}}{A_\ell^{\langle k\rangle}(\tau) r^{\gamma-\ell k}}\right| = \lim_{k\to\infty}\left|\frac{\frac{e^{-\gamma\kappa\tau}}{(k+1)!}\left(\frac{e^{\kappa\tau\ell}-1}{\kappa\ell}\right)^{k+1}\left(\prod_{j=0}^{k}\widetilde{Q}_\ell^{\langle j\rangle}\right) r^{\gamma-\ell(k+1)}}{\frac{e^{-\gamma\kappa\tau}}{k!}\left(\frac{e^{\kappa\tau\ell}-1}{\kappa\ell}\right)^{k}\left(\prod_{j=0}^{k-1}\widetilde{Q}_\ell^{\langle j\rangle}\right) r^{\gamma-\ell k}}\right|$$

$$= \lim_{k\to\infty}\left|\frac{\left(e^{\kappa\tau\ell}-1\right)\left(\gamma-\ell k\right)\left(\frac{1}{2}(\gamma-\ell k-1)\sigma^2+\kappa\theta\right)}{(k+1)\kappa\ell r^\ell}\right|.$$

The above expression is $\mathcal{O}(k)$ as $k \to \infty$; hence, the limit diverges. By ratio test, the series (15) diverges for all $(r,\tau) \in (0,\infty) \times (0,T]$. □

From Corollaries 3 and 4, and Theorem 4, we have the following result.

Corollary 5. *Assume that r_t follows SDE (3). Then, the series (15) converges for all $(r,\tau) \in (0,\infty) \times (0,T]$ if and only if:*

1. *$\frac{\gamma}{\ell} \in \mathbb{Z}^+$, or*
2. *$\frac{1}{\ell}\left(\gamma - 1 + \frac{2\kappa\theta}{\sigma^2}\right) \in \mathbb{Z}_0^+$.*

The convergent results for case 1 and 2 are given in Corollaries 3 and 4, respectively.

4. Probabilistic Properties

This section illustrates some usefulness of our results from Section 3 including the first, second and fractional conditional moments; conditional variance and central moments; conditional mixed moments; and conditional covariance and correlation.

Example 1 (The conditional moments). *From Corollary 1, the nth conditional moment of an IND-CEV process when the parameter $\ell = 1/L$ for some $L \in \mathbb{N}$ is given by:*

$$\mathbb{E}[r_T^n \mid r_t = r] = u_\ell^{\langle n\rangle}(r,\tau) = \sum_{k=0}^{nL} A_\ell^{\langle k\rangle}(\tau) r^{n-\frac{k}{L}},$$

where:

$$A_\ell^{\langle 0\rangle}(\tau) = e^{-\int_0^\tau P_\ell^{\langle 0\rangle}(T-\xi)d\xi},$$

$$A_\ell^{\langle k\rangle}(\tau) = \int_0^\tau e^{-\int_\eta^\tau P_\ell^{\langle k\rangle}(T-\xi)d\xi} Q_\ell^{\langle k-1\rangle}(T-\eta) A_\ell^{\langle k-1\rangle}(\eta) d\eta,$$

for $k \in \mathbb{N}$, where:

$$P_\ell^{(j)}(\tau) = \left(n - \frac{j}{L}\right)\kappa(\tau),$$

$$Q_\ell^{(j)}(\tau) = \left(n - \frac{j}{L}\right)\left(\frac{1}{2}\left(n - \frac{j}{L} - 1\right)\sigma^2(\tau) + \kappa(\tau)\theta(\tau)\right).$$

For constants κ, θ and σ, we use $u_\ell^{(1)}(r,\tau)$ and $u_\ell^{(2)}(r,\tau)$ in Corollary 3. Then, for $L = 1$, the first and second conditional moments are given by:

$$\mathbf{E}[r_T \mid r_t = r] = (r - \theta)e^{-\kappa\tau} + \theta \qquad (21)$$

and

$$\mathbf{E}\left[r_T^2 \mid r_t = r\right] = e^{-2\kappa\tau}r^2 + \frac{(\sigma^2/2 + \kappa\theta)e^{-2\kappa\tau}}{\kappa}\left(r(e^{\kappa\tau} - 1) + \theta(e^{\kappa\tau} - 1)^2\right). \qquad (22)$$

For $L = 2$, the first and second conditional moments are given by:

$$\mathbf{E}[r_T \mid r_t = r] = e^{-\kappa\tau}\left(r + \theta\left(e^{\frac{\kappa\tau}{2}} - 1\right)\left(2r^{\frac{1}{2}} + \frac{\left(e^{\frac{\kappa\tau}{2}} - 1\right)}{\kappa}\left(-\frac{\sigma^2}{4} + \kappa\theta\right)\right)\right) \qquad (23)$$

and

$$\mathbf{E}\left[r_T^2 \mid r_t = r\right] = e^{-2\kappa\tau}\left(r^2 + \left(e^{\frac{\kappa\tau}{2}} - 1\right)\left(\frac{\sigma^2}{2} + \kappa\theta\right)\left(\frac{4}{\kappa}r^{\frac{3}{2}} + \frac{6\left(e^{\frac{\kappa\tau}{2}} - 1\right)}{\kappa^2}\left(\frac{\sigma^2}{4} + \kappa\theta\right)r\right)\right)$$

$$+ e^{-2\kappa\tau}\frac{4\left(e^{\frac{\kappa\tau}{2}} - 1\right)^3}{\kappa^2}\left(\frac{\sigma^2}{2} + \kappa\theta\right)\left(\frac{\sigma^2}{4} + \kappa\theta\right)\theta r^{\frac{1}{2}}$$

$$+ e^{-2\kappa\tau}\frac{\left(e^{\frac{\kappa\tau}{2}} - 1\right)^4}{\kappa^2}\left(\frac{\sigma^2}{2} + \kappa\theta\right)\left(\frac{\sigma^2}{4} + \kappa\theta\right)\left(-\frac{\sigma^2}{4} + \kappa\theta\right)\theta. \qquad (24)$$

Additionally, for $\ell = 3/4$, the conditional moment with $\gamma = 3/2$ is given by:

$$\mathbf{E}\left[r_T^{\frac{3}{2}} \mid r_t = r\right] = e^{-\frac{3}{2}\kappa\tau}r^{\frac{3}{2}} + 2e^{-\frac{3}{2}\kappa\tau}\left(\frac{e^{\frac{3}{4}\kappa\tau} - 1}{\kappa}\right)\left(\frac{\sigma^2}{4} + \kappa\theta\right)r^{\frac{3}{4}}$$

$$+ e^{-\frac{3}{2}\kappa\tau}\left(\frac{e^{\frac{3}{4}\kappa\tau} - 1}{\kappa}\right)^2\left(\frac{\sigma^2}{4} + \kappa\theta\right)\left(-\frac{\sigma^2}{8} + \kappa\theta\right). \qquad (25)$$

Next, we propose the consequences of Example 1, which are the conditional variance and central moments, conditional mixed moments, and conditional covariance and correlation, as follows.

Example 2 (The conditional variance and nth central moment). *By applying Corollary 3, (21) and (22), the conditional variance of the IND-CEV process can be given by:*

$$\mathbf{Var}[r_T \mid r_t = r] = \mathbf{E}\left[(r_T - \mathbf{E}[r_T \mid r_t])^2 \mid r_t = r\right] = u_\ell^{(2)}(r,\tau) - \left(u_\ell^{(1)}(r,\tau)\right)^2,$$

where $u_\ell^{(1)}(r,\tau)$ and $u_\ell^{(2)}(r,\tau)$ are derived in (21) and (22) for the CIR process. In general, the nth central moment is presented by:

$$\mu_n(r,\tau) := \mathbf{E}\left[(r_T - \mathbf{E}[r_T \mid r_t])^n \mid r_t = r\right] = \sum_{j=0}^{n}(-1)^{n-j}\binom{n}{j}\left(u_\ell^{(j)}(r,\tau)\right)\left(u_\ell^{(1)}(r,\tau)\right)^{n-j}$$

where $u_\ell^{(0)}(r,\tau) := 1$.

Example 3 (The conditional mixed moments). *By applying the tower property for $0 \leq t < T_1 < T_2$, where $\tau_1 = T_1 - t$ and $\tau_2 = T_2 - T_1$ and Corollary 1, the conditional mixed moment of the IND-CEV process (2) with $\ell = 1/L$ is given by:*

$$\begin{aligned}
\mathbf{E}\left[r_{T_1}^{n_1} r_{T_2}^{n_2} \mid r_t = r\right] &= \mathbf{E}\left[r_{T_1}^{n_1}\mathbf{E}\left[r_{T_2}^{n_2} \mid r_{T_1}\right] \mid r_t = r\right] = \mathbf{E}\left[r_{T_1}^{n_1}u_\ell^{\langle n_2\rangle}(r_{T_1}, T_2 - T_1) \mid r_t = r\right] \\
&= \sum_{k=0}^{n_2 L} A_\ell^{\langle k\rangle}(\tau_2)\mathbf{E}\left[r_{T_1}^{n_1+n_2-\frac{k}{L}} \mid r_t = r\right] \\
&= \sum_{k=0}^{n_2 L} A_\ell^{\langle k\rangle}(\tau_2)u_\ell^{\langle n_1+n_2-\frac{k}{L}\rangle}(r, T_1 - t) \\
&= \sum_{k=0}^{n_2 L}\sum_{j=0}^{(n_1+n_2)L-k} A_\ell^{\langle k\rangle}(\tau_2)A_\ell^{\langle j\rangle}(\tau_1)r^{n_1+n_2-\frac{k+j}{L}}. \quad (26)
\end{aligned}$$

In addition, the general formula for conditional mixed moments $\mathbf{E}\left[r_{T_1}^{n_1}r_{T_2}^{n_2}\cdots r_{T_k}^{n_k} \mid r_t = r\right]$, where $n_1, n_2, \ldots, n_k \in \mathbb{Z}^+$ and $0 \leq t < T_1 < T_2 < \cdots < T_k$, for the process (3) can be analytically derived by using Corollary 3.

Example 4 (The conditional covariance and correlation). *The conditional covariance of the CIR process for $0 \leq t < T_1 < T_2$, where $\tau_1 = T_1 - t$ and $\tau_2 = T_2 - T_1$, is given by:*

$$\begin{aligned}
\mathrm{Cov}[r_{T_1}, r_{T_2} \mid r_t = r] &:= \mathbf{E}\left[(r_{T_1} - \mathbf{E}[r_{T_1} \mid r_t])(r_{T_2} - \mathbf{E}[r_{T_2} \mid r_t]) \mid r_t = r\right] \\
&= \mathbf{E}[r_{T_1}r_{T_2} \mid r_t = r] - \mathbf{E}[r_{T_1} \mid r_t = r]\mathbf{E}[r_{T_2} \mid r_t = r] \\
&= \sum_{k=0}^{1}\sum_{j=0}^{2-k} A_\ell^{\langle k\rangle}(\tau_2)A_\ell^{\langle j\rangle}(\tau_1)r^{2-k-j} - u_\ell^{(1)}(r,\tau_1)u_\ell^{(2)}(r,\tau_2). \quad (27)
\end{aligned}$$

Applying the results from (26) and (27), we obtain that the conditional correlation of the CIR process is given by:

$$\begin{aligned}
\mathrm{Corr}[r_{T_1}, r_{T_2} \mid r_t = r] &:= \frac{\mathrm{Cov}[r_{T_1}, r_{T_2} \mid r_t = r]}{\mathrm{Var}[r_{T_1} \mid r_t = r]^{1/2}\,\mathrm{Var}[r_{T_2} \mid r_t = r]^{1/2}} \\
&= \frac{\sum_{k=0}^{1}\sum_{j=0}^{2-k}A_\ell^{\langle k\rangle}(\tau_2)A_\ell^{\langle j\rangle}(\tau_1)r^{2-k-j} - u_1^{(1)}(r,\tau_1)u_1^{(2)}(r,\tau_2)}{\left(u_1^{(2)}(r,\tau_1) - \left(u_1^{(1)}(r,\tau_1)\right)^2\right)^{1/2}\left(u_1^{(2)}(r,\tau_2) - \left(u_1^{(1)}(r,\tau_2)\right)^2\right)^{1/2}}. \quad (28)
\end{aligned}$$

We can generalize (27) and (28) by using (26) as the closed forms of $\mathrm{Cov}\left[r_{T_1}^{n_1}, r_{T_2}^{n_2} \mid r_t = r\right]$ and $\mathrm{Corr}\left[r_{T_1}^{n_1}, r_{T_2}^{n_2} \mid r_t = r\right]$, where n_1 and n_2 are positive integers.

5. Unconditional Moments of the IND-CEV Process

This section provides the formula of the unconditional moments of the IND-CEV process with constant parameters as $\tau \to \infty$ reduced from the formula of conditional moments.

Theorem 5. *Assume that r_t follows SDE (3). Then, for all $\gamma/\ell \in \mathbb{Z}^+$,*

$$\lim_{\tau \to \infty} u_\ell^{\langle \gamma \rangle}(r,\tau) = \prod_{j=1}^{\gamma/\ell} \frac{2\kappa\theta + (\ell j - 1)\sigma^2}{2\kappa}. \tag{29}$$

Proof. Let $s = \gamma/\ell \in \mathbb{Z}^+$. By considering (18) in Corollary 3, the coefficient terms of $r^{\gamma-\ell k}$ converge to 0 as $\tau \to \infty$ for $k = 0, 1, 2, \ldots, s-1$. Thus, the summation (18) is reduced to only one term, where $k = s$,

$$\lim_{\tau \to \infty} u_\ell^{\langle \gamma \rangle}(r,\tau) = \lim_{\tau \to \infty} \frac{e^{-\gamma\kappa\tau}}{s!} \left(\frac{e^{\kappa\tau\ell} - 1}{\kappa\ell} \right)^s \left(\prod_{j=0}^{s-1} \widetilde{Q}_\ell^{\langle j \rangle} \right) r^{\gamma - \ell s}$$

$$= \frac{1}{s!(\kappa\ell)^s} \left(\prod_{j=0}^{s-1} \widetilde{Q}_\ell^{\langle j \rangle} \right) \lim_{\tau \to \infty} e^{-\gamma\kappa\tau} \left(e^{\kappa\tau\ell} - 1 \right)^s$$

$$= \frac{1}{s!(\kappa\ell)^s} \left(\prod_{j=0}^{s-1} \widetilde{Q}_\ell^{\langle j \rangle} \right) \lim_{\tau \to \infty} \left(1 - e^{-\kappa\tau\ell} \right)^s$$

$$= \frac{1}{s!(\kappa\ell)^s} \left(\prod_{j=0}^{s-1} \widetilde{Q}_\ell^{\langle j \rangle} \right),$$

where $\widetilde{Q}_\ell^{\langle j \rangle}$ is defined in (16). By expressing $\widetilde{Q}_\ell^{\langle j \rangle}$ to the above equation, it can be performed to

$$\lim_{\tau \to \infty} u_\ell^{\langle \gamma \rangle}(r,\tau) = \frac{1}{s!(\kappa\ell)^s} \prod_{j=0}^{s-1} (\gamma - \ell j) \left(\frac{1}{2}(\gamma - \ell j - 1)\sigma^2 + \kappa\theta \right) = \prod_{j=1}^{\gamma/\ell} \frac{2\kappa\theta + (\ell j - 1)\sigma^2}{2\kappa}. \quad \square$$

Note that the formula for unconditional moments does not rely on the initial value r, and these unconditional moments represent the moments of the stationary distribution of the process (3).

6. Experimental Validation

In this section, we validate the closed-form formulas presented in Theorem 2 and Corollaries 1 and 2. The Euler–Maruyama (EM) method was applied to simulate the process (2) and approximate the conditional moments based on the symmetry concept. For an interval $[0, \tau]$, let $\Delta = \tau/N$ for a fixed $N \in \mathbb{N}$ and $t_i = \Delta i$ for $i = 0, 1, \ldots, N$. We denote a numerical solution of the IND-CEV process at time t_i by $\hat{r}_{t_i}$. The EM approximation of (2) on the interval $[0, \tau]$ is defined as $\hat{r}_0 = r$ and

$$\hat{r}_{t_{i+1}} = \hat{r}_{t_i} + \kappa(t_i)\left(\theta(t_i)\hat{r}_{t_i}^{-(\ell-1)} - \hat{r}_t\right)\Delta t + \sigma(t_i)\hat{r}_{t_i}^{\frac{-(\ell-2)}{2}}\sqrt{\Delta}W_{i+1} \tag{30}$$

where $W_1, W_2, \ldots, W_N$ are N independent standard normal random variables. In this validation, the MC simulations based on the EM method (30) were conducted by MATLAB R2021a software on a quadcore Intel Core i5-1035G1 with 8 GB RAM.

Example 5. *In this example, we apply the MC simulations based on the CEV process [15]:*

$$dr_t = \kappa \left(\frac{\sigma_0^2 d e^{2\sigma_1 t}}{4\kappa} r_t^{-(\ell-1)} - r_t \right) dt + \sigma_0 e^{\sigma_1 t} r_t^{-\frac{\ell-2}{2}} dW_t \tag{31}$$

where κ and σ_0 are positive constants, σ_1 is a non-negative constant and d is a positive integer greater than 2. By considering (31) and (2), the parameter functions for SDE (31) are $\kappa(t) = \kappa$,

$\theta(t) = d\sigma_0^2 e^{2\sigma_1 t}/4\kappa$ and $\sigma(t) = \sigma_0 e^{\sigma_1 t}$. Note that Assumptions 1 and 2 hold for these parameter functions. By Theorem 2, we have that:

$$u_\ell^{\langle\gamma\rangle}(r,\tau) = e^{-\gamma\kappa\tau} \sum_{k=0}^{\infty} \xi_k \qquad (32)$$

where:

$$\xi_k := \frac{1}{k!}\left(\prod_{j=0}^{k-1}(\gamma-\ell j)(d+2(\gamma-\ell j-1))\right)\left(\frac{\sigma_0^2 e^{2\sigma_1(T-\tau)}\left(e^{2\sigma_1\tau+\kappa\tau\ell}-1\right)}{4(2\sigma_1+\kappa\ell)}\right)^k r^{\gamma-\ell k}. \qquad (33)$$

However, Formula (32) can be reduced to a finite sum for a particular situation. By Corollary 1, if $\gamma/\ell \in \mathbb{Z}^+$, then:

$$u_\ell^{\langle\gamma\rangle}(r,\tau) = e^{-\gamma\kappa\tau} \sum_{k=0}^{\gamma/\ell} \xi_k. \qquad (34)$$

By Corollary 2, if there exists $m \in \mathbb{Z}_0^+$ such that $\gamma = 1 - 2\kappa(\tau)\theta(\tau)/\sigma^2(\tau) + \ell m$, which is $1 - d/2 + \ell m$ in this example, for all $\tau \in (0, T]$, then:

$$u_\ell^{\langle\gamma\rangle}(r,\tau) = e^{-\gamma\kappa\tau} \sum_{k=0}^{m} \xi_k. \qquad (35)$$

Our experiments are classified into three cases: (i) $\gamma/\ell \in \mathbb{Z}^+$, (ii) $(\gamma-1+d/2)/\ell \in \mathbb{Z}_0^+$, and (iii) $\gamma/\ell \notin \mathbb{Z}^+$ and $(\gamma-1+d/2)/\ell \notin \mathbb{Z}_0^+$. The algorithm of our validation is given in Algorithm 1. The parameters $\ell = 2/3$, $\sigma_0 = 0.01$, $\sigma_1 = 0.02$, $\kappa = 0.03$ and $T = 10$ in the process (31) are set for all of these three cases. MC simulations were performed at each initial value $r = 0.1, 0.2, \ldots, 2$ and $\tau = 1, 2, \ldots, 10$.

Algorithm 1 MC validation for the process (31)

1: Set the values for parameters $\ell, \gamma, d, \kappa, \sigma_0, \sigma_1, T$
2: $N_0 \leftarrow \begin{cases} \gamma/\ell & \text{if } \gamma/\ell \in \mathbb{Z}^+ \\ (\gamma-1+d/2)/\ell & \text{if } (\gamma-1+d/2)/\ell \in \mathbb{Z}^+ \\ \text{the number of terms in (32)} & \text{if } \gamma/\ell \notin \mathbb{Z}^+ \text{ and } (\gamma-1+d/2)/\ell \notin \mathbb{Z}^+ \end{cases}$
3: Compute $u(r,\tau) = e^{-\gamma\kappa\tau} \sum_{k=0}^{N_0} \xi_k$ according to (33) for a refined grid of variables r and τ
4: Plot a surface of $u(r,\tau)$ representing the conditional moments from our formulas
5: Construct a grid of variables r and τ to perform MC simulation
6: For each initial value r and final time τ, apply the EM method with 1000 time steps to the process (31) to get $\hat{r}_\tau$ with 1000 sample paths and compute the average value of $\hat{r}_\tau^\gamma$
7: Plot the resulting values and compare them with the surface of $u(r,\tau)$

For the case when $\gamma/\ell \in \mathbb{Z}^+$, we set $d = 3$ and consider two different values of γ. Here, we choose $\gamma = 2$ and $8/3$. Figure 1 shows the comparison between Formula (34) and MC simulations. The results from MC simulations are presented by blue star markers, and Formula (34) is presented by the solid surfaces. All markers perfectly match with the surfaces. This indicates that our formula from Corollary 1 is correct. The validation runtimes for $\gamma = 2$ and $8/3$ were 23.82 and 22.30 s, respectively.

For the case when $(\gamma-1+d/2)/\ell \in \mathbb{Z}_0^+$, we set $d = 4$ and consider $\gamma = 1$ and $5/3$. Figure 2 demonstrates the comparison between Formula (35) and MC simulations. Evidently, the results from MC simulations and the surfaces from Formula (35) are completely coincident. Validation runtimes for $\gamma = 1$ and $5/3$ were 22.34 and 22.63 s, respectively.

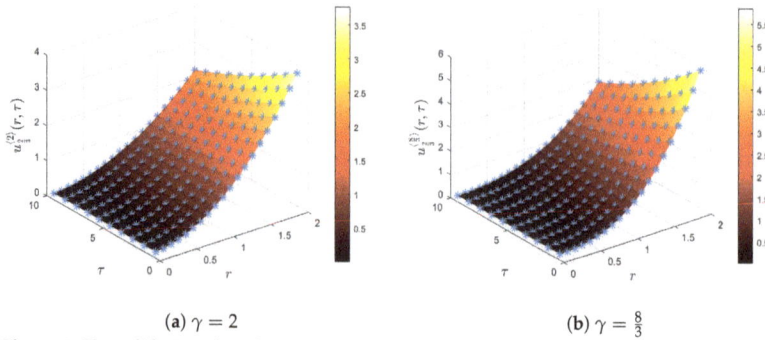

(a) $\gamma = 2$ (b) $\gamma = \frac{8}{3}$

Figure 1. The validation of conditional moments for process (31) where $\ell = 2/3$, $\sigma_0 = 0.01$, $\sigma_1 = 0.02$, $\kappa = 0.03$, $T = 10$ and $d = 3$ with MC simulations.

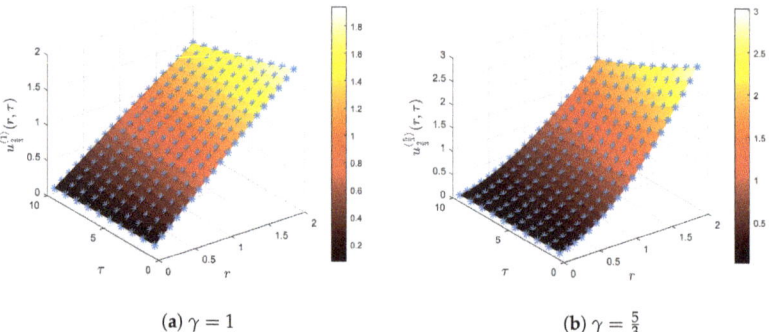

(a) $\gamma = 1$ (b) $\gamma = \frac{5}{3}$

Figure 2. The validation of conditional moments for process (31) where $\ell = 2/3$, $\sigma_0 = 0.01$, $\sigma_1 = 0.02$, $\kappa = 0.03$, $T = 10$ and $d = 4$ with MC simulations.

For the case when $\gamma/\ell \notin \mathbb{Z}_0^+$ and $(\gamma - 1 + d/2)/\ell \notin \mathbb{Z}_0^+$, we set $d = 5$ and consider $\gamma = 1$. Observe that from (33), $|\xi_{k+1}/\xi_k|$ is $\mathcal{O}(k)$ as $k \to \infty$; thus, $\lim_{k \to \infty} |\xi_{k+1}/\xi_k| = \infty$ for $(r, \tau) \in (0, \infty) \times (0, T]$. By the ratio test, the summation $\sum_{k=0}^{\infty} \xi_k$ diverges; hence, Formula (32) diverges for all $(r, \tau) \in (0, \infty) \times (0, T]$. This means that the conditional moment cannot be expressed in the form (5). However, our experiment shows that finite terms of the summation in Formula (32) can be used to approximate the conditional moment. Figure 3 shows the comparison between the formula

$$S_n(r, \tau) := e^{-\gamma \kappa \tau} \sum_{k=0}^{n} \xi_k \qquad (36)$$

for $n = 10, 1000$ and MC simulations. The results from MC simulations coincide with the surface from Formula (36) with $n = 10$. For $n = 1000$, the results from Formula (36) could not be computed by our machine. This supports our theory that Formula (32) diverges. Validation runtimes for $n = 10$ and $n = 1000$ were 22.76 and 26.98 s, respectively.

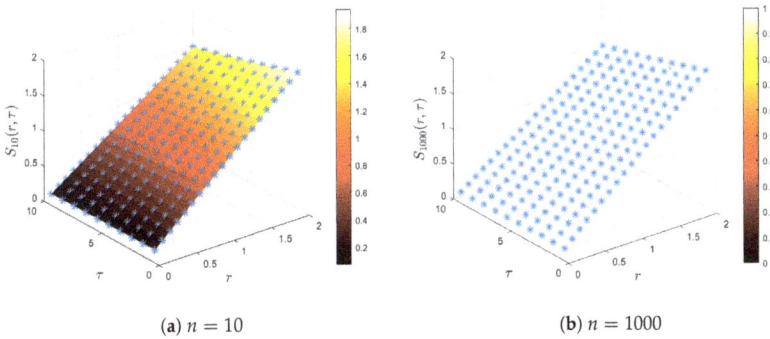

(a) $n = 10$ (b) $n = 1000$

Figure 3. The validation of conditional moments for process (31) where $\ell = 2/3$, $\gamma = 1$, $\sigma_0 = 0.01$, $\sigma_1 = 0.02$, $\kappa = 0.03$, $T = 10$ and $d = 5$ with MC simulations.

The next example shows a similar result of the third case in Example 5 for the IND-CEV process with constant parameter functions.

Example 6. For SDE (3) with $\ell = 2/3$, $\kappa = 0.03$, $\theta = 0.003$, $\sigma = 0.01$, $\gamma = 1$ and $T = 10$, we have that $\gamma/\ell \notin \mathbb{Z}^+$ and $(\gamma - 1 + 2\kappa\theta/\sigma^2)/\ell \notin \mathbb{Z}_0^+$. From Corollary 5, $u_{2/3}^{(1)}(r, \tau)$ cannot be expressed in the form (5). However, our experiment shows that finite terms of the summation in Formula (15) can be used to approximate the conditional moment. Let:

$$\widetilde{S}_n(r, \tau) := \sum_{k=0}^{n} \frac{e^{-\kappa\tau}}{k!} \left(\frac{e^{2\kappa\tau} - 1}{2\kappa}\right)^k \left(\prod_{j=0}^{k-1} (1 - 2j)\left(\kappa\theta - j\sigma^2\right)\right) r^{1-2k}. \quad (37)$$

Figure 4 shows the comparison for Formula (37) between $n = 10, 1000$ and MC simulations. All blue markers match with the surface from the formula with $n = 10$, even though $\widetilde{S}_n(r, \tau)$ diverges as $n \to \infty$. Validation runtimes for $n = 10$ and $n = 1000$ were 22.79 and 26.96 s, respectively.

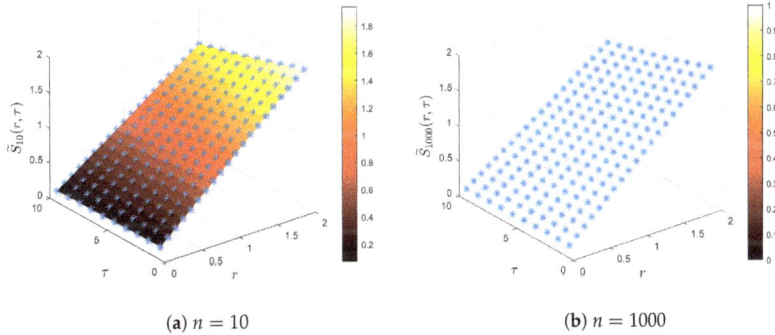

(a) $n = 10$ (b) $n = 1000$

Figure 4. The validation of conditional moments for process (3) where $\ell = 2/3$, $\gamma = 1$, $\kappa = 0.03$, $\theta = 0.003$ and $\sigma = 0.01$ and $T = 10$ with MC simulations.

7. Conclusions, Limitations and Future Researches

In this study, we focused on the IND-CEV process (2) and a special case when the parameter functions are constants, which leads to process (3). We gave the sufficient conditions for SDE (2) in order to have a unique positive path-wise strong solution. We have derived the explicit formulas of conditional moments for this process. The derived formula for process (2) is shown in Theorem 2 in terms of infinite series. The formula can be reduced from infinite sum to finite sum for two situations: (i) the case when $\gamma/\ell \in \mathbb{Z}^+$, and (ii) condition (13), which are shown in Corollaries 1 and 2. Furthermore, we have presented the formula for process (3), where the parameter functions are constant, in Theorem 3. As a consequence, formulas for special situations are expressed in Corollaries 3 and 4. The characterization for the convergence of the infinite sum in the formula for process (3) is discussed in Theorem 4 and summarized in Corollary 5.

The use of our results was illustrated. This includes conditional moments, conditional variance and central moments, conditional mixed moments, conditional covariance and correlation. In addition, the moments of the stationary distribution of process (3) were proposed in Theorem 5.

Moreover, we have validated our closed-form formulas for process (2) by comparing the calculated values of conditional moments from our formula with the MC simulations via a number of experimental examples in Section 6. Our results in each situation have completely matched with MC simulations. Moreover, for some moments γ whose formula cannot be reduced to a finite sum, we can approximate the conditional moments by displaying the numerical result of the finite sum with suitable order. It turns out that the obtained results have good accuracy when compared with the MC simulations.

One major concern is that our proposed formulas in Theorem 2 and Corollaries 1 and 2 are not in closed form when integral terms cannot be analytically computed. In this case, a numerical method can be applied to calculate the coefficients numerically; see [28,29].

In the context of future works, our proposed closed-form formulas under the IND-CEV process have further beneficial aspects for pricing financial derivatives, such as moment swaps and the asset whose payoff can be generated by the conditional moments, see more details in [23,30]. In addition, since the transition PDF of process (2) is complicated and does not exist in closed form, our closed-form formulas can also be applied for parameter estimations of the behavior and dynamic of observed data; see more details in [9].

Author Contributions: Conceptualization, K.C., R.T. and C.T.; methodology, K.C., R.T. and C.T.; software, K.C., R.T. and C.T.; validation, K.C., R.T. and C.T.; formal analysis, K.C., R.T. and C.T.; investigation, K.C., R.T. and C.T.; writing—original draft preparation, K.C., R.T. and C.T.; writing—review and editing, K.C., R.T. and C.T.; visualization, K.C., R.T. and C.T.; supervision, K.C. and R.T.; project administration, K.C., R.T. and C.T. All authors have read and agreed to the published version of the manuscript.

Funding: This research received no external funding.

Institutional Review Board Statement: Not applicable.

Informed Consent Statement: Not applicable.

Data Availability Statement: Not applicable.

Acknowledgments: We are grateful for a variety of valuable suggestions from the anonymous referees that have substantially improved the quality and presentation of the results. All errors are the authors' own responsibility. Thank the newborn son to make 24 June 2022 the best day of the first author's life.

Conflicts of Interest: The authors declare no conflict of interest.

Abbreviations

The following abbreviations are used in this manuscript:

CEV	Constant elasticity of variance diffusion
CIR	Cox–Ingersoll–Ross
ECIR	Extended Cox–Ingersoll–Ross
EM	Euler–Maruyama
IND	Inhomogeneous nonlinear drift
MC	Monte Carlo
MR	Marsh–Rosenfeld
ODE	Ordinary differential equation
OU	Ornstein–Uhlenbeck
PDE	Partial differential equation
PDF	Probability density function
SDE	Stochastic differential equation

References

1. Araneda, A.A.; Bertschinger, N. The sub-fractional CEV model. *Phys. Stat. Mech. Its Appl.* **2021**, *573*, 125974. [CrossRef]
2. Cao, J.; Kim, J.H.; Zhang, W. Pricing variance swaps under hybrid CEV and stochastic volatility. *J. Comput. Appl. Math.* **2021**, *386*, 113220. [CrossRef]
3. He, X.J.; Zhu, S.P. A closed-form pricing formula for European options under the Heston model with stochastic interest rate. *J. Comput. Appl. Math.* **2018**, *335*, 323–333. [CrossRef]
4. Nonsoong, P.; Mekchay, K.; Rujivan, S. An analytical option pricing formula for mean-reverting asset with time-dependent parameter. *ANZIAM J.* **2021**, *63*, 178–202.
5. Vasicek, O. An equilibrium characterization of the term structure. *J. Financ. Econ.* **1977**, *5*, 177–188. [CrossRef]
6. Cox, J.C.; Ingersoll, J.E., Jr.; Ross, S.A. A theory of the term structure of interest rates. In *Theory of Valuation*; World Scientific: Singapore, 2005; pp. 129–164.
7. Chapman, D.A.; Pearson, N.D. Is the short rate drift actually nonlinear? *J. Financ.* **2000**, *55*, 355–388. [CrossRef]
8. Jones, C.S. Nonlinear mean reversion in the short-term interest rate. *Rev. Financ. Stud.* **2003**, *16*, 793–843. [CrossRef]
9. Boonklurb, R.; Duangpan, A.; Rakwongwan, U.; Sutthimat, P. A Novel Analytical Formula for the Discounted Moments of the ECIR Process and Interest Rate Swaps Pricing. *Fractal Fract.* **2022**, *6*, 58. [CrossRef]
10. Duangpan, A.; Boonklurb, R.; Chumpong, K.; Sutthimat, P. Analytical Formulas for Conditional Mixed Moments of Generalized Stochastic Correlation Process. *Symmetry* **2022**, *14*, 897. [CrossRef]
11. Cox, J. *Notes on Option Pricing I: Constant Elasticity of Variance Diffusions*; Unpublished Note; Stanford University, Graduate School of Business: Stanford, CA, USA, 1975.
12. Marsh, T.A.; Rosenfeld, E.R. Stochastic processes for interest rates and equilibrium bond prices. *J. Financ.* **1983**, *38*, 635–646. [CrossRef]
13. Zhou, H. Itô conditional moment generator and the estimation of short-rate processes. *J. Financ. Econom.* **2003**, *1*, 250–271.
14. Hull, J.; White, A. Pricing interest-rate-derivative securities. *Rev. Financ. Stud.* **1990**, *3*, 573–592. [CrossRef]
15. Maghsoodi, Y. Solution of the extended CIR term structure and bond option valuation. *Math. Financ.* **1996**, *6*, 89–109. [CrossRef]
16. Sutthimat, P.; Mekchay, K. Closed-form formulas for conditional moments of inhomogeneous Pearson diffusion processes. *Commun. Nonlinear Sci. Numer. Simul.* **2022**, *106*, 106095. [CrossRef]
17. Sutthimat, P.; Mekchay, K.; Rujivan, S. Closed-form formula for conditional moments of generalized nonlinear drift CEV process. *Appl. Math. Comput.* **2022**, *428*, 127213. [CrossRef]
18. Feller, W. Two singular diffusion problems. *Ann. Math.* **1951**, *54*, 173. [CrossRef]
19. Sutthimat, P.; Mekchay, K.; Rujivan, S. Explicit formula for conditional expectations of product of polynomial and exponential function of affine transform of extended Cox–Ingersoll–Ross process. *J. Phys. Conf. Ser.* **2018**, *1132*, 012083. [CrossRef]
20. Sutthimat, P.; Rujivan, S.; Mekchay, K.; Rakwongwan, U. Analytical formula for conditional expectations of path-dependent product of polynomial and exponential functions of extended Cox–Ingersoll–Ross process. *Res. Math. Sci.* **2022**, *9*, 10. [CrossRef]
21. Nualsri, F.; Mekchay, K. Analytically Pricing Formula for Contingent Claim with Polynomial Payoff under ECIR Process. *Symmetry* **2022**, *14*, 933. [CrossRef]
22. Chumpong, K.; Mekchay, K.; Rujivan, S. A simple closed-form formula for the conditional moments of the Ornstein–Uhlenbeck process. *Songklanakarin J. Sci. Technol.* **2020**, *42*, 836–845.
23. Chumpong, K.; Mekchay, K.; Thamrongrat, N. Analytical formulas for pricing discretely-sampled skewness and kurtosis swaps based on Schwartz's one-factor model. *Songklanakarin J. Sci. Technol.* **2021**, *43*, 465–470.
24. Chumpong, K.; Sumritnorrapong, P. Closed-form formula for the conditional moments of log prices under the inhomogeneous Heston model. *Computation* **2022**, *10*, 46. [CrossRef]
25. Boonklurb, R.; Duangpan, A.; Treeyaprasert, T. Modified finite integration method using Chebyshev polynomial for solving linear differential equations. *J. Numer. Ind. Appl. Math* **2018**, *12*, 1–19.
26. Boonklurb, R.; Duangpan, A.; Gugaew, P. Numerical solution of direct and inverse problems for time-dependent Volterra integro-differential equation using finite integration method with shifted Chebyshev polynomials. *Symmetry* **2020**, *12*, 497. [CrossRef]

27. Duangpan, A.; Boonklurb, R.; Juytai, M. Numerical solutions for systems of fractional and classical integro-differential equations via finite integration method based on shifted Chebyshev polynomials. *Fractal Fract.* **2021**, *5*, 103. [CrossRef]
28. Duangpan, A.; Boonklurb, R. Modified finite integration method using Chebyshev polynomial expansion for solving one-dimensional nonlinear Burgers' equations with shock wave. *Thai J. Math.* **2021**, 63–73.
29. Duangpan, A.; Boonklurb, R.; Treeyaprasert, T. finite integration method with shifted Chebyshev polynomials for solving time-fractional Burgers' equations. *Mathematics* **2019**, *7*, 1201. [CrossRef]
30. Schoutens, W. Moment swaps. *Quant. Financ.* **2005**, *5*, 525–530. [CrossRef]

MDPI
St. Alban-Anlage 66
4052 Basel
Switzerland
Tel. +41 61 683 77 34
Fax +41 61 302 89 18
www.mdpi.com

Symmetry Editorial Office
E-mail: symmetry@mdpi.com
www.mdpi.com/journal/symmetry